Cultures of Masculinity

Cultures of Masculinity presents a survey of the social, cultural and theo-retical issues which surround and inform our understanding of masculinity. Beginning with an analysis of the so-called 'crisis' of masculinity – in which men are repeatedly reported to be experiencing employment, health and educational failings – Tim Edwards considers the validity of the concerns and anxieties which surround masculinity in the contemporary world.

Edwards then covers a range of key topics, including:

- The New Man, the New Lad and 'men's movements'
- Men, masculinity and violence
- Marginalised masculinities: black masculinity and gay male sexuality
- Queer theory, performativity and fashion
- Cinema, representation and the body

One of the most comprehensive and progressive studies of modern mas-culinity available, this book will be essential reading for students of gender, culture and sociology.

Tim Edwards is a lecturer in the Department of Sociology at the University of Leicester. His primary research interests include gender studies, partic-ularly analyses of masculinity, sexuality, fashion and consumer culture, the interface between social and cultural theory, and social divisions.

Cultures of Masculinity

Tim Edwards

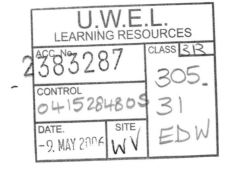

Routledge
Taylor & Francis Group

LONDON AND NEW YORK

First published 2006
by Routledge
2 Park Square, Milton Park, Abingdon, Oxon OX14 4RN

Simultaneously published in the USA and Canada
by Routledge
270 Madison Ave, New York, NY 10016

Routledge is an imprint of the Taylor & Francis Group

Typeset in Sabon by
Keystroke, Jacaranda Lodge, Wolverhampton
Printed and bound in Great Britain by
TJ International Ltd, Padstow, Cornwall

British Library Cataloguing in Publication Data
A catalogue record for this book is available from the British Library

Library of Congress Cataloging in Publication Data
A catalog record for this book has been requested

ISBN10: 0–415–28480–5   ISBN13: 9–78–0–415–28480–6 (hbk)
ISBN10: 0–415–28481–3   ISBN13: 9–78–0–415–28481–3 (pbk)

For Chris, with love

Contents

Acknowledgements

This particular baby has had a long, exhausting and difficult gestation and an even harder birth. I am thankful to the midwives along the way. In alphabetical order they are: Sam Ashenden, who helped me sort the Foucault from the chaff and the constructed from the inessential; Shirley Beller who loyally provided much in the way of feedback, books and cigarettes when needed; Jo Flannery for being the perfect student and helping me feel a little less queer; Peter Handford for simply being there; Philip Hoggar who commented usefully on the chapter on cinema and was a good sounding board; Jonathan Randall who provided me with much needed computer assistance at one stage; Liz Ringrose who taught me how to write a bit better; and Carla Willig who offered me breaks in London as well as her total clarity of vision – I am and will be eternally grateful to all of them for their friendship, hospitality and simply putting up with me. More formally I am very grateful to Chris Rojek, Mari Shullaw and – most particularly – Constance Sutherland, for their help, patience, and kicks up the backside when needed. Leicester University also usefully provided me with one semester's study leave. I am also most appreciative of Casper the cat for keeping me company and keeping me real. Lastly, but in no way leastly, I am most sincerely thankful and deeply indebted to Chris Marsh for both being an inspiration for how a man can be in the twenty-first century and for being quite simply everything this book's often bad tempered, exhausted and exhausting, and ceaselessly demanding mother could ever wish for.

Introduction

Cultures of masculinity

And so it goes – go round again
But now and then we wonder who the real men are.
(Joe Jackson)

Masculinity is at once everywhere and yet nowhere, known and yet unknowable, had and yet un-*have*-able. In fact, to paraphrase Richard Dyer, it is not male sexuality but masculinity *per se* that 'is a bit like air – you breathe it in all the time, but you aren't aware of it much' (Dyer, 1985: 28). Except perhaps that we are aware of masculinity in the twenty-first century like never before. Even Mrs Anybody gathering her shopping on a Monday morning knows that the fuss about David Beckham has something to do with his masculinity, or that Tom Cruise movies are often tied up with notions of what American manhood should be, or that magazine stands are full of men without their shirts showing off their six packs – beer bellies become beer cans – and, well, it's all a bit *odd* really. Of course such developments have not gone unnoticed more academically across the canon of critical studies of men and masculinity as well as some of their more media friendly variants. Yet it remains the case that far from forming anything homogenous or conclusive, all this talk about masculinity has often left the notion hanging and inconclusive. One of the reasons for this situation, I will suggest, is that the study of masculinity has itself fragmented into multiple parts, reflections from a shattered mirror even or, perhaps more accurately, an array of Petri dishes growing cultures of masculinity. So, to continue with the white-coated theme, this book sets about blowing off a few of their lids, giving them a spin and letting the professor loose in the laboratory of masculinities.

Synopsis of style, content and scope

This book aims to be reasonably inclusive but makes no pretence to be exhaustive. The canon of studies of men and masculinities is now vast, even sociologically, and the task of reviewing all of this is simply not within the scope of a single project. In particular, anyone expecting an interrogation of the biological bases of masculinity or a scientific analysis according to cognitive or behaviourist psychological models will be sorely disappointed. While a variety of approaches are utilised or critiqued along the way, the book remains a work of sociology or cultural studies, not biology or psychology, and I make no apology for this.

Throughout this work I refer to what I call a three-phase or 'wave' model of critical studies of masculinity. It is no coincidence that there is a slight pun on the terminology often used to describe the first, second and potential third waves of feminism, given the immense degree of indebtedness that studies of masculinity owe to feminist theory. The first phase or wave of critical studies of masculinity refers to the development of the sex role paradigm in the 1970s to apply more directly to questions of masculinity (David and Brannon, 1976; Farrell, 1974; Tolson, 1977). Though varied to some extent, the key emphasis of these studies was, first, to demonstrate the socially constructed nature of masculinity and its reliance on socialisation, sex role learning and social control; and second, to attempt to document how these processes were limiting and perhaps even harmful to men in terms of their own psychological and even physical health (Goldberg, 1976). The pressures of performance, whether in the bedroom or the boardroom, and an emphasis on emotional repression – or the commonly quoted syndrome of 'big boys don't cry' – were particularly common targets.

The second phase or wave of critical studies of masculinity emerged in the 1980s primarily out of immense criticism of the first wave. More particularly, the sex role paradigm was now commonly seen to be both dubious politically in implying some kind of level playing field between the sexes and limited theoretically in its purchase on masculinities in the plural sense rather than in the singular sense of one, often white, Western and middle-class, model. Fundamental in this was the work of Connell in developing the concept of hegemony to apply it to questions of masculinity (Connell, 1987). The primary sex role paradigm exposed in the first wave of studies was the most hegemonic and therefore dominant set of masculinities exerting influence, control and power over other more oppressed masculinities, particularly those commonly associated with the vectors of race, class and sexuality. Consequently, black, working-class and gay men and masculinities were seen to be subordinated to, and perhaps even exploited by, hegemonic white, Western, middle-class and heterosexual men and masculinities. As a result, the second wave of studies of masculinity is concerned, more than anything else, with *power* and its complex and polyvalent meanings and operations. Not surprisingly there were numerous variations on a theme here, from theoretical interrogations of prevailing philosophies of gender and society, through attempts to re-evaluate Marxist approaches to masculinity and gender, to interrogating the role of autobiography (Hearn, 1987; Morgan, 1992; Seidler, 1989). However, a common and often unifying theme here was more political, as most of the authors involved were overtly pro-feminist in their stance on most issues, in seeking an alliance with feminism, and indeed in defining themselves.

The third wave of studies of masculinity, rather like the potential third wave of studies of femininity, is clearly influenced by the advent of post-structural theory, particularly as it relates to gender in terms of questions of normativity, performativity and sexuality (Buchbinder, 1998; Butler, 1990; Simpson, 1994). As is also the case with feminism, it is less easy to define, often slipping across interdisciplinary lines and invoking literary, cultural and media studies alongside the work of social scientists (see, for example, Dollimore, 1991; Jeffords, 1994; Schoene-Harwood, 2000). A common theme, however, is the importance of representation and its connection with wider questions of change and continuity in contemporary, and in some more historical, masculinities and identities. In addition, many of these studies of cultural texts are relatively positive in their emphasis, whether more overt or covert, on the sense of artifice, flux and contingency concerning masculinities.

There is of course a strong sense of artifice in this discussion *per se* or, to put it simply, it's a case of attempting to draw lines in the sand, yet I wish to assert that what this highly figurative analysis at least starts to do is to open more widely a developing set of tensions within the study of men and masculinities. More directly, this relates to the conflict, or at least lack of integration, of more culturalist, poststructural or media-driven analyses of masculinity with those perceiving themselves as pro-feminist, structuralist or empirically driven or, to put it more simply and rather crudely, between the second and third waves of studies of masculinity. An interesting example is Kimmel, Hearn and Connell's excellent and exhaustive *Handbook of Studies on Men and Masculinities* that somehow also curiously completely omits almost the entire canon of cultural, literary and media-driven studies of masculinity (Kimmel, Hearn and Connell, 2004). Similarly, most of the aforementioned more culturalist, literary or media-driven analyses of masculinity seem oblivious to the enormous legacy of studies of masculinity that preceded them. Yet what unites them, and indeed all of these studies, is their emphasis on the social and cultural construction of masculinity and the challenge this provides to the more reactionary, or at least ongoing commonsense, tendency to see masculinity as something that is, has always been, and always will be, coming from men's testicles. Ultimately, then, this sense of dualism is indeed artifice, false even, yet not half as fake as it could be.

In addition, it is this sense of tension that informs my work here. More particularly, my selection of topics is driven according to an interrogation of cultural, poststructuralist or more media-driven studies, on the one hand, and those studies now defined as pro-feminist, critical studies of men and masculinities or more simply sociological, on the other. To be clear, it is precisely the sense of a frequently non-communicating, often differing, and perhaps even *opposing*, interface that drives this analysis. This also focuses, and in fact interferes with, the topic selection. To put it quite simply, cultural or media studies and sociology or sexual politics do not often even consider the same topics in relation to masculinity or ask the same questions, let alone come up with comparable answers. Consequently, my initial intention to take a selection of topics from both angles soon blew apart and became something nearer to a tale of two halves. The first half focuses on a series of topics in relation to masculinity that are – for the most part – more traditionally sociological, or at least more commonly studied under the auspices of social science and sexual politics: the crisis of masculinity, men's responses to feminism, men's violence and the violations of masculinity, and race or ethnicity and masculinity. The second half shifts attention towards a series of more contemporary topics that often invoke as much cultural if not necessarily media-driven attention: sexuality and queer theory, performativity and fashion, the cinema and viewing relations, and lastly the body.

Chapter 1, which might also have been aptly titled 'much ado about nothing', opens up what proves to be an unending confusion of men and masculinities. Consequently, it covers what I call the *crisis from without* or the perception that men as a group are somehow in crisis, and the *crisis from within*, or the feeling that men are somehow experiencing a crisis more personally. This in turn is seen to rest on the confusion of men and masculinities as, although some *men* in some situations are perhaps in some kind of crisis, often through structural changes such as unemployment, this does not equate with a crisis of *masculinity* as a set of characteristics, values or dispositions. Here, a more historical viewpoint clearly reveals that masculinity is often in crisis or, perhaps more accurately, it *is* crisis or at least contains crisis tendencies. Secondly, in Chapter 2, I explore the linked theme of men's responses to feminism, as some exponents of the crisis of masculinity thesis would clearly seem to blame second-wave feminism. However, another split develops here between what I call the *backlash against* feminism and the *lashed backs* of feminism, or between anti-feminist men's movements who align themselves *against* feminism, particularly in the United States, and strongly pro-feminist scholars who often align themselves *with* feminism. Neither perspective is satisfactory, however, due to their mutual failure to articulate precisely *what* they are aligning themselves with or against. In the second part of this chapter I address more media-driven analyses of men's responses to feminism, in the form of an analysis of contemporary men's style magazines and the iconography of the New Man and the New Lad. Though the New Lad has arguably been more successful than the New Man in setting up a more enduring response to feminism, I argue that neither the New Man nor the New Lad truly exists outside of its media invention. In addition, both of these media inventions are often connected more to patterns of consumption and marketing, or the commodification of masculinities, than to second-wave feminism and sexual politics. However, second-wave feminism and sexual politics do frequently inform contemporary discourses concerning men's violence. Yet, to return to the confusion between men and masculinities, what is frequently lacking here is an interrogation of the relations of violence and *masculinity*, rather than *men*, and this in turn often involves questions of the violation of men themselves as well as their violence against others. A similar political imperative underpins the discussion of race and masculinity in Chapter 4. The analysis of race and masculinity rests almost entirely on the thesis of black emasculation that is, for the most part, completely dismantled by black feminism. The formation of a growing analysis of whiteness, and the even more incipient development of studies of non-Western masculinities, has yet to form anything remotely approaching an analysis of race, ethnicity and masculinity. Thus, the analysis of race, ethnicity and masculinity remains in black and white and not in colour. In Chapter 5, I investigate the significance of gay masculinities, and thereby sexuality in relation to gender more widely. Ever since gay liberation, if not before, the gay male community has been beset with a series of sexual political struggles concerning its more gendered identity and its relationship to its sexuality, or what one might call the contradictions and contra-*directions* of identity and desire. Queer theory has started to offer some more sophisticated theoretical solutions to these conflicts but the gay male community, by and large, remains locked within its own temporary narcissistic resolution of these tendencies. The analysis of poststructural theory is extended in Chapter 6 where I consider the significance of the theory of performativity. However, while apparently offering much potential, performativity theory is seen as having limited purchase even on the analysis of fashion, let alone the future direction of understanding masculinities. Chapter 7, one of the longest and most involved, considers an alternative perspective on the importance and construction of masculinities, namely cinema and media studies. Mulvey's thesis of the gendered nature of looking relations is now widely critiqued yet leaves the analysis of the relationship of representation to contemporary masculinities open to wider interrogation. Via a consideration of several recent films, I conclude that cultural texts are indeed of relevance in understanding more contemporary masculinities at least and there is a need for more sociological, as well as media-driven, investigation of the questions they raise. This more culturalist theme is continued in Chapter 8 where I consider the role of the body in relation to masculinities and argue once again for greater dialogue between disciplines, if not necessarily a more interdisciplinary form of study of men and masculinities *per se*.

Some of this analysis is indeed provocative, if not controversial, and I make no secret of this. The second chapter on responses to feminism, for example, is not half as critical of the mythopoetic men's movement as some would like, and levels some critique at the often poorly articulated responses of some of its pro-feminist critics. Similarly, in considering violence in Chapter 3, I argue that men's violence against women is only part of the relationship of masculinity and violence. In later chapters, I am also critical of much of the work on performativity, representation and masculinity for its frequent cultural solipsism and more often implied authorial-textual elitism. My aim here is not to demonise, or even denounce, any of these studies, but rather to expose their partiality and their limitations and to encourage them to engage in more dialogue with each other.

Throughout the work I employ more than one writing style or approach and critical and academic, or long and extensive, reviews of prevailing literatures are often interspersed with shorter, more direct and more personal accounts. This is not just a case of trying to make things more interesting, but is premised on the recognition of the limits of many prevailing literatures, and indeed academic disciplines, that just don't, won't, and can't 'go there' – to where certain questions lie. A primary example here is the chapter on violence, which ends with a very personal and direct account of my own experiences. Similarly, the chapters on cinema and the body pivot on a far more direct and less abstracted interrogation of certain questions. In the final conclusion, I argue the need for integration not separation, dialogue not monologue, and for the articulation of experience rather than its abstraction.

1 'Crisis, what crisis?'
Sex roles revisited

It is now not uncommon in populist and academic circles alike to talk of a 'crisis' of masculinity, yet what this actually means remains unclear. One of the causes of this confusion is the sheer profusion of uses and applications of the concept. Consequently, it is seen to refer to factors as diverse as the impact of second-wave feminism on men, competition with women either at school or at work, the escalating levels of violent acts men are seen to commit, anxieties concerning how men should act within the home or within personal relationships, the representation of men in negative terms in the media, or the undermining of traditional male sex roles. What constitutes a crisis as such is equally unclear. In particular, the concept of crisis is used to incorporate a sense of panic or anxiety that on the one hand has already happened or on the other might happen, and is applied equally to masculinity as a concept or to the experiences of men themselves.

This chapter has three key aims: first to try to define what a crisis of masculinity actually means, second to document and assess some of the 'evidence' for and against its use, and third to consider where this actually leads us not only in terms of its sexual political implications but rather for its importance to our understanding of masculinity itself. My concern here is neither to unquestioningly accept the concept of a crisis of masculinity or what it implies, nor to dismiss it out of hand. There are, I will suggest, ways in which masculinity is, perhaps, in deep crisis yet not necessarily in accordance with how this crisis is often perceived. Consequently, there are three sections: first, a consideration of how the crisis of masculinity is most commonly defined and what it is predicated on; second, an evaluation of various explanations of its significance; and third, an analysis of what a crisis of masculinity actually means more widely in terms of the theory and practice of sexual politics.

The crisis from without, the crisis from within

Evidence for the masculinity in crisis thesis tends to come from two inter-linked sets of concerns. The first I call the crisis from without. This includes some partially empirically documented concerns relating to the position of men within such institutions as the family, education and work. A specific concern here is the perception that men have lost, or are losing, power or privilege relative to their prior status in these institutions. The second I call the crisis from within. This is far less easily documented as it centres precisely on a perceived shift in men's *experiences* of their position *as* men, their maleness, and what it means. Most importantly, this often refers to a sense of powerlessness, meaninglessness or uncertainty. The continuity concerning the importance of *power* here highlights not only its significance for masculinity *per se*, but rather the sense that this is a key factor that informs the entire masculinity in crisis thesis. More particularly, it also highlights the way in which the crisis from without and the crisis from within connect or how the crisis from without can also be a crisis from within and vice versa. Consequently, in this section I will consider these two levels of crisis in relation to seven key areas of concern. These include work, education, the family, sexuality, health, crime and representation, which, when taken together, may then inform an overall masculinity in crisis thesis.

(handwritten margin note: men. loosing power they ha always had.)

Work

Historically, work has often stood as the most fundamental foundation of masculine identity, particularly in relation to modernity or, more specifically, advanced Western industrial capitalism. Moreover, it was a key thesis of many of the earliest critiques of masculinity working within the sex role paradigm that work was seen to be the most fundamental element in the formation of successful masculine identity (see, for example, David and Brannon, 1976; Farrell, 1974; Tolson, 1977). The primary point here was that work not only matters *to* men, but is also part *of* them as a key dimension of their identity and masculinity. Consequently, successful masculinity was equated directly with success at work whether in middle-class terms of a career or in more working-class terms of physical labour. The more contemporary problem in many Western societies is that this ethos is argued to be severely undermined on several fronts, usefully summarised by Beynon (Beynon, 2002). First, the decline of manufacturing has meant that many working-class men have found themselves unemployed, sometimes later in life and with little prospect for improvement. Second, downsizing and increasingly market-driven policies in many Western societies have led to rising occupational insecurity and a sense of precariousness across many service-oriented, professional or financial sectors and this in turn has meant that some middle-class men have similarly found their positions undermined. In addition, studies of unemployment tend to show a marked stigma concerning men who feel emasculated without work and, more particularly, the loss of 'men's work' or manual labour in later life (Cockburn, 1983; Gaillie, Marsh and Vogler, 1994; Willott and Griffin, 1996). Third, all of this has taken place alongside the increasing participation of women in the workforce combined with a greater emphasis on sexual equality, thus tending

(handwritten margin note: Job = your mascu-linity.)

societies is in a state of flux and opens up opportunities for reform as well as reinforcement of gender relations (Connell, 2000; Francis, 1998, 2000; Mac an Ghaill, 1994). However, this would hardly seem to constitute evidence for an overall crisis of masculinity in education. It would seem, then, that the perceived gender disparity in terms of educational attainment means little, at least in isolation. What does still seem to retain some significance is the linking of this factor with concerns relating to employment as previously outlined or indeed in relation to crime.

Crime

Crime remains a profoundly gendered phenomenon. To put it simply, the vast majority of crimes and particularly violent crimes are committed by boys or men and not by girls or women (see also Chapter 3). While there is some evidence to support the claim that women's crime is increasing or is simply under-represented, the committing of crimes remains profoundly linked to the male sex (Bowker, 1998; Heidensohn, 1996; Messerschmidt, 1993, 1997; Smart, 1978; Stanko, 1994). This is, in essence, nothing new. What is newer here, however, is the sense in which this may relate to a wider crisis of masculinity. The concern is that crime, and particularly violent crime as committed by young and working-class males, is strongly related to rising unemployment and an increasing sense of despair among these groups, which finds expression or outlet through aggression and violence. Of particular concern is the recent wave of violent crime in depressed and impoverished areas, such as council estates in the UK since the late 1980s, often accompanied by new forms of crime such as ram-raiding, joy-riding and the rise of alcohol-induced brawling in towns and cities. The problem has also received some feminist as well as media attention, further highlighting its connections with a crisis of masculinity (Campbell, 1993).

There are, though, some points of scepticism worth raising here. First and foremost, crime remains notoriously difficult to measure, let alone relate to any simple cause and effect model as complex as a crisis of masculinity. Secondly, the immense media attention often now paid to matters of violent crime has in all likelihood also escalated and distorted its significance in a manner not dissimilar to the moral panics surrounding the mods and rockers in the 1950s (Cohen, 1972). As already stated, violence among lower-class young males is not necessarily new and therefore not necessarily indicative of any particularly contemporary crisis of masculinity. Thirdly, and most significantly, any recent or current escalation of violent crime in impoverished areas in all likelihood may be due as much, if not more, to rising social divisiveness and economic inequality, most particularly the widening gap between rich and poor, than to gender or masculinity. On top of this, the often strongly racialised dimension of such crimes is also frequently wholly neglected (Bowker, 1998). What remains of concern here, however, is the sense that such tendencies towards a crisis of masculinity from without, while often vastly overstated, may still relate to a wider crisis from within. There is some reason to assume that *some* young men are turning to crime as an alternative way of life when faced with a lack of opportunities elsewhere. This point is endorsed by Ian Taylor in *Crime in Context* where he attempts to interrogate the connection of questions of crime and masculinity to wider developments in the market and capitalist society, noting, in particular, the connection of crime and crises of masculinity at 'lower levels of opportunity' (Taylor, 1999: 79). As violence is still an activity associated more with masculinity than with femininity, then it is also logical for the despair and frustration of *some* groups of young men to take this form. What remains clear, however, is the sense that this remains demographically and geographically quite specific and not particularly indicative of any *overall* crisis of masculinity.

Family

The family is perhaps the most complex arena within which the greatest sense of concern relating to a perceived crisis of masculinity resides. In the first instance this most fundamentally relates to the world of work. Given — increased insecurity at work, if not unemployment, coupled with the rising participation of women in paid work and the commonality of dual-income households, there is much reason to assume that the image and indeed practice of men as providers, and the breadwinning ethic that goes with it, have been severely undermined if not displaced. On top of this the rise in rates of divorce, more commonly filed by women than by men, further undermines any mythic, or indeed real, status the stereotypically gendered nuclear family may have had or still has (see Beynon, 2002).

Moreover, the status of fatherhood has also suffered on several fronts. First, there has been increased coverage of such issues as domestic violence, child abuse and men's general abandonment of the role of fatherhood. Though all of these issues are very worthy of significantly greater attention than they received previously, this has had the unintended consequence of representing *all* men as potential violators of their position as fathers and partners. Second, the masculine provider ethic and the role of the father may also be potentially undermined through advances in technology such as IVF that render the need for fathers increasingly redundant, though again this is easily overstated. Third, it is now well known that the judicial process tends to favour women or mothers as primary carers of children according to what are now perhaps outdated modes of parenting. Recent high-profile campaigns by Fathers for Justice in the UK and similar pressure groups concerning men's rights are a prime example that has attracted much media attention. Taken together these factors would seem to present a somewhat pessimistic future for the position of men within the family.

However, such a view is undermined on several fronts: first, it often over-simplifies the view of fatherhood and tends to marginalise very fundamental variations according to class, race and sexuality (for a useful summary see Marsiglio and Pleck, 2004). Similarly, Adams and Coltrane (2004) highlight the tendency to collapse into anxieties concerning the implosion of gendered differences or the biological stereotypes concerning both children and parenting. Second, men often remain reluctant fathers and resistant to change and to taking their domestic responsibilities and commitments seriously, as men's participation in child care and domestic work has not increased particularly significantly and often remains pitched at the secondary level of 'helping out' (see for example, McMahon, 1999). Consequently, while fathers are often relatively poorly supported through employment practices and state legislation, they also often appear equally slow to force change. Third, and more widely, men's position within the family is not necessarily undermined *per se*, rather it may be perceived as adapting to changing circumstance which may work to men's advantage as well as women's, giving them both the opportunity for more loving relationships with their children and a sense of equality and commonality with their partners.

Sexuality

Concerns relating to the family and men's position within the domestic sphere relate strongly to underlying anxieties surrounding men's sexuality. There are essentially two dimensions to this issue. The first of these concerns men's ongoing difficulties in relation to emotional expression or communication and interpersonal intimacy. Though the New Man promised a new dawn in men's inner emotional happiness and expression, as typified in the now overly common imagery of men holding babies, this often proved to be little more than a media invention and myth. Men's difficulties with emotional expression are also not new historically and are well documented, yet what is newer here is the sense of increasing pressure surrounding men's personal development and capacities in these areas (Clare, 2000; Horrocks, 1994; Seidler, 1989). Of particular importance here is the perception of women's rising expectations sexually and emotionally in the wake of second-wave feminism, often linked with a greater sense of their sexual and emotional independence from men.

Allied to this, the contemporary plethora of near pornographic representations of muscular men, oiled and gleaming, in everything from Hollywood movies to pop music and adverts for soft drinks, has led some to argue that a culture of anxiety and low self-esteem is now growing among men not dissimilar to that experienced in relation to women for many years (Pope, Phillips and Olivardia, 2000; Bordo, 1999; Wolf, 1991). An additional difficulty here, however, is the sense of slithering into the altogether different territory of gay sexuality and it is decidedly unclear whether some of this overtly sexual representation of men is related to women's expectations of heterosexual men at all or rather to the proliferation of dual marketing and implicitly 'gay' representations of male sexuality. In particular, concerns around men's sexuality often focus precisely and exclusively on the heterosexual and many stereotypes concerning both black and gay male sexuality remain. In sum the issue here seems to centre on a lack of resolution to a not very new set of problems.

Health

Concerns relating to men's health exist on several well-documented levels. A particularly useful summary is provided by Lee and Owens in *The Psychology of Men's Health* (Lee and Owens, 2002). First, men's mortality rates are generally higher than women's across advanced Western industrial societies. One frequently quoted statistic concerns the gender gap in life expectancy which, although actually now closing, remains significant (Beynon, 2002; Connell, 2000; Watson, 2000). Explanations for this situation are numerous, yet mostly centre on a mixture of genetic and social considerations varying from the influence of testosterone to men's greater participation in many forms of life-threatening activities including sport, drinking and smoking, violence and road accidents, which account for many young male deaths (Lee and Owens, 2002). A second factor concerns comparisons in relation to morbidity rates, where men are sometimes perceived as over-represented, and in connection with a whole series of diseases and afflictions that men, purely by virtue of being male, are prone to or which are exclusively male afflictions. The most glaring example of this was Goldberg's sensationally titled work *The Hazards of Being Male* originally published in 1976 and reprinted in 2000. Goldberg assaulted the notion of male privilege with vigour in documenting men's health risks over a wide range of both major concerns such as various cancers as well as more minor issues such as colour blindness (Goldberg, 1976). A third, and particularly problematic, consideration is men's comparative neglect of their own health. Most of this is explained simply as a result of men's disassociation from their own physical needs, often regarding themselves as machines that perform functions rather than as corporeal realities that need care and attention. The male tendency to solve such issues through competitive sport and pounding sessions at the gym rather than in personal check-ups and trips to see the doctor are examples of such gendered practices (Messner and Sabo, 1994; Sabo, 2004; Sabo and Gordon, 1995). Consequently, men's health remains a significant concern on several fronts. The difficulty here is that none of this constitutes anything new with one exception: the near epidemic level of young male suicides (Sabo, 2004). It is common to explain this as the result of a crisis of masculinity, in that many young men are perceived as increasingly prone to a sense of despair, particularly in relation to employment and the undermining of traditional male roles. As stated earlier, this is in itself a fairly geographically and demographically specific phenomenon that has as much to do with wider economic trends as with any shift in the understanding or practices of masculinity. Consequently, claims here have a tendency towards exaggeration. However, men's comparative ill health relative to women's and their overriding inattention to caring for it remains a significant if not particularly new area of concern.

Representation

All of the aforementioned issues in relation to a perceived crisis of masculinity have gained added credence due to their increased prevalence in a variety of forms of media coverage. On one level at least, the crisis of masculinity is a crisis of representation. There are in essence two sides to this question: first, the extent to which the crisis of masculinity exists simply as a matter of its representation as such; and secondly, the extent to which contemporary representations of masculinity fuel the sense that masculinity is itself in crisis. In the first case, this question is mostly answered with respect to the previous empirical documentation of shifts in relation to masculinity and the experiences of men which provide at least *some* evidence of at least *some* concern for at least *some* men, though very little which supports an *overall* crisis of masculinity thesis. In the second case, there is equally conflicting evidence concerning the ways in which men are represented. Though it is true that male incompetence and inadequacies with everything from household cleaning (advertisements for Mr Muscle) to personal relationships (a famous Volkswagen Golf advert) now form a key target in much television advertising and that many UK and US situation comedies now depict men as either emotionally inept (*Men Behaving Badly*) or simply less important (*Sex and the City*), the image of the heroic male in whatever form still dominates the movie industry, adorns magazines from *Men's Health* to *GQ*, and fuels a myriad of aspirational desires from sport to corporate success.

A key factor of shift here is comedy and the sense in which men are now often laughed *at* in a variety of formats, yet once again this is not entirely new. One only has to think of the slapstick foolery of *Laurel and Hardy* or Tony Hancock, the classic 1970s situation comedies such as *Dad's Army* or *Fawlty Towers*, and the comedic ambivalence of some Hollywood icons such as Cary Grant, to know that the male as comic spectacle is hardly without precedent. The only really conspicuous shift here seems to centre on the apparent rise in women's participation within comedy in a variety of forms from *French & Saunders* and Victoria Wood and Jo Brand in the UK to *Ally McBeal*, Joan Rivers and *Rosanne* in the US, to mention only some. Much of this development would seem far more positive in promoting the experiences and careers of women than it is negative in undermining or excluding men. In short, what one seems left with is merely the crudity of some advertising campaigns, itself explained by Goldman in Marxist terms through the power of marketing in creating 'false needs' or what he calls 'commodity feminism' (Goldman, 1992). Once again this hardly constitutes a wholesale crisis, whether real or representational.

Having summarised at least some of the concerns underpinning the contemporary notion of a crisis of masculinity, it is worth making some more general comments. First, and foremost, there is little real evidence of anything that might constitute a crisis of masculinity within the terms of how this is most commonly specified. While changes in employment and the family are significant and even radical in some respects, their effects on men remain hard to measure and almost certainly highly uneven according to wider criteria of class, ethnicity, age, geography or sexuality. Second, and consequent from this, is the sense that there is in all likelihood a growing set of concerns relating to some specific groups of men who have fallen victim to wider economic trends. The decline of manufacturing, increased economic inequality, and deprivation in many inner city and or rural areas alike provide the focus for much attention here. Third, and perhaps most pessimistically, is the sense that many of the issues raised here are simply not new at all, coupled with the fact that, despite increased attention to matters of men's emotional difficulties, health concerns and their often contradictory position within the domestic sphere, few solutions are forthcoming. All of this leads us to reconsider exactly on what level the crisis of masculinity may exist and how it is explained.

Sex roles revisited: theorising the crisis

Having surveyed some of the empirical evidence surrounding the commonly perceived contemporary crisis of masculinity, the situation appears confused and uneven and there is little support for any *overall* crisis of masculinity thesis. Part of the explanation for this confusion centres on the level at which any crisis of masculinity is perceived to exist. On the one hand, the crisis of masculinity may refer to the *position* of men, often perceived as being undermined in relation to institutions such as work, the family, education or even representation. On the other hand, the crisis of masculinity refers more precisely to men's *experience* of these shifts in position. So far I have called these aspects the crisis from without and the crisis from within. They do of course strongly interlink and, as I have argued, evidence for the crisis from without is patchy to say the least and centres on a series of mostly culturally and demographically specific phenomena that are not necessarily new. However, in relation to these phenomena more specifically, some contemporary concerns are in all likelihood, very valid if not necessarily quite as overwhelmingly gendered as they appear. Consequent from this, some men are suffering or will in all likelihood suffer some experience of crisis on some level, whether in relation to loss of employment prospects, despair as to their future, rising demands from women in their personal lives, frustration at perceived inequalities with other men, or all of these. None of

h, would seem to constitute an *overall* crisis of masculinity so
.s *tendencies towards* crisis for some men.

Any wider crisis of masculinity tends to rest on an entirely different set of
propositions. First, masculinity as a set of values, practices or dispositions
may be suffering crisis in so far as it is being undermined and devalued or,
moreover, that masculinity *per se* is now to a greater or lesser degree equated
with a series of negative rather than positive associations and connotations
(MacInnes, 1998). Secondly, masculinity may be in crisis due to its perceived
tendency to, as it were, implode into femininity, whether through an overall
undermining of any gender role distinctions or through feminisation of some
forms of masculinity as, for example, in the case of the rise of contemporary
consumerist, fashion-conscious or sexually uncertain masculinities such
as metrosexuality (Simpson, 1996). Thirdly, and most fundamentally, the
crisis of masculinity may relate to the sense that masculinity in terms of
the male sex role is itself *ipso facto* crisis-inducing. In this sense, masculinity
is not *in* crisis, it *is* crisis. In this final section, I will consider the validity
of these propositions and will assert that it is on these levels, rather than
on those discussed in previous sections, that the crisis of masculinity truly
exists.

The sociological literature on the so-called crisis of masculinity thesis is
arguably a ragbag of partly theoretically informed and partly politically
prescriptive assertions that can be grouped in roughly three perspectives: first,
historical perspectives that argue in essence that the contemporary crisis of
masculinity is not without precedent; second, psychoanalytic perspectives
that, while seeing the crisis of masculinity as resulting from wider social and
economic developments, also see its ramifications in primarily psychological
terms; and third, poststructural or discursive perspectives that seek to
deconstruct the notion of a crisis of masculinity in more theoretical terms
while often allying this with certain sexual political standpoints.

The historical perspective is essentially premised on the idea that the
contemporary crisis of masculinity is nothing new. Chief among these is the
work of Connell (1995). Connell's starting point is a critique of the concept
of crisis *per se* and its application to masculinity:

> As a theoretical term 'crisis' presupposes a coherent system of some
> kind, which is destroyed or restored by the outcome of the crisis. [. . .]
> It [masculinity] is rather a configuration of practice within a system of
> gender relations. We cannot logically speak of a crisis of configuration;
> rather we might speak of its disruption or its transformation. We can,
> however, logically speak of the crisis of a gender order as a whole, and
> of its tendencies towards crisis.
>
> (Connell, 1995: 84)

This leads Connell to analyse what he calls 'crisis tendencies of the gender
order' (Connell, 1995: 84). These are seen to relate to three prevailing

structures of gender relations – power relations, production relations, and relations of cathexis or, to put it more simply, a primary emphasis on and consideration of patriarchy, work and sexuality. These three areas are seen in historical terms as sites of change and development. Thus, the prevailing order of patriarchy is seen as being undermined by – if not necessarily under threat from – the emancipation of women; shifts in the worlds of technology and work are also seen to rupture stereotypical notions of gender divisions in employment, and the rise of gay and lesbian sexualities is also seen to undermine patriarchal dominance. Connell draws on the work of Kimmel and Theweleit in attempting to expose and document earlier crisis tendencies (Kimmel, 1987a; Theweleit, 1987). Despite this, he fails to develop such ideas and turns instead towards small-scale qualitative data concerning a rather different set of issues. The more immediate difficulty with Connell's approach is that we are thrown back on the empirical dimension to the notion of a crisis of masculinity as well as the controversy concerning such notions as the decline of patriarchy.

Kimmel's evidence concerning the historical longevity of concerns relating to masculinity and indeed the masculinity in crisis thesis *per se* is more convincing (Kimmel, 1987a). In documenting the immense and indeed ongoing anxieties concerning masculinity during the turbulent history and formation of the United States, particularly pertaining to notions of the 'effeminisation' of men and rumbling concerns relating to the perceived rise in their sexual ambiguity, Kimmel argues that the so-called contemporary crisis of masculinity goes back well over two hundred years and is, to be sure, anything but new. Similarly, Mosse argues that concerns with masculine degeneration and decadence are indeed historical constructs and that the formation of the 'manly ideal' and modernity are inextricably interlinked and mutually interdependent concepts (Mosse, 1996). Consequently: 'The manly ideal corresponded to modern society's felt need for order and progress and for a countertype that would serve to increase its self-confidence as it emerged into the modern age' (Mosse, 1996: 77). More critically, this also depended on a series of other processes including the rise of bourgeois society, the role of the body and patterns of racism and homophobia in setting up types and countertypes to the manly ideal. Fletcher also documents a much earlier perceived crisis of masculinity in Tudor and Stuart England relating to the rise of women's supposed sexual independence and voracity (Fletcher, 1995). The sense of repeating echoes concerning the 'threat from women' or the 'implosion' of gender differences is strong here and worthy of more investigation and synthesis.

The psychological approach, however, makes much of the perceived emotional crisis of masculinity. Primary within this is the role of psychotherapy and indeed the perspectives of psychotherapists on masculinity. Of principal importance here is the work of Roger Horrocks whose book *Masculinity in Crisis: Myths, Fantasies, Realities* attempts both to document the empirical realities and to theorise the fundamental tenets of the masculinity in crisis thesis (Horrocks, 1994). Underpinning this, though, is his concern with men's emotional difficulties or what he calls male autism:

> I have found in my work that in fact many men are haunted by feelings of emptiness, impotence and rage. They feel abused, unrecognised by modern society. While manhood offers compensations and prizes, it can also bring with it emotional autism, emptiness and despair.
>
> (Horrocks, 1994: 1)

Ultimately, then, we are on the familiar terrain of masculinity premised on emotional repression. In addition, however, Horrocks seeks to provide a theoretical overview of work on masculinities and then to consider more empirical evidence of the perceived crisis of masculinity. In so doing he draws on an eclectic range of sources including Freud and Marxism, Robert Bly and repeated reference to D. H. Lawrence, as well as a diversity of topics covering everything from patriarchy and violence to castration and media representations of masculinity (Bly, 1991). Perhaps not surprisingly, Horrocks' work often suffers not only from lack of coherence but also from his frequent collapses into personal eulogiums. For example, his penultimate chapter is purely autobiographical, going into the author's upbringing in Lancashire and commenting: 'How rich it is to be a man, how difficult, how confusing' (Horrocks, 1994: 181). Well, quite. The difficulty here, however, is that Horrocks' scattershot of issues and perspectives is often more controversial than it is convincing. Consequently, his consideration of men's violence as being socially and psychically constructed is well meaning, yet he ends up hoisting himself with his own petard in arguing that Peter Sutcliffe's activities are explained merely through reference to the inadequacies of his father.

Rather similar difficulties beset Anthony Clare's book _On Men: Masculinity in Crisis_ (Clare, 2000). As a psychotherapist, Clare attempts to critique the literature on male aggression and testosterone and then takes on a kind of psychological explanation similar to the men in crisis thesis previously developed in the work of Horrocks:

> The origin of so much male anger, rage and violence lies within the very way in which we conceptualise ourselves as men and women and the very way we negotiate the difficulties and obstacles of human love and hate.
>
> (Clare, 2000: 37)

Clare then launches into an assault on the usual range of suspects: men's health, the impact of divorce on the family and men, men's suicide, the lack of social support for men and the problems of balancing work and home life commitments. Of particular concern is his notion that fatherhood is increasingly in danger of redundancy due to media misrepresentation of men as monsters as much as to men themselves. Moreover, he concludes that 'At the heart of the crisis in masculinity is a problem with the reconciliation of the private and the public, the intimate and the impersonal, the emotional and the rational' (Clare, 2000: 212). Clare's perspective centres on a perceived dualism between the public and the private on which masculinity, and indeed gender, is often predicated. Of particular significance here is the way in which this public–private division is configured in relation to masculinity more specifically or, to put it more simply, the problem for masculinity and men becomes precisely the difficulty of reconciling public and private needs, or career success and aspiration with emotional warmth and intimacy. This tension does of course exist for women, yet successful femininity is perhaps less predicated on one *or* the other and centres on the difficult path of *combining* both, albeit often deeply problematical. Conversely, the perceived problem for men is precisely the sense that successful public masculinity and private happiness cannot be combined as they are quite literally antithetical parts of masculine identity and practice. The frequent lack of state – let alone commercial – support for working fathers is Clare's prime example here. Of critical importance, however, is the sense in which this entire psychological perspective on masculinity in crisis has become something of a media friendly invention beloved by daytime TV and promoted through the worlds of cod psychology or psychotherapeutically and or religiously informed self-help books that are now becoming legion. Moreover, much of the terrain exposed by these authors starts to blur into that of the new so-called men's movements and literatures concerning men's responses to second-wave feminism (see Chapter 2).

The inadequacies of the historical and psychological perspectives on the question of a crisis of masculinity lead us to consider more theoretical work and, in particular, more poststructural perspectives. The poststructural approach to the crisis of masculinity is premised primarily on extending the logic of social constructionist theory onto a more philosophical, if not existential, terrain. Of central significance here is the work of John MacInnes provocatively titled *The End of Masculinity* (MacInnes, 1998). At the core of MacInnes's perspective is the idea that masculinity is not only socially constructed but is – as it were – an 'invention' of modernity that is now increasingly becoming obsolete. This leads MacInnes into considerable discussion of both seventeenth- and eighteenth-century philosophy, particularly the work of contract theorists such as Thomas Hobbes and Rousseau, as well as the construction of gender difference under modernity more widely. In addition a recurrently posited idea here is that 'sexual genesis', or the formation and construction of sexual difference, is confused with – or imploded into – 'sexual difference' *per se*. This in turn rests on two fairly controversial assertions: first, that 'modernity systematically undermines patriarchy'; and second, that gender is 'an ideology people use in modern societies to imagine the existence of differences between men and women on the basis of their sex where in fact there are none' (MacInnes, 1998: 1). Apart ti-essentialism implied here, the more debateable point to which such assertions, though provocative, are ..ole, for which MacInnes invokes the philosophy of social ..∪ι, arguing that the rise of modernity rendered an understanding of sexual difference problematic on the basis of the fact that people were now increasingly understood as fundamentally equal. Thus modernity, and the Enlightenment more particularly, in challenging the 'naturalness' of sexual difference and inequality – previously seen to be ascribed purely on the basis of family and kinship – opened up a new problematic of gender inequality that remains unsolved both by contract theorists and by more contemporary feminists and masculinity theorists. Thus, in turning to the question of a crisis of masculinity, MacInnes argues:

> This is because the whole idea that men's natures can be understood in terms of their 'masculinity' arose out of a 'crisis' for all men: the fundamental incompatibility between the core principles of modernity that all human beings are essentially equal (regardless of their sex) and the core tenet of patriarchy that men are naturally superior to women and thus destined to rule over them.
>
> (MacInnes, 1998: 11)

Thus, there is within more contemporary culture a contradiction, or at least an irreconcilable tension, in our understanding of gender: namely that men and women are the same socially and therefore equal and that they remain naturally or fundamentally different and therefore unequal. The former idea is the outcome of modernity and the philosophy of contract while the latter notion is the legacy of the ongoing history of patriarchy, in itself seen as originally premised on the idea of natural difference and the superiority of men. MacInnes then goes on to interrogate a range of theorists including contemporary feminists such as Pateman and Rubin, as well as the more long-standing tradition of Freud and Hobbes, arguing that there is much unfinished business within all of these theorists' works (Pateman, 1988; Rubin, 1975).

MacInnes also considers the crisis of masculinity specifically in his third chapter, where he reiterates his earlier points concerning the confusion of sexual genesis with sexual difference and asserts that masculinity is essentially a fluid category that cannot be properly grasped or defined. Thus, masculinity the concept *per se* is in perpetual crisis. The increasing lay and academic recognition of the social and historical construction of masculinity leads to a sense in which it is seen to evaporate or at least become more unstable. More fundamentally, however, MacInnes argues that the very 'material forces' of modernity undermine the notion of sexual difference and with it masculinity's already precarious status. Thus, much of what follows is then premised on the ideas of the perceived 'feminisation' of employment, the achievements of women within contemporary societies, moves towards legislative equality for the sexes, and the death of the ideology of the bread-winner. Consequently, he concludes: 'It is a bad time to be a man, compared to the supremacy men have enjoyed in the past' (MacInnes, 1998: 55).

There are a number of problems with the approach to the subject of masculinity being in crisis that MacInnes adopts. First and foremost, it is hard not to feel that his assertions of the perceived frailties of masculinity premised on his exposure of the falsity of the notion of sexual difference are overstated and, while given some credence conceptually or theoretically, this is a point that requires more empirical documentation. Secondly, given MacInnes's ample deconstruction of the hegemony of masculinity at least hypothetically, it is a little ironic that he constantly invokes modernity as an equally *un*problematic if not reified concept. Thirdly, and more crucially, MacInnes' near prediction of the end of masculinity is premised not so much on the philosophy of contract as existentialism, and the terrain opened up here is not dissimilar to that considered in Chapter 6, namely masculinity and performativity, or the sense in which masculinity is quite literally no more than a costume identity to be donned, or not, at will. While MacInnes clearly recognises the untapped potential and indeed limits of many other analyses, he is a lot less convincing in seeing the implications of his own assertions. In addition – and of particular concern here – is the sense in which MacInnes continues to conflate, confuse and mix a crisis of masculinity with a crisis of men. This is a point to which I will return shortly, but first it is necessary to consider a few other variations on the theme of masculinity and poststructural theory.

Alan Petersen's work *Unmasking the Masculine* is a similarly theoretically and philosophically driven text that seeks to question the very foundations of gender and indeed masculinity (Petersen, 1998). Consequently, the notion of a crisis of masculinity is once again seen as a historical construction. Petersen draws on the work of both Badinter and Kimmel to draw parallels between the contemporary emancipation of women and feminisation of men, and previous perceived disruptions to the gender order both within pre-revolutionary France and more widely across Europe at the end of the nineteenth century (Badinter, 1995; Kimmel, 1987a). While these two earlier periods of crisis were in essence resolved or at least attenuated by cataclysmic events such as revolutions and world wars, the contemporary crisis of masculinity is more widespread. What underpins this for Petersen, like MacInnes, is 'a broader "crisis of modernity", involving a questioning of the grand synthesising of theories of the nineteenth century and the progressionist impulse of science' or, to put it more simply, postmodernity (Petersen, 1998: 21). Consequently, Petersen interrogates at length the perceived epistemology of masculinity and the move from essentialism to scepticism, drawing heavily on poststructural theory, including the work of Butler (Butler, 1990). This leads Petersen to provide an extended critique of the essentialism of the male body and the Cartesian dualisms concerning masculinity and rationality, as well as 'sex' and 'gender', and to provide support for the perceived rise of queer theory and the fall of identity politics. Underpinning all of this is Petersen's assertion that studies of masculinity have yet to properly interrogate their own epistemology or, more simply, to take seriously the work of poststructural theorists and their feminist variants in particular. This is a starting point one can easily accept, yet Petersen's analysis ends on a cliff edge without further, more empirical, documentation. While one can politically support the open-ended questioning of masculinity, premised on poststructural theory that Petersen adopts, he provides precious little in the way of answers or direction for further investigation. To return to the question of a crisis of *masculinity*, then, such perspectives tend to support such a notion in principle yet by entirely omitting its connection to the question of a crisis of *men* have precisely nowhere to run with it.

This tends to return us to the question of sexual politics, and the perceived crisis of masculinity's relationship to it, a point explored more fully in the work of Arthur Brittan (1989). In *Masculinity and Power*, Brittan seeks to question where the social construction of masculinity, and indeed the recognition of a plurality of masculinities, takes us in terms of sexual politics. In recognising the apparent fluidity of masculinities in concept and practice alike, Brittan is keen to assert the continuity and perhaps even fixity of masculinity as an ideology of power and domination, for which he coins the term 'masculinism', arguing: 'Masculinism is the ideology that justifies and naturalizes male domination' (Brittan, 1989: 4). This leads him to interrogate the naturalness, and moreover the ideological justification, of masculine identity, masculine sexuality and men's violence, prior to attacking the question of masculinity and crisis in his final chapter. In asserting that 'a crisis of masculinity is only a crisis in so far as the "relations of gender" are perceived and experienced as problematic by a significant proportion of men' he effectively inverts the analysis of Petersen and others into a more pragmatic notion where there cannot be a crisis of masculinity without a crisis of men (Brittan, 1989: 181). Though Brittan accepts that such crisis tendencies exist for some men in some contexts some of the time, he is unconvinced that any wider crisis of masculinity exists, suggesting that: 'what we are witnessing today is some kind of "legitimation crisis"' (Brittan, 1989: 184). In supporting this and his ideological thesis more generally, Brittan returns to Connell's notion of hegemonic masculinity, linking it to his own notion of masculinism and arguing that this effectively defuses any wider crisis tendencies. Consequently, in concluding, he re-endorses the need for feminist-informed praxis:

> The real crisis of masculinity is that men have come to believe that the distinction between reason and desire, the intellect and the body, the masculine and the feminine, is not only real, but necessary as well. The tragedy is that we have not really understood the connection between the personal and the political, between sexuality and power.
>
> (Brittan, 1989: 204)

In sum, what we are left with here is limited evidence for the perceived crisis of *men* and far more – yet entirely theoretical and purely conceptual – support for the notion of a crisis of *masculinity*.

Conclusions: Crisis, what crisis?

It would seem slightly odd that the crisis of masculinity thesis should at once be both so pervasive and yet so unsubstantiated. I have considered this thesis both from the perspective of the experiences of men and the concept of masculinity and at the level of empiricism as well as theory. Much of the support in either case concerns, either explicitly or implicitly, what is itself often an outdated notion of the male sex role paradigm that is in turn seen as undermined by, or muddied in with, the feminine sex role and femininity, or – in its latest invocation – increasingly exposed as pure artifice. Though there is some evidence to support the notion of demographically or geographically specific 'crisis tendencies' for some men, there is very little to endorse any overall masculinity in crisis thesis other than to say that masculinity is perhaps partially constituted *as* crisis. In short, there is no crisis of masculinity as it is commonly portrayed – would, perhaps, that there were.

2 Femenism
Men, masculinity and feminism

It is arguable that the entire canon of critical men's studies of masculinity constitutes little more than a reaction to second-wave feminism. From the 1970s onwards, many men working in political and academic circles alike were exposed to, if not forced to confront, feminism and indeed feminists whether in their working, academic, political or personal lives. Simultaneously, the rise of small networks of men's consciousness-raising groups seeking to address some of these issues and perhaps more fundamentally to explore what it meant to be a man galvanised many men's early enquiries into masculinity more academically (Farrell, 1974; Tolson, 1977; Seidler, 1991). Equally, the growth of gay liberation led some men to question further the foundations of white, Western – and straight – masculinities. As Tim Carrigan and his colleagues pointed out all too painfully, however, any such alliance between gay and straight male activists around masculinity often proved short-lived and woefully inadequate to the task of addressing the heterosexism and homophobia of many men's studies, let alone men themselves (Carrigan, Connell and Lee, 1985).

Nonetheless, the embattled relationship between second-wave feminism and men's studies of masculinity was to prove more resilient and indeed came to inform much of the development of more contemporary men's studies of masculinity (Connell, 1987, 1995; Hearn, 1987; Hearn and Morgan, 1990; Pease, 2000; Stoltenberg, 2000). Despite this, conflicts and anxieties concerning resources, and particularly the potential depletion or undermining of women's studies, were never very far from the surface and were increasingly addressed head on as time progressed (Canaan and Griffen, 1990; Segal, 1990). The reaction of many men to second-wave feminism remained divided and in fact became even more split, a fracture that deepened during the 1980s and 1990s and led to the development of various men's movements, often implicitly and sometimes overtly opposed to the advancement of second-wave feminism, particularly in the United States in the wake of the rise of the mythopoetic and similar men's movements (Bly, 1991). As a result, a highly entrenched dualism emerged within men's studies of masculinity between what one might call a backlash *against* feminism and the lashed backs *of* feminism.

Similarly, the rise of a new crop of men's lifestyle magazines from the 1980s alongside the iconography of the New Man and later their invention of the New Lad in the 1990s has led to considerable debate about their sexual political implications for both women and men, particularly in relation to the near exponential growth of 'laddism' centred – at face value at least – on a negative reaction against second-wave feminism and the New Man (Benwell, 2003; Chapman and Rutherford, 1988; Jackson *et al.*, 2001). Accordingly, this is a chapter with two halves: the first considers responses to feminism in terms of the politics of men's movements and their critique. The second discusses the significance of the new so-called 'men's magazines' and the iconography of the New Man and the New Lad as potential responses to second-wave feminism.

From backlash to lashed backs and back again: Robert Bly and the politics of men's movements

Robert Bly's book *Iron John: a Book about Men* was, relatively speaking at least, a runaway bestseller in the early 1990s and in the United States in particular (Bly, 1991). The question that has beset academics in the field of men's studies ever since, is why. As an almost wholly un-academic text centred on a reinterpretation of ancient folklore and myth mixed in with an adaptation of Jungian theory and the ideas of Maria von Franz, it was clearly wholly at odds with the entire current of sociologically informed and second-wave feminist-derived men's studies of the 1980s (von Franz, 1981). Indeed, at the end of the book Bly denounces the way '(p)owerful sociological and religious forces have acted in the West to favour the trimmed, the sleek, the cerebral, the non-instinctive, and the bald' (Bly, 1991: 247–8). His entire premise is clearly anti-sociological and arguably anti-feminist, although he dismisses this claim in his preface. Bly's starting point is to identify a certain crisis of masculinity or, to put it another way, the grief of men and modern man. Thus he starts:

> We are living at an important and fruitful moment now, for it is clear to men that the images of adult manhood given by the popular culture are worn out; a man can no longer depend on them.
>
> (Bly, 1991: ix)

And he continues:

> The grief in men has been increasing steadily since the start of the Industrial Revolution and the grief has reached a depth now that cannot be ignored.
>
> (Bly, 1991: x)

Thus, one might therefore expect an historical analysis of changing forms of masculinity, which admittedly one does get in the most generalised and unsubstantiated form imaginable, or some kind of documentation of men's grief through interviews or use of secondary sources. However, what Bly gives us instead is an 'initiatory path in eight stages' centred on his translation and application of the 1820 Brothers' Grimm story of Iron Hans or Iron John. The story tells the tale of a young boy's encounter with a local Wild Man that leads him, rather in parallel with the notion of the prodigal son, to make a series of valiant achievements of manhood, though this is often far more implicit in the story than Bly's interpretation would have us believe. He then returns to take his place with the King and claim the princess as his wife and requires that the Wild Man be freed from his original ostracised status as a pariah. Bly's work otherwise forms a series of chapters which unpack the story and then adapt it into a more modern-day notion of initiation. The underlying theme is the need for modern men to reclaim their Wild Man, 'who has examined his wound [and] resembles a Zen priest, a shaman, or woodsman' and therefore is distinct from Savage Man, who motivates the 'dark side' of masculinity exemplified in expressions of violence and war (Bly, 1991: x). Lurking underneath all this is a perception of modern men as, in essence, emasculated, passive, lacking in self-esteem and out of touch with nature and their instincts. This in turn is linked strongly to the undermining of the father–son bond and men's inability to stand up against the demands of modern women. The motor driving this shift is the industrial revolution, which creates fatherhood as Saturnine, and feeds the growth of the greedy entrepreneur, the reckless settler and the 1950s model of the provider (perceived by Bly as a 'bluff') as more contemporary and acceptable forms of masculinity, which in turn dissolve into the Soft Man in touch with his feminine side. None of this exists separately from Bly's participation in, and development and leadership of, the mythopoetic men's movement, itself centred on consciousness-raising, vague notions of therapy centred on story-telling, and all male gatherings at retreats, Wild Man weekends and similar 'back to basics' types of events involving men bonding with each other and living with nature in the outdoors. In addition, more theoretically, most of Bly's analysis centres on a plasticised hotchpotch of Jungian psychoanalytic theory with a dash of Reich and even a dose of Gurdjieff thrown in. The concepts of unconscious archetypes, the animus–anima, shadow personalities and the move from the mother's side to the father's side lurk in various confused and implicit forms under the surface.

Despite the reader's initial tendency towards laughing disparagement, there is a very immediate sense here in which Bly is clearly appealing to a not entirely mythic sense of 'outdoorsy', particularly North American, masculinity associated with everything from the Wild West to going hunting. It should also be noted that Bly has received extensive support elsewhere and other North American writers, including Warren Farrell, a former men's liberationist, have similarly spoken out about the perceived crisis of contemporary North American manhood and masculinity, often linked to a wider critique of second-wave feminism or the need for healing and psychotherapy

(Farrell, 1993). Farrell's recent works seek increasingly to expose men's feelings of powerlessness, while Goldberg in *The Inner Male* asserts the importance of fundamental gendered differences in the emotional make-up of men and women and provides a series of case studies of the emotional damage to men by liberated women (Goldberg, 1976). Sam Keen similarly attempts to weld such assertions of emotional damage and Jungian mythopoetic concepts linked to wider environmental and political concerns relating to the welfare of the planet (Keen, 1991).

It should be pointed out, however, that there are variations both within and between these perspectives. For example, Farrell's *The Myth of Male Power* (1993) – while drawing on Bly's *Iron John* for some of its inspiration – is rather different. As a former member of the board of directors for NOW (National Organization for Women), Farrell's work is both more heavily based on a more sociological understanding of sex roles and more heavily and directly premised on a – very negative – response to second-wave feminism. Farrell's overwhelming concern is with the idea that men have become victims or what he consistently calls 'the disposable sex'. Fundamental in this is the idea that while feminism has benefited and liberated women, it has done so at the expense of men. Where he differs from Bly and the mythopoetic men's movement, however, is in arguing that men need to, as it were, 'catch up' with women rather than return to some prior state of masculinity prior to feminism. Thus, while *The Myth of Male Power* is a self-defined 'self-improvement' book like *Iron John*, Farrell claims 'it loves women in a different way' (Farrell, 1993: 14). Interestingly, Farrell invokes the same Jungian influenced concepts here arguing that: 'Feminism articulated the shadow side of men and the light side of women. It neglected the shadow side of women and the light side of men' (Farrell, 1993: 15). Like Bly, Farrell also advocates the role of support groups for men and sees men getting together with each other to discuss their feelings as the primary way forward.

However, the main thrust of Farrell's work is to launch into an assault on the second-wave feminist-inspired 'myth' of male power. Within this are a series of assertions, complete with comic book style illustrations, of how this myth operates to the detriment of men. Number one on the list is war which is seen as 'male-killing', and Farrell argues that women should also be on the front line when wars occur. A second set of concerns relates to men's lower life expectancy and the significant gender skew in suicide rates, which Farrell sees simply as an indicator of men's powerlessness. Similar arguments relate to the question of the perceived invisibility of men as victims of violence. More controversially, Farrell then seeks to expose men's lack of economic power, asserting that they are exploited through the spending obligation gap, for example in paying for dinner and playing the role of provider more generally, and the ways in which men are seen to work more hours than women outside the home. He also makes more familiar points concerning men's lack of entitlement under divorce law. Most controversial of all, however, is his assertion that men have essentially become modern-day 'niggers' or slaves who are in no uniform way oppressors to the oppressed, namely women. Though these claims are controversial to say the least, Farrell seeks to link them to a more sociological notion of changing sex roles, arguing that Stage I sex roles, centred on more traditional patterns of ascription and the sexual division of labour linked to the need for production and survival, have been supplanted by Stage II sex roles centred on issues of individuality, achievement, choice, openness, self-expression and mutual love. Farrell stirs into this concoction the idea that although women have begun to reap the benefits of Stage II men are still stuck in Stage I.

What is interesting, or at least significant, here is the sense in which Farrell uses and invokes, or perhaps more accurately *distorts*, wider and more sociological concerns relating to rising individualism into an assault on second-wave feminism. More specifically, there is an implicit link with the more recent work of Giddens on high modernity (Giddens, 1991). Also lurking under the surface are some slightly more valid claims concerning the misrepresentation of men or patterns of gendered representation more widely. His exposé of the media coverage of the Tyson trial, for example, as effectively eclipsing the role of men as carers and workers such as fire fighters in its gory obsession with the 'monstrosity' of Tyson as a male rapist, is telling and worthy of more sustained investigation. Yet this is not what we get. In his aggressively toned and argued conclusion, Farrell casually dismisses the critique of Bly's men's movement, stating baldly that 'Men were socialized to save women, not blame women' and concluding: 'Not to worry' (Farrell, 1993: 360). He then asserts that the real challenge is to 'care enough about men' to liberate them from what he calls 'the death professions', namely war mongering and combat and, conversely, to militate against the battering of men by their wives and to give them more rights over their children. In addition, he then argues that men need more outlets and spaces in which to express their feelings, and that we all need to stop seeing men as 'success objects' (Farrell, 1993: 370–371).

Perhaps not surprisingly, the reaction of many of those working with more critical and sociological studies of men and masculinity has been both bemused and hostile. By way of example, Connell provides a particularly stinging critique and visceral dismissal of Bly's work and indeed the entire mythopoetic men's movement. The main thrust of Connell's analysis is that Bly is unoriginal, arguing that '*Iron John* has been so widely thought a striking novelty that it is worth noticing how much ground it shared with earlier Books About Men', by which he means the earliest men's studies centred on the problems of the male sex role, often linked in practice to the rise of consciousness-raising groups. More importantly he asserts that Bly's 'blind spots – race, sexuality, cultural difference, class – are much the same' (Connell, 1995: 209). Apart from the fact that nearly *all* critical men's studies of masculinity are guilty to some degree on these counts, Connell's real axe to grind is one of political difference as he asserts that 'the main tendency of masculinity therapy is to replace a politics of reform rather than support it'

(Connell, 1995: 210). Connell is also unflinching in his critique of the work of Farrell in particular, seeing him, in essence, as a traitor to the original cause of second-wave feminism of which Farrell was once a part. This is, I think, a slight misreading of Farrell's early work, and similar proponents of what I have called the first wave of men's studies, as Farrell's ideas in his later work are for the most part consistent with his – and others' – critique of the male sex role as limiting to men (see Introduction). The real source of Connell's ire against Bly, Farrell, Goldberg and others is that he perceives them, perhaps correctly, as unilaterally against the pro-feminist and anti-sexist stance taken by Connell, Hearn, and Kimmel, to mention only some (Connell, 1987, 1995; Hearn, 1987; Kimmel, 1987a). That said, Connell does make the rather more considered point that any movement centred on male solidarity runs the risk of siding itself up *against* other groups, and more specifically women's groups, if it does not more consciously try to work *with* them, even if this is unintentional. This is in some senses a more valid point to make, yet it rests on the unproven assumption that men's and women's politics *can* work alongside each without conflict and that this is an unprob-lematic project, a claim that I wish to consider shortly.

One of the more thorough-going critiques of the work of Robert Bly and his followers in various men's movements is provided by Kimmel and Kaufman (Kimmel and Kaufman, 1994). Having noted the popularity of Bly's book in topping the United States bestseller list for over 35 weeks in 1991, they also note that '(t)he movement has certainly come in for its share of ridicule and derision' (Kimmel and Kaufman, 1994: 260). This is a point which leads other authors such as Whitehead to question the extent to which these new men's movements constitute any kind of threat to feminism, given what he calls their 'increasingly freakish quality' (Whitehead, 2002: 69). Kimmel and Kaufman then proceed to link the rise of the men's movement to a supposed crisis of masculinity linked to wider structural changes and their psychological impact on white middle-class heterosexual men. Bly's work is then deconstructed and severely critiqued on four counts: first, for its reconstruction of essentialist understandings of masculinity; secondly, for its inversion of feminist psychoanalytic theory on masculinities including the work of Chodorow and Dinnerstein; thirdly, in relation to its 'anthropological androcentrism' and 'historical hokum' or, to put it more simply, its highly selective use and indeed misuse of temporal and spatial evidence from other cultures; and fourthly, for its retreat to a lost image of boyhood and homosocial bonding. In sum, the bottom line for Kimmel and Kaufman is that Bly and the politics of the mythopoetic and similar men's movements constitute a 'flight from feminism' and a retreat from the nurturance of mothers, historical and anthropological specificity and above all responsibility for male domination, concluding that: 'Only by fighting for equality, side by side, as equals [with women], can men realize the best of what it means to be a man' (Kimmel and Kaufman, 1994: 286). This last sentence speaks volumes in invoking a notion of an alliance with second-wave feminism or a wider project of equality that requires, to say the least, further explication. More particularly, there remains a lack of any wholesale questioning of exactly what feminist project these authors claim to ally themselves with and why. It also raises the question of what exactly constitutes the difference between a group of predominantly white hetero-sexual middle-class middle-American men struggling to define masculinity in the wake of second wave feminist-derived critical studies of men and masculinity and a group of predominantly white heterosexual middle-class middle-American men struggling to define masculinity within a mythopoetic or any other men's movement. In sum, in savaging the blind spots of Robert Bly and his followers, his critics also sometimes inadvertently start to reveal their own.

A slightly different perspective is provided by Fred Pfeil in his cultur-ally informed work *White Guys: Studies in Postmodern Difference and Domination* (Pfeil, 1995). In a chapter humorously titled 'Guerrillas in the Mist', Pfeil links the North American mythopoetic men's movement to wider developments in United States international politics leading up to the Gulf War in particular. Like Connell, he notes an historic shift from a more pro-feminist to a more anti-feminist stance with the men's movement, yet sees this as the outcome of a growing interaction of contingent social events such as the Reagan era with overarching archetypes typified in Jungian-informed perspectives. This is in turn also seen to hinge on the shifting sands of articulating the relationship between the private and the public world in relation to masculinity. Where Pfeil differs from Connell and others is in his critique of second-wave feminism and his questioning of the direction of left-feminist political cultures, citing 'the failure of many versions of feminist theory . . . to allow for the possibility of any more or other than a single, unitary mode of masculinity in a given society at a given time (or, in some of the more extreme variants, anywhere on the planet, anytime' (Pfeil, 1995: 222). Thus Pfeil at least implicitly makes the point that the second wave feminist-informed analyses of masculinity fail to articulate the experience of men or acknowledge that 'redefining masculinity is men's work' while still recognising the difficulties of patriarchal influences and complicity (Pfeil, 1995: 228).

As I think is clear by now, most of the preceding critique of Bly's work and the rise of men's movements more widely is centred on the perception that they are anti-feminist if not anti-women. Though I do not necessarily want to question its validity, there are a number of problems with this assertion: first, though many of Bly's ideas are unsubstantiated and clearly motivated by purely subjective experiences of disempowerment that are indeed as mythical as they are real, this does not necessarily constitute an anti-feminist backlash so much as something plainly and simply at odds with at least some aspects of some more structurally focused feminist projects; second, though the experiences and perceptions of many working within the men's movements may well be falsifiable if not totally wrong-headed, they are nonetheless in some sense real and not so easily disregarded; and third, it is at least arguable that all men's studies of masculinity are to some extent inevitably at odds with feminism and indeed to do their job properly perhaps even *should* be. As some feminists have pointed out explicitly, the rise of critical studies of masculinity, if not necessarily in direct conflict with second-wave feminism, certainly does not make for a happy marriage with second-wave feminism, not least due to the potential divisions of academic resources (Canaan and Griffen, 1990). There is also now an influential collection of feminist work considering the relationship of critical studies of men and masculinities with feminism, displaying a wide range of responses and indeed *feminisms* as forms of interrogation that are not so easily assumed or assimilated as they are here (Gardiner, 2002; Jardine and Smith, 1987; Segal, 1990).

All of this leads to me to provide a rather different form of critique of the work of Bly and the men's movements' attending it. There are perhaps three main problems with the work of Robert Bly and his followers, whether inside or outside of his 'mythopoetic men's movement': first, it is a perspective almost entirely dependent on psychoanalytic, if not necessarily Jungian, theory and therapy. Whether intentionally or not, this has the consequence of re-essentialising masculinity into some kind of unconscious or at least subconscious essence that has to be, on occasions quite literally, *unearthed*. This not only renders masculinity problematic politically in terms of removing it from any kind of wider social, economic or cultural context to which it may be responsible, but more sociologically it also makes many of the claims made by these theorists impossible to demonstrate in any meaningful way empirically. Within the dimensions of the mythopoetic men's movement, masculinity simply becomes an *a priori* assumption, no more and no less. Secondly, and following on from this, its chief weakness is its lack of attention to any questions of social or historical or cultural variation. Asian men, black men, gay men, working-class men, aristocratic men and indeed white middle-class North American men are all thrown together into one great pot of masculine wounding that is seen to originate with the industrial revolution. To boil down all of these highly significant cultural and histori-cal variations into one singular conception of masculinity is quite simply nonsensical. More theoretically this perhaps follows on from some of the problematic dimensions of Jungian theory in setting up universal archetypes that tend to elide any wider cultural interrogation. A third problem is that such an approach politically is at best laughable, contradictory or suspect and at worst downright reactionary. Bly repeatedly slides around the slippery distinction of the 'wild man' versus the 'savage man' and just what defines the 'dark' side of men as distinct from anything else that is 'deep' and, as it were, 'hairy'. The issue of sexuality is particularly revealing here, as Bly admits that he addresses heterosexual men but does not exclude homosexual men, a piece of doublespeak in itself, and then conjures up a vision of return-ing to an all-male untamed masculine bonding, initiation and celebration of hairy-chestedness that would see many gay men salivating at the thought and which indeed shows marked parallels with gay male leather culture in particular (Mains, 1984).

That said, the work of Bly and his followers, and moreover its very popularity, demonstrates something further, namely that there *is* a more personal problem with masculine identity for at least some men. Some men are indeed suffering, whether through lack of prospects for themselves or feelings of being left behind in a race they have no control over, some or even many men do feel powerless and some men are living with women who demand too much of them or who do better at work and earn more than they do for reasons they cannot understand, and they do get confused and it does hurt and they do feel guilty for wanting to be sexually aggressive or even just getting erections on the wrong occasions and they do get laughed at and they don't know how to articulate their feelings, and they don't know how to get help and they don't know what to do about any of it and – more particularly – little, if any, of the barrage of pro-feminist books on the subject of masculinities offers much engagement with this. While various authors offer small and qualitative empirical studies centred on interviews and dis-cussions with small groups of men in differing positions, these are frequently utilised as adding grist to an already given mill. Examples include Connell's empirical work in *Masculinities* and Hearn's similarly qualitative study of men's sexual violence in *The Violences of Men* (Connell, 1995; Hearn, 1998). In each case, the men's experiences and stories are only partially told and then held up to judgement as examples of good, indifferent or often 'bad' male attitudes or behaviours. It is hardly surprising, then, that some men are turning to therapy and finding solace in some kind of 'men's movement' as, whatever their shortcoming and failings – and they are many and massive – they are arenas in which men are at least partially listened to and they are at least to some extent predicated on the very real articulation of men's often deeply felt and personal experiences. In short, it gives some men and indeed some men's experiences a *voice*. Thus, though Bly and his followers may offer wholly the wrong answers, the questions they raise remain pertinent and not so easily dismissed.

Adding further credence to this thesis is, rather ironically, the work of Susan Faludi who, in *Stiffed: the Betrayal of Modern Man*, controversially completely overturns her prior critique of the backlash against feminism to endorse the problems of men. Fundamental in this once again is the importance of men's more personal experience, and North American men's disillusionment in particular. She claims that 'If men are mythologized as the ones who *make things happen*, the how can they begin to analyse what is *happening to them?*' (Faludi, 2000: 13). Faludi's mammoth work is jour-nalistically informed through a series of discussions and interviews with North American men, juxtaposed with her reinterpretations of North American history and studies of North American culture. Particular concerns tend to centre on the decline of manufacturing, rising unemployment and crime, the Vietnam War, the Waco massacre, and the increasing importance of men's empowerment. Faludi's exposure of American manhood 'under siege' is lurid and heartfelt, yet ultimately seems to peddle a myth as much as it unpacks one, namely the idea of masculinity in crisis.

Of course, on the other side of this divide are what I have called the lashed backs of second-wave feminism or those men who go so far as to actively and politically support feminism and indeed label themselves pro-feminist. There is of course something of a continuum of responses here from mild endorsement through to unquestioning servitude. At the latter end of this scale is the work of John Stoltenberg summarised in his book *Refusing To Be a Man* (Stoltenberg, 2000). In the introduction to the revised edition, Stoltenberg claims to be 'translating radical feminist ideas into a worldview and a moral identity that could be claimed and embodied unabashedly by people born with a penis' (Stoltenberg, 2000: xi). Hence, there is a near existential denouncing of masculinity, to the point of renouncing the term 'man' *per se*. Alternatively, Stoltenberg claims the label of being a radical feminist following his long-term alliance with anti-pornography campaigner Andrea Dworkin and his co-founding of the group Men Against Pornography. Starting with the dubious assertion that radical feminism was borne out of the black civil rights movement, Stoltenberg goes on to produce a series of essays on topics such as sexual justice, rape, the sexual binary, sexual objectification, pornography, war and abortion. It should be pointed out immediately that most of these essays were written as public lectures, and either were or are meant to be read aloud. His style, not unlike Dworkin's, is polemical with often scant regard for evidence or substantiation. He claims to speak to those 'men [who] have made a vow to stand beside her and not abandon her, to wholeheartedly be her ally' (Stoltenberg, 2000: 1). He then mixes and muddles the legal ethics of sexual justice with social constructionist theory, asserting on the one hand that the 'idea of the male sex is like the idea of the Aryan race' (Stoltenberg, 2000: 26), before returning to more essentialist notions on the other hand whereby 'our bodies have learned many lies. If we dare to be ruthlessly honest, we can perhaps recover the truth' (Stoltenberg, 2000: 100). What is perhaps most interesting here is the sense that Stoltenberg's writing develops an increasingly sermonising zeal and hysteria that almost starts to complement Robert Bly's counter-attempt to reclaim the deep masculine, and it is perhaps not entirely coincidental that both writers are working within a North American context that has itself historically been most directly affected by radical feminism (Bly, 1991).

A rather more reasoned consideration of the difficulties and resolutions of masculinity and feminism is found in the work of Bob Pease. In his work titled *Recreating Men* Pease takes an entirely explicit and overt stance of being pro-feminist, stating at the outset:

> I believe that men's subjectivity is crucial to gender domination and that changing the social relations of gender will necessitate the transforming

of men's subjectivities as well as changing their daily practices . . . by focusing on the subjectivities and practices of profeminist men, of whom I am one.

(Pease, 2000: 1)

Pease was active in men's consciousness-raising groups in the 1970s and co-founded the group MASA (Men Against Sexual Assault). His self-declared aims are to theorise masculinities and to enact pro-feminist political strategies. Methodologically, his analysis is strongly informed by the work of Harding and Frankenberg in developing a feminist standpoint and in grounding theorising in the experience of oppression (Harding, 1987; Frankenberg, 1993). Consequently, his work includes an empirical study of pro-feminist men's subjectivities through consciousness-raising and memory-work. Pease's analysis is also informed by the rise of poststructural and postmodern forms of feminism, which both problematise subjectivity and attempt to deconstruct any kind of unitary gendered identity. There are three sections to the work: the first covers more theoretical attempts to document the relationship of masculinity and feminism; the second is more empirically driven, showing a variety of insights into masculine subjectivities; and the third focuses on the transformation of masculinity politics. Not surprisingly, Pease is highly critical of men's movement politics for their anti-feminist stance, whether explicit or implicit. In particular, he critiques various cultures of blame, counter-blame and victimisation that he perceives as endemic in much men's movement politics. More specifically, he attacks their perspectives on violence as anti-feminist, claiming that men and women are not equals in relation to questions of violence given men's greater physical size and their dominant role in relation to domestic and sexual violence, and he endorses feminist perspectives on provocation used to justify women's violence in retaliation against men's violence. However, there is much in common here with the work of Hearn, considered critically in Chapter 3. Interestingly, Pease's analysis turns on an invocation of the work of Connell on exit politics and his undermining of hegemonic forms of masculinity and indeed Stoltenberg's strategic 'refusal' to be a man, arguing that such politics to be successful need to engage with more postmodern interrogations of subjectivity in order to destabilise masculine identity more directly. Consequently, in returning to the question of subjectivities, Pease exposes a series of considerable confusions and fragmentations within pro-feminist men's movements, let alone between straight and gay men or men and women more widely, and his final chapter on postmodern masculinity politics becomes almost wholly prescriptive.

Though such staunchly politically motivated attempts to amalgamate the critique of masculinity with feminism are perhaps to be applauded, they are nonetheless problematic on several counts. First and foremost, any attempt to weld men's studies and feminism is flawed by the very diversity of feminisms and indeed feminist projects. Without exception all of these authors and their contemporaries who similarly call themselves pro-feminist fail to articulate exactly what feminist project they support or more simply how their own work connects with it or supports feminism. The more fundamental point here is that there is no real agreement *within* feminism concerning what is pro-feminist or a feminist project, of which the current conflicts surrounding the rise of poststructural and postmodern forms of feminism are a prime example. More importantly, a second point here concerns *why* any of these men should wish to ally themselves with feminism or call themselves pro-feminist. Moreover, the oft-quoted and commonly spelled out answer that the feminist project does, or at least will, benefit men runs counter to the argument made by the same theorists that men are overwhelmingly privileged by their current relation to women and indeed older, more traditional and non-feminist forms of masculinity. Though I do not refute that some men may well see advantages for themselves as well as women in supporting feminism, the unpacking of the often contradictory motivations necessarily involved is far from satisfactory. Finally, an often telling point here is of the alliance, or lack of it, between gay men and feminism. On the face of it gay men and feminists have much in common, namely a hegemonic heterosexual male oppressor, yet as is now well documented, little such alliance exists and indeed the relationship between gay men and feminism has often been conflicting, exposing both the misogyny of some gay men and the implicit homophobia of some forms of feminism (see Chapter 5). If one is then to assume that pro-feminist men are for the most part also heterosexual men, then the question of their relationship to women becomes all the more complex and the gap left by these authors in not exposing these complexities is, frankly, huge.

The commodification of masculinities: the iconography of the New Man and the New Lad and men's lifestyle magazines

In this section, I discuss the significance of the new so-called 'men's magazines' as one potential response to second-wave feminism and, more widely, as one more contemporary vehicle for understanding masculinities. The focus is primarily, though not exclusively, on the UK and wider comparisons are drawn where appropriate. More specifically, I analyse the sense in which men's lifestyle magazines have formed the focus for the wider significance of the iconography of the New Man and the New Lad, and the extent to which these may be perceived as responses to second-wave feminism or, more simply, as part of a wider process of the commodification of masculinities.

The seemingly meteoric rise of men's lifestyle magazines in the UK has created much interest in academic and media circles alike (Benwell, 2003; Edwards, 1997; Jackson *et al.*, 2001). As measured in terms of circulation through annual Audit Bureau of Circulation (ABC) studies or readership figures through National Readership Surveys (NRS), the market for men's magazines in the UK has grown from a mere four titles in 1990, each with a circulation of well under 100,000, to more in the region of at least a dozen titles, depending on one's definition of a 'men's magazine', with top sellers such as *FHM (For Him Magazine)* hitting circulation figures of 500,000, although there seems to be some evidence to suggest these figures are now falling (Beynon, 2002; Benwell, 2003). Only two titles – *Arena* launched in 1986 and *GQ* launched in 1988 – existed in the 1980s. The accuracy of such figures, particularly those related to readerships, is open to question but the overall expansion of this particular market has been undeniable.

To reinforce its dominance, the market has also tended to subdivide into health-oriented titles such as *Men's Health* and *Men's Fitness*, up-market glossies such as *GQ*, *Esquire* and *Arena*, and the slightly more down-market yet nonetheless consumerist world of the re-vamped *FHM*, *Front*, *Loaded* and *Maxim*. Similarly, many of the titles exist in differing formats across the world. *FHM*, *Loaded* and *Maxim* now exist in markedly similar form in the United States, while *Esquire* and *GQ* also remain true to their older North American origins and retain a distinctive, and for the most part more conservative and corporate if not necessarily more status conscious, dimension. Most recently, the UK has seen the launch of two weekly titles – *Nuts* and *Zoo* – that rework the theme of the New Lad yet again.

What is questionable here of course is what all this actually *means*. Though in no way wishing to take away from what is clearly an easily quantifiable impact, there are certain initial qualifying factors to take into account when assessing the importance of men's magazines. First, men's magazines have a longer history than is often suggested, as *Playboy* and *Esquire* for example date back to the 1950s in the USA. In addition, what one might call 'men's interest' magazines including titles for motoring, hobbies and pornography generally have a far longer history still (Osgerby, 2001). Second, the rapid expansion of men's lifestyle magazines is in some ways a peculiarly English phenomenon. Other parts of Europe and the USA have a history of producing lifestyle magazines for men, such as the French *Vogue Hommes*, and have not developed the same exponential cult of 'laddism' as in the UK. Third, this expansion also depends on a question of definition. While magazines organised around 'masculine' themes such as cars, technology or sports may be classifiable as 'men's magazines', or perhaps more aptly as men's interest magazines, the current crop of men's magazines has more to do with the rise of a whole new genre of lifestyle titles in the 1980s such as *i-D* and, most famously, *The Face* launched in 1984. The new men's magazines, then, are precisely men's *lifestyle* titles as opposed to men's *interest* magazines.

Questions of definition notwithstanding, what remains constant and interesting here is the ongoing promotion of magazines through which men can affirm their sense of masculinity without necessarily recognising or confronting it. Historically, this was achieved most simply and directly by constructing the magazines around assumed 'men's interests' rather than men themselves – whether cars, women or sport – while never fully addressing men as consumers or consciously acknowledging their role in constructing a masculinity for them. The problem for the new crop of men's style titles in the UK from the 1980s onwards lay precisely in trying to square the circle of producing a 'men's magazine' that somehow wasn't one at all. In short, 'men's magazines', past and present, have often been *for* men but rarely *about* men, other than male celebrities.

Men's lifestyle magazines are most fundamentally cultural texts and, as such, any analysis of their significance in terms of masculinity is essentially an analysis of representation. As is now well known, sociological and cultural understandings of representation have grown almost exponentially in recent decades (see, for example, Hall, 1997). When applying this analysis to the expansion of men's style magazines in the UK several important points arise. First, the question of supply and demand is contentious, as it is not necessarily clear that men's style magazines were *either* merely commercial initiatives in the market place *or* solely something men were demanding or wanted. Second, it is difficult to determine what they mean for the men who read them, who may take them very seriously or alternatively view them ironically. Third, and as a result, their importance for an understanding of contemporary masculinities is therefore tentative and contingent rather than demonstrative and fixed.

This situation is complicated further when one also considers that most of the early literature on men's magazines was theoretically led rather than research-driven and yet tends to postulate a series of fairly grandiose points related to the sexual politics of the 1980s and 1990s. These include: first, the notion that men's style magazines have arisen due to various cultural and historical developments and, in particular, entrepreneurial and commercial initiatives rather than as any direct result of shifts in sexual politics; second, that the images presented are often pluralistic and polyvalent in their importance, with the implication that the magazines tend to blur various boundaries relating to masculinity, particularly in relation to sexuality; and third, that men's style magazines are then understood most fully as part of a series of wider developments in visual or consumer culture (Chapman and Rutherford, 1988; Mort, 1996; Nixon, 1996). This literature provides important understandings of men's style magazines as a *cultural phenomenon*. What tends to remain lacking is an engagement with them more as representations or *cultural texts*. In particular, the absence of analysis of the audience or the consumption patterns of men themselves is problematic precisely because it tends to assume a pre-given set of meanings. Conversely, however, an analysis of men's style magazines as cultural texts alone runs the risk of missing their significance as a far wider cultural phenomenon. The key difficulty that remains is precisely that of trying to reconcile the two.

The prevailing literature on men's lifestyle magazines has also been conducted almost entirely within the framework of the iconography of the New Man and the New Lad. As I have stated previously, and as John Beynon has also elaborated more recently, the New Man has been and perhaps continues to be an oddly dualistic or two-sided phenomenon, being about nurturance and caring on the one hand, as in the infamous imagery of men holding babies, or narcissism and grooming on the other, as in the endless advertising campaigns for everything from Levi's jeans and Calvin Klein underwear to Clinique skin care and an endless array of aftershaves (Beynon, 2002; Edwards, 1997). Perhaps not surprisingly, most of the more academic literature on the New Man slithers between these two poles of sexual politics and sexual marketing, with varying outcomes. Chapman and Rutherford's pioneering collection *Male Order: Unwrapping Masculinity* primarily framed its analysis in terms of responses to feminism yet ended up mostly admitting that the development was far from positive (Chapman and Rutherford, 1988). The journalist Jon Savage similarly wrote that the New Man was simply the same old wolf in designer clothes (Savage, 1996). Frank Mort's *Cultures of Consumption* (1996) considered the phenomenon of the New Man in terms of cultural history while Sean Nixon's analysis similarly centred more on developments in visual culture and the construction of masculinities at the level of advertising itself, which in turn was often facilitated through the expansion of flexible specialisation in mass production (Nixon, 1996). My own work challenged some of these analyses, particularly in relation to the supposed pluralism of some of the imagery, yet it remained an analysis of men's lifestyle magazines in relation to a much wider set of developments in fashion, consumer culture and masculinity (Edwards, 1997).

The New Lad, and with it 'laddism', are seen to develop with the launch of *Loaded* magazine in 1994. The magazine carried the tag line 'for men who should know better' and, as is now well documented, was a full-on slap in the face to both the New Man and the journalism of preceding titles such as *Arena* and *GQ* (Benwell, 2003; Beynon, 2002; Edwards, 1997). The magazine quickly outsold its competitors and spawned a series of imitators including *Front*, *Maxim* and – most famously – the revamped *FHM*. While the New Man was apparently a fairly *pro*-feminist, if still narcissistic, invention, the New Lad represented a return to reactionary *pre*-feminist values of sex, sport and drinking and the relatively male-only worlds of pubs, pornography and football. It is perhaps not surprising, then, that more recent attention to the question of men's lifestyle magazines has been concerned mostly with the perceived shift from New Man to New Lad iconography as a *prima facie* example of 'what's going on with men and masculinity today' or, more simply, as a potential response to second-wave feminism.

One key text here is the recent work of Nick Stevenson, Peter Jackson and Kate Brooks (Jackson *et al.*, 2001). This provides an empirical investigation, via interviews and group discussions, into men's consumption of the new crop of men's lifestyle magazines in the UK. Though limited to a fairly small sample, the work strongly undermines any simplistic or deterministic understanding of men's relationship with the magazines. Moreover, it often highlights the key factors of men's ambivalence towards them, and indeed the wider phenomenon of laddism, as well as their sense of almost simultaneous engagement and disengagement with both the existence and content of the magazines. Interestingly, the authors are also critical of what they call the moral or judgemental tone of some analyses, including my own, that – in their opinion – attempt to over-simplify the consumption of men's lifestyle magazines. As I will explore shortly, this rather confuses the production, or perhaps even intention, of the magazines with their consumption. Nevertheless, they reiterate the important point that analyses of men's lifestyle magazines have mostly constituted discussion of them as an overall cultural phenomenon rather than as specific cultural texts.

The most recent, and indeed inclusive, addition to the discussion of men's lifestyle magazines is Benwell's edited collection *Masculinity and Men's Lifestyle Magazines* (Benwell, 2003). The collection highlights the growing sense in which the field of analysis of men's lifestyle magazines is both expanding and diversifying. While sticking with the overall iconography of the New Man and the New Lad, the volume also illustrates the growing tension between perspectives providing an analysis of men's lifestyle magazines as specific cultural texts and those concerned more with men's magazines as a general cultural phenomenon. The volume also raises some newer dimensions. First, a number of authors highlight the increasing sense in which cultural intermediaries such as editors and advertisers may play a key role in developing the direction, and indeed identity, of any given magazine and perhaps the market for men's magazines more widely (Crewe, 2003; Stevenson, Jackson and Brooks, 2003). The role of James Brown and Tim Southwell, as co-founders of *Loaded* magazine, is a critical example here; particularly in the work of Crewe, which extends Nixon's earlier and more generic analysis of cultural intermediaries (Crewe, 2003; Nixon, 1996). Second, feminists remain divided and indeed concerned as to the role of New Lad culture as potentially producing what Benwell calls 'new sexism', either though *incorporating* feminism, in the sense once used by Hebdige in his analysis of subculture, or – worse still – an actual backlash against feminism (Benwell, 2003; Faludi, 1992; Hebdige, 1979). Crucial within this is the role of irony, particularly in relation to the often overt sexism of New Lad culture that somehow might still not be taken seriously. Outside of this collection, Imelda Whelehan in *Overloaded* remains severely critical of New Lad culture, calling the response reactionary or retreatist retro-sexism, a point endorsed in Germaine Greer's often fierce critique of contemporary popular culture in *The Whole Woman* (Greer, 2000; Whelehan, 2000). Clearly the difficulty here is the sense in which readings of cultural texts *vary*, which leads on the third theme of Benwell's volume, namely, the increasing use of more discursive or linguistic analysis of men's lifestyle magazines (Benwell, 2003; Taylor and Sunderland, 2003; Wheaton, 2003). Most of these forms of analysis tend to argue, perhaps inevitably, that the magazines illustrate a degree of ambiguity, contradiction, and uncertainty or merely 'constructed certitude' (Benwell, 2003). As mentioned previously, this also tends to be supported in Stevenson, Jackson and Brooks' (2003) investigation into men's consumption of the magazines. Most convincingly, however, Osgerby's analysis of the cultural history of *Esquire* in the US within the framework of shifting conceptions of masculinities, which is in some senses also a consideration of the history of masculinity in microcosm, demonstrates that men's magazines in the twenty-first century are nothing new at all (Osgerby, 2003).

This discussion tends to highlight a tension between an analysis of the *production* of men's magazines, which in turn tends to inform an analysis centred more on the importance of them as a cultural phenomenon, and an analysis of the *consumption* of men's lifestyle magazines, which in turn tends to lead to an analysis centred more on them as cultural texts. As I state elsewhere, this is a tension that also dominates and undermines discussion of fashion *either* as a template of design and dress *or* as a phenomenon of style and taste (see Chapter 6). This ultimately leads to the ongoing sense of dividing fashion into differing disciplines – art and design (fashion as dress or cultural text) and social science (fashion as style or cultural phenomenon) – when, quite clearly, if one is really to get to grips with what is going on in the worlds of haute couture or street culture alike one needs a least a sense, if not a synthesis, of both. Thus we are returned to the wider terrain of this entire work, namely the tension of more culturalist or media-driven analyses of identities and masculinity on the one hand and more traditionally socio-logical, or at least social scientific, investigations of masculinity and identities on the other.

One slightly differing concern here is the sense that the iconography of the New Man and the New Lad may now co-exist. The difficulty here, however, is that whereas New Man iconography existed primarily at the level of various forms of media journalism, New Lad culture became a far wider phenomenon found in prime time television and mainstream film as well as in the press and magazines. The BBC situation comedy *Men Behaving Badly*, as well as movies such as *Reservoir Dogs*, *Snatch* and *Lock, Stock and Two Smoking Barrels*, in very different ways can be seen to play on the theme of the New Lad. There is also, perhaps, as much a sense of continuity here as there is change, as all these representations of masculinity are intensely media-driven and more 'hyper-real' than 'real' (Baudrillard, 1983). They all also crucially depend on, and are indeed constructed around, a series of commodity signifiers and consumerist practices, whether in the form of sharp suits and designer-label culture or classic cars and smoking. Similarly, in many ways, the new men's lifestyle magazines, whether in the form of the older, glossier and fashion-conscious *Arena* or newer and laddish *Loaded*, are similar to the original men's interest titles and are still organised according to the same assumed 'men's interests' of cars and alcohol or sport and women except, precisely, for their emphasis on a more *visual* style. As I have illustrated previously, a simple content analysis of the magazines tends to demonstrate that most of these newer and more 'feminine' concerns with fashion and grooming are concentrated within advertising or heavily promotional content while the assumed and traditional men's interests still dominate features and articles (Edwards, 1997). More widely, this also illustrates a tension within all the titles, namely the extent to which they are more progressive in re-defining new content for men's magazines or the extent to which they retain or maintain more traditional sexual divisions. Headline discussion of, for example, how men may look younger has yet to exist on a scale parallel to the prominence of fashion and adornment in women's magazines. More importantly, the development of parallel biannual fashion oriented titles such as *Arena Homme Plus* and *FHM Collections* illustrates not only the commercial success of the sector overall, but also an increased tendency to separate potentially more gender transgressive areas. In the final instance, then, it seems that the New Man and the New Lad are niches in the market more than anything else, often defined according to an array of lifestyle accessories.

We are left, then, with the question of what is still distinctive here concerning the rise of the New Lad or the expansion of men's lifestyle magazines more generally. In particular, no mainstream magazine of any kind is invented, exists or survives without the commercial revenue of advertising. The success of New Lad iconography therefore is at least partly due to its provision of a vehicle for securing advertising revenue, which in turn raises the question of what has caused the iconography of the New Lad to succeed where that of the New Man had previously failed. The success of New Lad culture would still seem to centre precisely on *how* consumer culture is sold to men, which in turn depends on the matter of masculinity. As I have argued previously, at least one of the reasons why the New Lad has succeeded so well where previous invocations of consumerist masculinity failed is precisely because it reconciled, at least artificially, the tension between the playboy and the narcissist or, to put it more simply, it reconstructed personal consumption and grooming as acceptable parts of working-class masculinities (Edwards, 2003). Where the iconography of the New Man failed in reaching a wider audience of men due to its overly upmarket and aspirational emphasis, the New Lad succeeded in appealing – apparently – to the more ordinary man. Similarly, whereas the New Man was potentially easily perceived as 'namby pamby' or at least as sexually ambivalent, the New Lad was all too certain of his often downright adolescent sexual orientation.

Interestingly, it is this question of sexual orientation that never really goes away, now returning in the guise of the metrosexual. This term was coined by Mark Simpson in the *Independent* to describe 'the most promising consumer market of the decade' when reporting on the first men's style exhibition 'It's a Man's World' held at the Design Centre, London and organised by GQ magazine in 1994 (Simpson, 1996: 225). Interestingly, Simpson also takes a dig at *Loaded*, arguing that it too is metrosexual – its anti-style stance is still style, its heterosexuality so studied that it's camp, and new lads are just as narcissistic as new men. What Simpson documents so amusingly – and so accurately – is the sense of the increasingly fudgy boundary between gay and straight masculinities when both are equally interested in keeping up appearances and when what unites them is narcissism: 'Metrosexual man might prefer women, he might prefer men, but when all's said and done nothing comes between him and his reflection' (Simpson, 1996: 227). What is also clear here, and in the repeated echoes of metrosexuality across the media – particularly in discussions of its so-called epitome: football superstar, family man, and fashion icon David Beckham – is that in discussing metrosexuality we are on remarkably similar territory to the New Man and, what is more, what unites them, and indeed the New Lad, is commodification. As Ellis Cashmore has pointed out, Beckham is not so much a new form of masculinity as a brand selling everything from Dolce & Gabbana to Gillette shaving products (Cashmore, 2002). Masculinities now are not so much something possessed as an identity as something marketed, bought – and sold – in men's lifestyle magazines, style programmes like *Queer Eye for the Straight Guy*, and across the world of visual media culture more generally. Though this could, just about, still be seen as some sort of defensive response against second-wave feminism, most of these iron-pumping, primping, preening, high-spending and hard-shopping men are far more engaged with themselves and other men than they are with women. This is of course not necessarily homosexual at all but rather homosocial, centred on men looking at other men, competing with other men, and stacking themselves up almost like shelves in the supermarket. And aiding and abetting them all the way to the bank and back are the armies of cultural intermediaries: the editors, the advertisers, the retailers, the image consultants and men's lifestyle magazines themselves in the almighty 'ka ching' that is the commodification of masculinities.

Conclusions: femenism

In this chapter, I have attempted to interrogate two domains of analysis often considered potential sites of men's responses to feminism – men's movements and men's lifestyle magazines. In neither case is the connection with second-wave feminism that clear-cut nor is its critique any more so. What constitutes men's relationship with feminism, or what one might call 'femenism', remains complex to say the least, though, as I have suggested, it is increasingly commodified.

3 Violence and violation

Men, masculinity and power

It remains a sad yet well-known fact that crimes of violence are still a significant, if not often growing, problem in many contemporary societies and that the vast majority of violent acts across the world, past and present, are committed by men. From pub brawls to building bombs, and from forced prison buggery to battered wives, the problem seems to be men: men swearing, men punching, men kicking, men smashing, men bashing, men destroying things, other men, women, themselves, even the world. Little wonder then that the answer to the question 'Is violence masculine?' is commonly a resounding 'Yes'. Even when women thump men or other women, throw pans across the room in frustration, or take part in more formalised crimes of violence, there seems to be very little that is 'feminine' about it. So violence is 'masculine' – or is it? And, more to the point, does that mean masculinity is violence? These are some of the questions, among others, which I will attempt to answer in this chapter.

Three central questions are raised in this discussion that form three sections to the chapter: first, the nature of violence, its definitions and the difficulties involved in making assessments of it; second, the question of whether violence is 'masculine' and its wider causes and explanations; and third, the violations of men and a concern as to whether masculinity *per se* is, quite simply, violence. Sociological, cultural and sexual political literatures, including the work of feminists and those who work in 'men's studies', are drawn on throughout, but it should be pointed out that no one perspective addresses all of these questions, let alone has all the answers.

The nature of (men's) violence: definitions and difficulties

Crimes or even acts of violence are a notoriously difficult area to research for the following reasons: first, evidence of violence relies on the *reporting* of violence and therefore reflects only that for which people are prosecuted or prepared to own up to, whether as perpetrators or victims and, as feminist work has often highlighted, this is particularly problematic in relation to sexual violence and violence within a domestic context; second, violence is particularly difficult to study in relation to questions of gender due to

fundamental differences in perception, as physical violence in particular is
predominantly more socially acceptable as a practice for men or boys rather
than for women or girls while, conversely, men or boys are often acutely
embarrassed if they become *victims* of violence and particularly if that
violence comes from girls or women, whereas the fear of violence remains
a dominant factor in many women's lives; and third, violence *per se* is
an emotive topic for men and women alike, often invoking and even depending on strong feelings, personal relationships and underlying questions of
power, fear and inequality (Bowker, 1998; Connell, 1995; Hearn, 1998;
Heidensohn, 1996; Newburn and Stanko, 1994; O'Connell-Davidson and
Layder, 1994; Smart, 1978).

A more fundamental question, however, is what constitutes or defines
violence in the first instance? With this in mind it is worth discussing the
various forms and types of violence in more detail. An initial distinction
centres on differentiating between violence that is directly physical and that
which is more verbal or psychological. Hitting, punching, pulling, tearing,
smashing, stamping, slamming and similar activities are clearly all forms of
physical violence whether against another person or property. What constitutes psychological violence is, however, a good deal less clear. Taunting and
personal verbal attacks clearly make up varieties of more psychological
intimidation or violence. However, whether an argument constitutes violence
is potentially more controversial, as a heated debate in the boardroom
may not be seen as violence, though one might argue it possibly should be,
whereas a husband and wife yelling at each other and waving their arms
probably would be construed by many as a form of violence though the
parties themselves may regard it as normal.

What is raised here are questions of perception, intention and context.
Though at any one point in space and time there may be some significant
consensus as to what does and does not constitute violence, there remains
a sense that what constitutes violence for one person may not constitute
violence for another. Furthermore, it is important to recognise that perceptions of violence change over time and vary from one culture to another.
This often informs more historical perspectives, as we shall see shortly.
Similarly, destroying one's own property for the purpose of disposal is
different from smashing it in a rage or vandalising someone else's property.
More specifically, perceptions may well vary within a particular culture and
time according to such factors as class, ethnicity and geographical location.
For example, one stereotyped assumption is that southern European cultures
are more vocal and demonstrative than northern ones and that many
working-class communities will often sanction some forms of violence such
as arguing and fighting. I will explore these points more fully shortly.

However, what is also raised here is a more immediate difficulty concerning what we may or may not include within our terms of reference
of what constitutes violence *per se*. Staring, joking, or even looking may
constitute psychological violence or intimidation within certain contexts

or, more particularly, if perceived as violence by the person being looked at or joked about. More subtly still, not doing something or doing something which is otherwise entirely socially acceptable may still be perceived, perhaps correctly, as violence. For example, a manager who repeatedly behaves differently towards one member of staff as opposed to another, in terms of offering favours or compliments or alternatively withdrawing them, may be perceived as intimidating that member of staff or being subtly and psychologically 'violent' in some way towards them. This is of course the point at which waters can become extremely murky and resolutions to situations, or even exact knowledge of them, teeter on the impossible and become a matter of interpretation. A prime and popular example here is the film *Gaslight* (dir. Dickinson, 1940; Cukor, 1944) which is set in late Victorian society and tells the story of a wife who is both terrorised and led to question her own sanity by the activities of her husband in moving items around the house, manipulating the lighting and making noises in the attic at night. No act of physical or even verbal violence takes place but the psychological intimidation involved is brutal. The problem that tends to emerge here is the sense that almost any human act or interaction may potentially constitute a form of violence, particularly if one considers more subjective perceptions of its more psychological forms such as harassment, intimidation or bullying; whereas physical violence, being sometimes both more overt and objectively measurable, is perhaps less problematic. However, to ignore the ramifications of more psychological and subjective experiences of violence, though they are amorphous and awkward to assess, does much disservice to the suffering of many, past and present.

Of profound and continuing importance here is the question of power, which undercuts many of these issues. For example, the manager mentioned previously is potentially violent precisely through being in a position of power. Similarly, the tormented wife, like many women in the late nineteenth century, suffers as she lacks the position or power to escape her tormentor. More particularly, a more external or structurally overt *position* of oppression or powerlessness often links strongly with a more internal or covert *experience* of helplessness, so that women, sexual and racial minorities, the elderly and frail may feel a sense of the potential threat of violence that often connects with their wider oppression. Underpinning this is a more implicit connection with questions of gender, as many feminists have documented explicitly women's frequent disempowerment within the home as well as the workplace, and the more nefarious role of interpersonal as well as institutional forms of violence (Daly and Wilson, 1988; Dobash and Dobash, 1979, 1992; Dobash *et al.*, 2000; Hanmer and Saunders, 1984). However, whether women *en masse* constitute a violated group *per se* is still a contested point, as the structural and interpersonal positions of women vary significantly according to questions of class, race, age and geography. Conversely, children, racial and ethnic minorities, gay men and lesbians, or indeed anyone engaged in externally or structurally unequal relationships with others such as students with teachers, patients with doctors or simply the poor with the wealthy, may clearly experience not only violence *per se*, but also the fear or threat of its *potential*. This makes assessment of interpersonal violence particularly difficult due precisely to its subjective or internal intangibility rather than objective or external measurability.

Such problems are compounded further in considering sexual violence or relationships where sexual expression is either potential or real. Violent and forced penetrative sex without consent is clearly and commonly perceived as rape and indeed as a form of violence and it clearly conflates with physical violence more widely. Yet, as is well known, many rape cases do not involve anything as clear cut as evidence of forced physical penetration but centre on differing understandings of what was and was not consented to and under what conditions (Mooney, 2000). These difficulties are often compounded still further when considering the relationships and potential for violence between adults and children. Children's understandings of the world are necessarily different from adults and arguably considerably more limited and less empowered (Ennew, 1986; LaFontaine, 1990; Millett, 1984). Thus, there are difficulties in assessing violence against children, whether parental or sexual, physical or psychological, and these in turn conflate with wider issues of perception, as children's inner worlds are often neither the same as, nor necessarily clear to, the adults surrounding them.

One often more neglected form of violence within our frame of reference here, however, is what one might call political violence. Wars, acts of state or similar institutions that lead to the sanctioning of death, exile or the undermining of the most fundamental human needs of particular individuals or groups or, conversely, unsanctioned acts of terrorism such as bomb attacks and similar forms of destruction whether to persons or property, are all clearly forms of violence that are perhaps more nefarious and destructive in their consequences than any other. The clear difficulty here is that in the years since the Second World War, the experience of such violence of the vast majority of populations in advanced Western industrial nations is often not only second-hand but mediated by, and indeed subject to, the media in their many forms. Similarly, organised and gang violence such as mafia and mob practices are relatively rare for many people yet pervasively represented and aestheticised in the media, for example in the famous Hollywood trilogy *The Godfather* (dir. Coppola 1972, 1974, 1990). While most people in the West have experienced or know of others who have been affected by many other forms of violence, political or organised violence for many still remain both considerably more abstracted and media-driven. A prime example here is 9/11, an act of terrorism that was experienced directly by only a few thousand yet has indirectly, and primarily through the media, affected the entire world population.

On top of these variations in forms of violence, as well as the issues involved, it is also necessary to consider the contexts in which they take place. In the first instance, one might assert that violence can, at least potentially, happen anywhere at any time. More importantly, this perception also perhaps fuels the often escalating rates in the fears of violent crime. However, though it is hypothetically true that violence can happen anywhere at any time it remains the case that it still tends to relate to some contexts more than others (Ainsworth, 2000; Box, Hale and Andrews: 1988; Hough, 1995). More significantly, certain arenas or institutions would seem to condone or at least tolerate at least some forms of violence more than others. For example, places of work and education, plus many similarly formal or state-run institutions from libraries to swimming pools, actively seek to control, if not establish sanctions against, most forms of violence, particularly physical forms of violence such as fights or more overt psychological forms of violence such as loud arguments. Similarly, many commercial organisations will also actively militate against the use of violence, whether in shops, restaurants or other service areas, though they rarely possess powers to legislate against it other than simply to protect staff or customers from acts of violence by invoking the powers of the police or similar state-run or commercial security services. However, the extent to which any institution, whether state-run or commercial, may undermine, or perhaps even perpetuate, other more subtle forms of violence remains a moot point, particularly in the case of issues such as sexual harassment (Hearn and Parkin, 1987, 2001).

Most importantly perhaps, some state institutions may actually endorse violence and the use of physical force, weapons or acts of destruction within certain arenas and contexts: for example, within the police, the military and armed forces, or in situations of war and protest. This leaves us with the generally public worlds of bars and clubs, underground and illegal 'fight clubs', and various team sports such as football and rugby, which some have argued form one means of legitimating violence within modern societies (Elias and Dunning, 1986). The one remaining domain here is the home, a supposedly safe haven from the violence of elsewhere and yet now well known to be a central arena for many more sexual and gendered forms of violence that often go on unregulated (Hanmer and Saunders, 1984).

What this brief consideration would seem to make clear, then, is the sense that some contexts or institutions will actually sanction some forms of violence at least within some situations such as in the police or armed forces; while others will actively attempt to undermine or control most if not all forms of violence as in most educational establishments, workplaces or service institutions, whether commercially or state run. Similarly, though many formal institutions continue to regulate or intervene in many forms of violence, many other more informal institutions, and particularly the family, remain relatively unregulated. Given the commonsense assumption that violence, of whatever form in whatever context, is at the very least often undesirable if not necessarily perceived as wholly destructive, the considerable variability in its handling is of some concern and worthy of some investigation. I will explore this matter further shortly. In the meantime, however, how does of any of this relate to questions of masculinity?

Aside from major difficulties concerning the reporting of crime and the accuracy of crime statistics, most evidence tends to suggest at the very least that the majority of violent crime is committed by males rather than females (Bowker, 1998). This would clearly seem to relate violent crime to questions of masculinity *per se* and this is a point I will explore more shortly. However, given the above variations in the nature, perception and contexts of violence, there are some caveats to this: first, though more physical forms of violence are clearly associated with men rather than women, verbal and more psychological dimensions of violence are not necessarily so restricted or one-dimensional in gendered terms. Some studies have in fact indicated that, to the contrary, women may be more violent than men in terms of verbal abuse or more psychological forms of domination, perhaps due precisely to their relative under-representation in terms of more physical forms of violence (Chesney-Lind, 1997; Kirsta, 1994; Liddle, 1993). Secondly, due to women's relative lack of representation in positions of power within the state or other formal institutions, their involvement in perpetuating more political forms of violence is clearly less active while conversely, and given the added difficulties involved in reporting domestic crimes of violence, women's involvement in more private forms of violence is potentially, though not necessarily, more significant. Thirdly, women's involvement in crimes of sexual violence is often rendered near to non-existent given the tendency of many Western laws to define sexual violence according to limited conceptions of rape or assault that are often solely defined in relation to vaginal penetration which tends to exclude other forms of enforced sexual activity such as oral and anal sex, to the detriment of both male and female victims (Ginsburg and Lerner, 1989; Gregory and Lees, 1999; Lees, 1996; 1997). All forms of sexual violence are also complicated further when considering acts of sadomasochism, which may seek to endorse violence, whether heterosexual or homosexual, male or female, through consent. The question often raised here concerns the point at which notions of consent are insufficient, particularly in cases of sexual activity that either involve torture and long-term suffering or are in some way life-threatening as in the case of exposure to sexual diseases such as HIV or, most famously, the case of Operation Spanner when sixteen gay men were arrested and charged in Manchester in 1987 for engaging in sadomasochistic sexual activities. Their defence centred on their use of consent yet was overruled both by the British Courts and later in the European Court of Human Rights (Furlong, 1991).

At the end of this short yet wide-ranging discussion we are left with the following conclusions: first, that violence is neither a uniform phenomenon nor easily defined but is multi-dimensional, dynamic and open to interpretation; second, that questions of context and perception are of profound significance in deciding what constitutes violence and, moreover, how it is handled; and third, that there is not necessarily any unilateral or one-dimensional connection of violence with *men*. This does not mean, however, that no such connection exists between violence and men more widely and or indeed violence and *masculinity*.

Is violence masculine? Questions, causes and explanations

What is the relationship between violence and masculinity? The preceding discussion highlighted the extent to which violence is not a uniform or simple phenomenon and therefore that its connection to questions of masculinity is potentially multidimensional and complex. None of this of course rejects or even undermines the sense in which much violence is still strongly *associated*, or indeed statistically correlated, with men or masculinity rather than women or femininity. What it does do, however, is undermine any one-dimensional analysis that seeks to explain violence as a consequence of maleness *per se*, which leads to the first and perhaps most fundamental debate concerning men's violence.

Natural men vs. nurtured men

The most immediate and basic debate concerning men's violence concerns the extent to which it is a biological or otherwise inherent phenomenon versus the sense in which it is a social or more simply learned phenomenon. From the point of view of commonsense, for many people men's propensity towards violence is a direct outcome of their maleness or in short their biology: men have always been more violent than women and always will be: it's in their nature. Moreover, a range of scientists have sought to prove a connection with the natural, whether in the form of aggression, instinct or genetics. A useful summary and critique of this evidence is provided in Hearn's work *The Violences of Men* (Hearn, 1998). For Hearn, these studies have taken roughly three forms: first, an emphasis on instinct or territoriality; second, links with chromosomal factors and the role of the Y chromosome in particular; and third, hormonal differences and the role of testosterone in raising levels of aggression in particular. In all three cases, scientists have used animal studies to demonstrate or extrapolate connections between practices in the animal kingdom and those in the human world. In addition, some studies have also been carried out on humans directly, particularly concerning the role of the Y chromosome and the importance of testosterone. Clearly the validity of such research varies in accordance with the study in question, yet the following questions are raised regardless of the specific study. First, results from animal studies do not in any easy or straightforward way necessarily equate with human behaviour and in particular, though the genetic inheritance between some members of the ape family and humans is very largely shared there remains, for humans alone, the fundamental significance of language and the social world. Second, chromosomal studies are frequently centred on the role of a minority of men, namely those with the XYY chromosome. Though these men are shown as statistically more likely to commit violent crimes, they remain a minority group from which findings cannot easily be extrapolated to the male population in general. Third, studies of the role of testosterone often see testosterone in essence as a 'male' hormone, yet it remains present within females to lower levels and also varies enormously within males. Therefore, while increased testosterone tends to lead to increases in aggression, it does so in anyone and does not explain the propensity of men's violence more particularly. More fundamentally, as Hearn notes, various wider problems with most if not all biological or 'natural' explanations remain:

1   Such explanations tend to fail to account for the variations within men's violence across time and space. Though testosterone, the Y chromosome or instincts may account for some men's violence in certain contexts, they cannot account for why some men are not violent, why others are only violent under certain conditions, or why men's tendencies to commit violence may change over time, let alone why some women are violent.
2   Such explanations tend to fail to explore precisely the *interconnection* between the body and the social world, as the former is often seen to determine the latter in a unilateral fashion.
3   These studies tend to lead to an asocial and apolitical view of men's violence that often removes the sense of agency involved and indeed the capacity of men to change or improve. Put most simply, these are often simplistic 'hydraulic' models of human practice where men simply become 'victims' of their 'maleness'.

In sum, though 'natural' accounts of men's violence cannot be discounted entirely, particularly in terms of their application to genetic minority populations, they remain severely limited in terms of their explanatory power as applied to the full scope of men's violence.

The chief form of opposition to these 'natural' accounts of men's violence comes from sex role theory that explains violence as a result of socialisation or sex role learning. There is again much commonsense thinking involved in such a perspective, leading some, primarily North American, authors to actively campaign against elements of the socialisation of boys such as prohibiting using toy guns or dressing up in militarily clothing or restricting boys' exposure to the more violent competitive sports as well as questioning the media's involvement in promoting violence as a socially acceptable or even glamorous activity for young men (Miedzian, 1991). The primary factor in all such analyses is the theory of socialisation, or the process through which humans are perceived to learn socially appropriate responses, actions and attitudes. This is seen to work on three, implicitly chronologically ordered, levels: first, primary socialisation or the role of family and infancy in social learning; second, secondary socialisation or the role of the school, peers and childhood; and third, tertiary socialisation, which is seen to primarily refer to the mass media and more particularly adolescence. The role of gender as a primarily mechanism or ordering device through which such processes are seen to operate differently for males and females is of course fundamental. Bandura has extended such a model to analyse the conditions under which aggression and violence are most commonly encouraged, perpetuated or regulated (Bandura, 1973, 1977). Goldstein also highlights the roles of the home, the school and the mass media as both potential perpetrators or inhibitors of aggressive and violent behaviours (Goldstein, 1989). The problems of such perspectives are now well known (Edley and Wetherell, 1995). However, it is worth reiterating some of these points here as they apply to men's violence:

1   Socialisation and sex role theories tend to differentiate insufficiently *within* the genders as opposed to *between* them, that is to say they tend not to be able to account for the differences within groups of boys and girls as opposed to between boys and girls as homogenous groups. Consequently, it is difficult to explain why some males are more violent than others purely through reference to differential patterns in socialisation, as many aspects of parenting, schooling and the mass media are widespread rather than individually specific.
2   Socialisation and sex role studies are largely under-theorised in their explications of gender *per se*. In particular, if parental violence is seen to influence boys' violence then why does it not do so equally for girls? Similarly, there are wider difficulties of agency and causation, as one has to ask how the parents learned their own violent tendencies other than from their parents. Thus, the end result is often essentially circular or teleological.
3   Sex role theories are problematic more politically in several key respects: first, for their emphasis on notions of voluntarism that ignore the wider significance of social structures and indeed the structured nature of gender differences; second, for their undermining of the role of human agency and the implied passivity of human beings in simply absorbing their backgrounds; and third, in the implicitly often white, middle-class, heterosexual and in some cases even 'WASP'-driven distortion of many North American studies.

In sum, though there is much evidence to commend the importance of social learning in understanding patterns of gendered violence, socialisation and sex role theory remains too simplistic as a tool to explain the full extent and practices of violence.

More fundamentally, 'nature' and 'nurture' perspectives tend to form an unhelpful mutually reinforcing and polarised dualism that is often seen to achieve little more than self-perpetuation, a point highlighted in another set of studies, namely those from an Eliasian standpoint.

An Eliasian solution?

The Eliasian perspective is based on the work of Norbert Elias and his followers, including Eric Dunning in particular (Dunning, 1999; Elias, 1994; Elias and Dunning, 1986). The perspective overall is deeply opposed to the promotion of dualisms of any kind and indeed dualistic or what they call 'diachronic' thinking, of which the nature vs. nurture controversy is a prime example. The approach taken by Norbert Elias and his followers has been termed 'figurational' sociology as, rather than separating the individual and the social, it sees the two elements as mutually constitutive. Consequently, violence is seen neither as an individual phenomenon and the result of some kind of natural or nurtured idiosyncrasy nor as structurally and socially determined, as the two elements are argued to be inseparable. Human beings are thus biologically social and socially biological and, similarly, structures create their individuality and their individuality creates social structures. However, the entire thrust of the Eliasian analysis of violence depends more particularly on the theory and concept of the civilising process, summarised by Dunning as follows:

> The central elements of this civilising process have been: state formation, that is to say increasing political and administrative centralization and pacification under state control, a process in which the monopolization by the state of the right to use force and impose taxes has been a key component; a lengthening of interdependency chains; an equalising change in the balance of power between social classes and other groups, that is to say a process of 'functional democratisation'; the elaboration and refinement of manners and social standards; a concomitant increase in the social pressure on people to exercise self-control over sexuality, aggression, over the emotions generally and in more and more fields of social relations; and, at the very level of personality, an increase in the importance of conscience ('super-ego') as a regulator of behaviour.
>
> (Elias and Dunning, 1986: 13)

It is not within the scope of this chapter to evaluate such a statement fully, though one can easily assert that such claims are, at the very least, controversial and not necessarily the statements of fact that they may appear. Nevertheless, the theory and concept of the civilising process has had much purchase on the Eliasian study, both theoretical and empirical, of violence, particularly as it pertains to such phenomena as fox hunting, seen more as an exercise in social control and an upper-class system of manners, the rise of the parliamentary system in England and a panoply of sports from boxing to rugby and football. The rise of modern sports is, in particular, seen as a prime example of a civilising process, or growth of civility and control of violence, that is seen to start in the sixteenth century with various shifts in the class system and the rise of court society most prominent. Elias, Dunning and others are at pains to point out that this does not constitute a one-directional shift from barbarism to civilisation, but an ongoing and complex process that is furthermore perpetually undermined by the possibility of 'de-civilizing spurts' and through the unintended and unknown outcomes of the aforementioned 'figurations' (Dunning and Rojek, 1992).

Much of this wider analysis is applied more specifically to sport, a topic often otherwise rather neglected within sociology, and here seen in sum as the 'controlled decontrolling of emotions' or, to put it another way, sport allows people to let off steam within a regulated environment of rules and controls rather than allowing people to engage in random fighting, and indeed violence, towards the same end. Dunning in particular also notes the importance of many more 'violent' sports as an often male and specifically lower working-class male domain. However, Elias and Dunning are at pains also to point out that there has not, as has often been perpetuated by the media, been an escalation in violence but, conversely, the growth of sports such as football and rugby follows in tandem with the rise of the civilising process more widely. Of course the obvious thorn in their side is the rise of football hooliganism, explained both as a possible 'de-civilizing spurt' or throwback to 'segmental bonding' and, more generally, as the result of young male working-class feelings of exclusion or what Elias calls 'outsider syndrome' (Elias and Dunning, 1986).

So where does such an analysis leave us in relation to questions of masculinity and violence? In the first instance, it has to be said that this analysis does little to further understandings of the connections of masculinity and violence other than in very limited and perhaps pejorative and stereotypical notions of working-class masculine identity, due mostly to its wholesale lack of engagement with feminism or gender studies more widely (Hargreaves, 1992, 1994). Secondly, and more significantly, Eliasian analysis is prone to collapse into essentialism in asserting the significance of an asocial 'need' for excitement and the de/controlling, or not, of human 'impetuous instinctual drives'. Indeed, within this analysis, violence is ultimately and simply the result of not controlling the human 'animal'. Most problematically of all, however, the two world wars and similar atrocities of the twentieth century, the rise of terrorism and the now pervasive aestheticisation of violence within many parts of the media are not easily dismissed as mere 'de-civilising spurts' or 'unintended outcomes'. Similarly, the ongoing significance and perpetuation of more interpersonal forms of violence within the home, or violence related to gender and sexuality more directly, are completely omitted in this analysis. In sum, though Eliasian theory offers some interesting insights into some more specific forms of violence, and perhaps the potential for application to others, its role in understanding the gendered dimensions of violence more widely remains severely limited.

The feminist imperative

Perhaps not surprisingly, feminist work has long been concerned with the problem of men's violence against women, arguably since its inception in the late eighteenth century (Wollstonecraft, 1992 [1792]). Feminists have consistently invoked wider questions concerning gender and, most importantly, its relationship to sexuality when considering questions of men's violence, starting most prominently with the Purity Campaigns of the late nineteenth century in the UK that sought to regulate male sexuality and parallel developments concerning prostitution in the US (Jeffreys, 1985). Nevertheless, it was not until the second wave of feminism, following the rise of the women's movement in the 1960s, that women's fundamental right to freedom from men's violence became a cornerstone of feminist enquiry *per se*. Early second-wave feminist texts varied in the extent to which they prioritised questions of sexual violence and more still in their explanations for its occurrence (Firestone, 1970; Friedan, 1963; Millett, 1971; Mitchell, 1971). Indeed, Greer in her earliest analysis of female sexuality tended to denounce the role of men's violence almost entirely (Greer, 1971). Yet from their attacks on the sexual objectification of beauty contests to their attempts to theorise wider problems of male dominance as patriarchy, feminists were often united in asserting that violence was both an under-acknowledged and under-represented problem for women. Perhaps the most fundamental of these analyses was Susan Brownmiller's powerful polemic *Against Our Will* which placed men's violence, particularly the problem of sexual violence and rape, at the epicentre of the feminist cause (Brownmiller, 1975). The growth of some forms of radical feminism, often centred on the politics of separatism and the Woman Identified Woman particularly in the United States, also did much to fuel the furore that broke out concerning sexual violence and the role of pornography in particular in its perpetuation (Eisenstein, 1984). The combined work of Andrea Dworkin and Catherine MacKinnon forced the problem of the eroticisation of dominance onto the map of gender oppression, most prominently as the linchpin around which men's power over women revolved (Dworkin, 1981; MacKinnon, 1987). However, this debate quickly became deeply polarised and feminists remain divided over just how far women's oppression is explained in relation to men's violence (Rubin, 1984; Segal and McIntosh, 1992; Vance, 1984). Moreover, a range of increasingly diverse perspectives on such issues have developed since the late 1980s, to such a point that it would be both wrong and naïve to assert that there is any one feminist perspective on the problem of men's violence or indeed any one feminism. There are, to be clear, feminisms (Kemp and Squires, 1997). Feminist work on men's violence towards women is now vast and varied, covering a range of issues from domestic violence to sexual harassment and rape (Dobash and Dobash, 1979, 1992; Hanmer and Maynard, 1987; Hanmer and Saunders, 1984; Russell, 1984). It is neither the purpose, nor within the scope of this chapter, to consider this work in detail. Nevertheless, certain common points of interest or themes do tend to emerge:

1   Men's violence against women is often unacknowledged or under-represented and its significance is often underestimated, particularly in terms of the culture of fear that it creates and the ways in which it controls and limits many women's lives.

2   The extent of men's violence against women remains somewhat unknown, yet feminist studies commonly indicate that it is far more extensive than commonly thought and often significantly underreported due to women's fears of reprisals from their assailants. Similarly, the lack of support or insensitivities of the police and similar state interventions and services are often off-putting for many women.

3   The range of forms of men's violence against women is extensive, ranging from leering and derogatory language to harassment and intimidation, and from misappropriations of power and manipulation to rape, assault and physical attacks. For some feminists this constitutes a 'continuum' of violence against women and the significance of wide-ranging abuses of women is often lost in separating them (Kelly, 1988).

4   There exist interpersonal and institutional resistances to recognising and indeed dealing with men's violence against women, ranging from men's own personal excusing of their behaviour to the inherent sexism of the courts and many other formal institutions that either explicitly or implicitly condone or at least tolerate men's violence against women and thereby also potentially become part of its perpetuation rather than its negation. The often low rates of prosecution and convictions for crimes of violence against women is testimony to this and further undermines women's willingness to report acts of violence against them.

5   In relation to matters of men's sexual violence against women more particularly, women do not ask for it, want it or lead men into it in any way. 'No' simply means 'no'.

6   The home and the family are particularly problematic sites for women, as they may operate as sources of violence rather than protection from it, particularly in terms of more interpersonal forms of violence such as wife-beating and rape. Furthermore the disempowerment of women within the home as either economically dependent and or primary child carers often aids and abets men in committing such acts of violence against women and limits women's capacity to resist or escape.

7   Most fundamentally, *all* varieties of men's violence against women, including sexual violence, are a form of men's power over women in either asserting or maintaining dominance.

Accordingly it is not surprising that most feminists engaged in the analysis of men's violence against women are deeply politically committed to the wider project of the recognition of the problem and indeed its eradication.

Where feminists differ is in their interpretation of these issues and the explanations they offer to understand them. While for some, mostly radical, feminists these points reflect the more or less universal domination of women by men in the form of patriarchy, others are more concerned with the significance of particular cultural and historical variations (Segal, 1987). It is not my intention here to evaluate these perspectives or to extrapolate any wider generalisations, but to offer some observations more relevant to the analysis of masculinity. First, though feminist work on men's violence against women goes some considerable way to engender its analysis it does not, of necessity at least, consider gendered differentials in the *experience* of violence or *men's* experiences of violence more particularly. Second, there remains some concern as to the extent to which some forms of feminist analysis at least may essentialise or homogenise the question of sexual difference such that variations *within* the genders are often overlooked (Connell, 1995). More particularly, questions of class, race, ethnicity and sexual orientation are seen to be neglected in some accounts. Third, feminists remain deeply divided concerning the causes and solutions for men's violence against women, advocating understandings which vary from socio-biology to capitalism and policies that vary from separatism to socialism (Daly, 1979; Jeffreys, 1990; Segal, 1994).

In sum, feminist enquiry has done much to problematise violence in gendered terms and it remains a powerful reminder of its inequities and its effects on women's lives. Moreover, some feminists have begun to interrogate these connections more theoretically (Hatty, 2000). This does not, however, entirely 'engender' violence, and violence against women, though a major problem, does not equate fully with violence *per se*. Thus it is worth considering men's own critical studies of violence in trying to address some the wider ramifications of masculinity and violence.

Masculinity in question: men's studies

If feminist theory and studies perhaps remain limited in their applications to men and masculinity more widely, then men's own and critical studies of masculinity may offer the potential to form a more successful alternative in this respect. In the first instance, however, it is necessary to point out that many, if not all, of these studies and analyses of masculinity in relation to questions of violence are heavily informed by, if not more simply following in the footsteps of, second-wave feminism. Nevertheless there are some variations and it is worth considering some of these perspectives in more detail, in particular the work of three key authors: Connell, Hearn and Messerschmidt.

Connell is perhaps the leading theorist of masculinity and it is not surprising therefore that the matter of violence should form some part of his analysis (Connell, 1995, 2000). There are perhaps three core elements to his perspective. The first of these concerns the significance of men's violence *per se* which he explains in terms of its role in male domination more widely, which in turn is seen primarily as a social, historical structural phenomenon related to wider patterns of inequality. More particularly, Connell is critical of what he calls the 'categoricalism' of some forms of feminism which see gender as a homogenous category that supersedes other social structures such as class, race or sexuality. Consequently, violence is seen as a key part not only of men's maintenance of power over women but rather more in terms of men's power over the entire planet. Secondly, one of Connell's key concerns is the role of the state in perpetuating men's violence including in particular wars, which are seen as crucial in the history of the formation of the modern nation state and, more recently, within contemporary patterns of Western domination under globalisation. More problematically, Connell also interrogates masculinity and gender more widely as a key factor in political movements and mobilisation towards world peace. This is, perhaps necessarily, as grandiose as it is prescriptive, yet a third area of Connell's enquiry, namely hegemony, is also relevant to the study of men's violence. Connell is at some pains to point out that men do not constitute a homogenous category and more particularly that men have the capacity to oppress, and indeed violate, other men as well as themselves and women. Most importantly, he highlights the roles of race, ethnicity, class and sexuality in constructing hegemonic and subordinated masculinities and argues, most fundamentally, that hegemonic masculinity depends on the domination of working-class and particularly gay and black masculinities as well as women for its supremacy. His empirical study of four groups of men – environmentalists, gay men, unemployed working-class men, and middle-class men working in newer professions – that forms the central linchpin of *Masculinities* shows some of these processes in operation (Connell, 1995). In addition, it also opens up the extent to which individual men and groups of men may be seen to actively perpetuate, openly resist or passively follow the dictates of hegemonic masculinity. More recent developments in Connell's work have, however, shown a marked tendency to move away from more interpersonal questions of violence against women (or men) towards more macro-structural concerns of globalisation and war (Connell, 2000). Though Connell's work remains some of the most nuanced in critical studies of men and masculinity, it perhaps starts to suffer under the weight of supporting an increasingly unwieldy wider project concerned with world order.

The work of Jeff Hearn is more specifically focused on the question of men's violence, particularly in terms of its more interpersonal forms within the home and elsewhere. In particular, his work in *The Violences of Men* reports in-depth research into men's violence against women (Hearn, 1998). Hearn has long supported wider feminist projects of not only women's emancipation but men changing other men towards feminist ends. It is not surprising, then, that his three-year in-depth study of around 75 men coupled with a questionnaire and linked to some allied analyses tends to take the form of an interrogation of the violent behaviours of men and the various discursive constructs, or ways of talking about their violence, that they invoke to excuse it, explain it or generally exonerate it. Hearn is at pains to point out the political imperatives involved in addition to trying to demonstrate the structural and institutional as well as individual nature of violence as something embedded in wider patterns of domination or, in short, patriarchy. Consequently, Hearn's theorising and politics are almost entirely at one with that of Dobash and Dobash, MacKinnon, and similar radical feminist analyses of men's violence against women, which see it as emblematic of a wider form of male domination (Dobash and Dobash, 1992; MacKinnon, 1987). More particularly Hearn also links what he calls 'heteroviolence' directly to wider questions of heterosexuality and argues that they are mutually constructed in relation to one another. It is unfortunate, then, that Hearn almost entirely neglects questions of race, class and indeed sexual variation more widely. Where the analysis is more telling is in his discussion of how men talk about and justify their violence and how, following this, agencies supporting victims of violence or working towards its prevention may become more effective.

Perhaps not surprisingly, one of the key aspects of work or studies on men's violence comes from criminology. Within the framework of reference of masculinity, of particular importance here is the work of Messerschmidt in attempting to reconceptualise the relationship of masculinity and crime (Messerschmidt, 1993, 1997). As Messerschmidt emphatically points out, the history of criminology has, rather ironically, largely been one of gender blindness, where being male has simultaneously been the largest predictor of criminal activity and yet wholly unproblematised in gendered terms. As often seen elsewhere, feminist research since the 1970s, and particularly the work of Frances Heidensohn (1996), Carol Smart (1978) and Elizabeth Stanko (1994), has successfully begun to problematise the masculine in relation to crime and also to expose and explore the position of women who have largely been left out of any previous discussions of crime. Messerschmidt it must be said, however, is not overly sympathetic towards feminist enquiry and a large chunk of his work in *Masculinities and Crime* is taken up with dismantling many of the tenets of second-wave feminism (Messerschmidt, 1993). Nevertheless this acts primarily as a forerunner to setting up his theory of structured action to account for men's involvement in all kinds of criminal activity. In crude terms, this takes on Connell's understandings of hegemonic and subordinated masculinities and attempts to weld them to a Giddens-driven notion of structuration. Consequently, Messerschmidt argues: 'masculinity must be viewed as structured action – what men do under specific constraints and varying degrees of power' (Messerschmidt, 1993: 81). These constraints and variations of course centre in turn on the structures of class, race and sexuality. This somewhat unoriginal analysis takes on a new twist, however, when Messerschmidt argues that criminality, and indeed violence, are potentially invoked as a *resource* for successfully accomplishing masculine identity particularly when, as it were, all else fails. Consequently, Messerschmidt provides a useful tool that potentially starts to explain much of the variation in, and indeed function of, men's crime and violence. Nevertheless, three problematic concerns arise: first, how to explain the violence of men who are otherwise successful and privileged rather than 'subordinated'; second, how to counter the implication that, if violence forms a resource for accomplishing masculinity, then how does it become functional rather than destructive; and third, Messerschmidt's analysis, rather like Connell's, leads him to analyse the state as playing a key role in the historical construction and contemporary perpetuation of men's crime and violence and yet, in so doing – to invoke the work of Hearn – it takes away the initiative from men themselves in moving towards a wider and indeed more abstract field of enquiry and politics (Connell, 1995; Hearn, 1998; Messerschmidt, 1993, 1997).

Is masculinity violence, or the violations of men?

If violence, as previously illustrated, is strongly connected to questions of masculinity, then can one, potentially at least, also assert that masculinity is predicated on questions of violence? Moreover, if masculinity is connected with, or even dependent on, the internalisation and expression of violence, then does masculinity necessarily also lead to the violation of men themselves?

These are moral as well as political questions that are, for the most part, rarely addressed in any of the literature on masculinity and violence, which consistently frames the analysis in terms of the violence of men as perpetrators rather than victims and tends to avoid discussion of men's experiences of violence or indeed violation. While such an analysis is important, in common with similar points I have made earlier, these studies do not easily or simply equate with a correlation of violence and masculinity. A simple and perhaps very direct point here is that, although still very much a minority of the full extent of violence, some *women* are violent at least on some occasions. To say that violence is predicated on *maleness*, therefore, cannot explain this, though to say that violence is predicated on *masculinity*, as a quality that women may also possess, may still hold. Indeed, with the exception of the often ludicrous and media-driven notion of 'cat fights', few would call violent women 'feminine'. Many forms of violence would seem to undermine femininity and this, as some feminists have highlighted, may also explain why women's violence is often unknown or unacknowledged and why it is often reacted to so strongly when it does occur (Heidensohn, 1996). This, in turn, is due partly to women's far lesser propensity to commit acts of violence yet is also due partly to the fact that, quite simply, there is nothing very 'feminine' about it. The highly publicised examples of child murderer Myra Hindley, and more recently Maxine Carr, both often portrayed by the British media as inhuman monsters, arguably has much to do with their implied deviation from female gender roles including those related to care, service and motherhood. In addition, what evidence on women's violence there exists also suggests that it is often different in nature and kind from men's violence and is frequently far more bound up with both more 'feminine' matters of interpersonal relationships and sexuality and stereotyped attitudes concerning women, crime and deviance (Chesney-Lind, 1997). Women's violence is often, in short, gender deviant as it tends to negate traditional notions of femininity.

Of course what also negates femininity, and indeed often relies on its negation, is masculinity *per se* and if violence is one means of negating femininity then there is clearly a connection between violence with masculinity. Messerschmidt's analysis of violence as a resource either for the formation or maintenance of masculine identity has some purchase here, yet it is perhaps simplistic to see violence as a functional practice for identity or men and masculinity (Messerschmidt, 1993). More fundamentally, however, it also implies at least potentially that negating femininity may itself form violence and, moreover, that this may affect men as well as women though in an entirely different way, namely violation.

One way of addressing this question is to consider men's experience, rather than their perpetration, of violence. As I have already illustrated, this a very under-researched area yet what few studies there are tend to indicate that when men become victims of violence, their masculinity is also called into question (Connell, 1995; Messerschmidt, 1993, 1997; Stanko and Hobdell, 1993). Some more recent studies have similarly expanded on the idea of men's violence against other men as a form of resource or 'hyper-masculinity' for the violator (Bowker, 1998). Consequently, this very much ties in with the previous point concerning femininity since, whereas *perpetrating* violence remains 'masculine', *suffering* violence tends to have a 'feminising' or emasculating effect. What is curiously still lacking here, however, is an interrogation of the violations of masculinity *per se*. Thus, what is *not* called into question is the sense that some forms or practices of masculinity at least may *constitute* violence in themselves. A primary example of such a phenomenon is the repression and repudiation of femininity that forms a major part of many contemporary Western forms of masculine identity, in which hardness, insensitivity to pain and an unflinching willingness to inflict it when deemed necessary are key aspects of successful masculinity, and indeed seen as vital to many forms of heroism. Practices, contexts and outcomes range from minor and mundane including the stigma on crying, suffering in silence and the promotion of the stiff upper lip, to the major and life-threatening such as training for war and military combat. The notable failure of many of early writers on masculinity to be taken seriously when raising such problems and the ambivalence that still surrounds much discussion of New Man models of masculinity as 'namby-pamby' arguably has much to do not only with problematic questions of power and inequality but also the unease that still surrounds any man or form of masculinity that might be seen to be a bit 'soft'. Indeed, softness is not an adjective often used to describe men other than in negative terms. Even soft or flaccid penises are seen as inferior to their erect or hard counterparts. The common notion that men may, or may not, be in touch with their 'feminine side' similarly underlines the point that it still remains far more common for it to be drummed out of them. More empirically, some studies have indicated that men's violence is potentially connected to their difficulties in finding other and far less harmful ways of communicating or expressing their feelings of anger, hurt or frustration (Horrocks, 1994; Miedzian, 1991; Morgan, 1992). Of course the difficulty here is that one can all too easily fall into the trap of sympathising with male experience to the extent that the importance of their power to resist is lost (Hearn, 1998). There are, furthermore, many other ways to be 'masculine' even in terms of the hegemonic models of white Western masculinity that Connell has described (Connell 1987, 1995, 2000).

What remains problematic, however, is the sense that violence still correlates with some forms of masculinity more than with others. There is, one suspects, much correlation between sexist, racist or homophobic attitudes and practices of violence more generally and one hardly expects more 'feminine' or sensitive men to take up careers in the police, the military or certain sports. It is, in sum, the more traditional and 'unreconstructed' models of masculinity that tend to correlate most strongly with patterns and practices of violence and, moreover, these are precisely the models of masculinity that are also often most repressive to men themselves as full and complete personalities rather than just well trained thumping machines. Thus, it is precisely this sense of correlation or connection between *violent* models of masculinity and the *violation* of certain forms of masculinity against men themselves that remains under-researched and unresolved.

Conclusions: violence and violation

When I initially started to work on this topic it seemed rather alien to me personally, and then the more I thought about it, the more relevant it seemed to become. Much of my life has, at least implicitly, often been informed by the fear of violence – I still avoid football grounds and, living in Leicester, I am regularly intimidated by both the throngs of testosterone- or alcohol-fuelled fans spilling onto the streets and the policemen on horseback who try to overpower them. I also make detours around pubs, bars and clubs that are likely to be frequented by large groups of men and purposefully avoid any kind of confrontation with any kind of gang of men in any public situation. Much to the recent bafflement of my female students, I also informed them that I do not walk through dark parks alone at night either.

Most of this, to some perhaps 'wimp-like', behaviour would seem to be explained by two factors: first, my homosexuality; and second, the fact that, at the age of 22, I was beaten up and put in hospital with my nose broken by five football fans (they wore scarves and similar paraphernalia) on leaving a pub with my boyfriend at the time on the Euston Road in London. Whether it was queer-bashing remains a moot point as none of them actually engaged in any verbal abuse, it just seemed to be 'done for the fun of it'. Yet this is not really the root or even the entire range of my experiences of violence. In the past five years I have also twice been the victim of what is now commonly called 'road rage' – one man kicked in the door of my car at the traffic lights when I beeped him for carving me up and another followed me home when he couldn't get past on a single lane highway until I made it clear to him that I was calling the police. I also once had to call the police to deal with a landlady's possessive boyfriend's violence towards me and later had to cope with the fact that a girlfriend's (now ex) boyfriend got jealous of our friendship and thumped me.

Far more fundamentally, however, my fear of violence grew in my childhood when I was bullied, though not very severely, and taunted for being academically bright but not very sporty. I also remained perpetually utterly baffled by why anyone should want to endure the pain of being kicked in the shins on the football field, even accidentally, or being knocked over on rock hard ground in a rugby match despite the evident sadism of the sports tutors. Like many children, however, I enjoyed the rough and tumble of the playground otherwise and received my fair share of injuries in the process. In particular, I still remember the agony of grazing great lumps of skin off my knees and elbows on the concrete and gravel. My mother was no lover of machismo, but still managed to adopt an attitude of 'stop wailing and get on with it' on occasions that I am sure she would not have taken so easily with a girl with four square inches of skin missing. Moreover, my first and my most ongoing experiences of violence came from my mother, not so much physically, though I was given the odd smack, but psychologically in terms of her often fierce and aggressive temper that saw doors slammed off their hinges, crockery broken and many a sore throat from the sheer volume of yelling. She was unhappily married and frustrated in other ways so I understood it, yet I had to leave home to avoid being caught in the loop of it any further. I have inherited her hot-headed temper and have, over the years, caused numerous injuries to myself and my own property, though never to anyone else. Although my mother often insisted I was born with it, I believe I learned it from her. While I have no intention of blaming her or indeed anyone else, my point is this: none of the now vast literature on violence, or indeed men's violence more specifically, even encompasses, let alone explains, these experiences or the sense in which many men are often as much the victims of violence as they are the perpetrators, that some, although in all likelihood very much a minority, of that violence comes from women. In sum, the experience of being male or masculine may often be as much about violation as it is violence.

4 In black and white

Race, ethnicity and masculinity

It is at least *possibly* the case that the complete catalogue of critical men's studies of masculinity constitutes little more than one extremely extended male, middle-class, straight, Western – and white – complaint. This bad situation is, furthermore, arguably made worse by the lack of attention often given to questions of masculinity by many black theorists. The vast majority of studies of race and ethnicity pay little, if any, attention to questions of masculinity, often discussing developments in, and patterns of, colonialism, imperialism and racial discrimination in ungendered terms while placing more emphasis on wider patterns of social construction, deviance, identity and otherness (Anderson, 1983; Gilroy, 1987, 2000; Hall *et al.* 1978; Hall and Du Gay, 1996; Said, 1995). Consequently, and perhaps not surprisingly, the study of masculinity remains marginal within the analysis of race and ethnicity more widely and, thereby, mirrors or even directly parallels the marginalisation of the interrogation of masculinity within sociology and the social sciences more generally, which have, for well over a hundred years now, often failed to problematise concepts such as industrialisation, capitalism and modernity in terms of gender (Barrett, 1980; Marshall and Witz, 2004; Smith, 1988). The rise of second-wave feminism has of course done much to redress this balance, but often more in terms of its impact on women and the feminine rather than on men and the masculine. More particularly, some developments within the newer critical studies of men and masculinity have started to reveal the importance, if not the interdependence, of the relationship of masculinity to modernity (MacInnes, 1998; Petersen, 1998; Seidler, 1994). Yet, in so doing, they often tend to create a caveat about unexplored connections with race or ethnicity. The study of whiteness, as we shall see, offers one – as yet still very tentative – form of connection of these issues (Bennett, 2000; Dyer, 1997a; Frankenberg, 1997).

Consequently, in order to address the question of the connections – rather than separations – of race, ethnicity and masculinity we are forced to consider slim pickings, or a marginal part of an already marginalised set of studies, namely a handful of studies by black male theorists considering black masculinity and the work of some black feminists. Most of this, as we shall see, focuses on the thesis of emasculation posited by some black male theorists, the critique of this thesis that comes from black feminism, and the development of alternative structures of analysis, particularly concerning whiteness, within wider poststructural theorisations of identity. Consequently, there are three sections in this chapter considering each of these areas of study.

Ain't I a man? The emasculation thesis

The emasculation thesis broadly states that black men have been and or continue to be somehow 'emasculated' through processes of racism, colonialism and Western imperialism. This forms the fundamental basis of most work by black male theorists on questions of masculinity and the position and experiences of black men more particularly. The difficulty here, however, is defining quite what this process of emasculation means and indeed what it implies for sexual politics more widely. In addition, accounts of the thesis vary significantly and these have been subject to immense critique, particularly from black feminists. It is consequently the purpose of this section to unpack what is meant by the emasculation of black men and, more simply, what this means for black men, black women and the study of masculinity.

Perhaps the earliest and most influential, if somewhat implicit, account of the emasculation thesis comes in Fanon's impassioned study of black masculinity in his extended essay *Black Skin White Masks* (Fanon, 1970). He starts: 'At the risk of arousing the resentment of my coloured brothers, I will say that the black is not a man' (Fanon, 1970: 7). Rather: 'The black is a black man; that is, as the result of a series of aberrations of affect, he is rooted at the core of a universe from which he must be extricated' (Fanon, 1970: 8). Thus, Fanon sets up a binary opposition between black men and white men, between black and white masculinity, and indeed between black and white cultures more widely, through which that which is black is denigrated, defiled and all but destroyed. In addition, he considers it 'fact': first, that white men consider themselves to be superior to black men; and second, that black men are caught up in a process of catching up with white men. More importantly, this is seen to have two mutually reinforcing dimensions: one 'primarily economic' and the other a process of 'internalization' (Fanon, 1970: 9). Thus the historical juxtaposition, or more simply exploitation, of Afro-Caribbean men by white Western men over recent centuries 'has created a massive psycho-existential complex' or, to put it in lay terms, an inferiority complex amongst black men (Fanon, 1970: 11). As a result black men are rendered both literally and symbolically schizophrenic as structural patterns of *external* annihilation are seen to affect personal or *internal* security. Fanon draws heavily on his experience of growing up in Martinique as well as the work of Lacanian psychoanalyst Mannoni. Ultimately though, if perhaps understandably, Fanon neither truly engages with psychoanalytic theory nor fully explores his own autobiography but plunges into a powerful and near-existential polemic. Though Fanon's thesis has been immensely influential in studies and analyses of race and ethnicity more widely ever since, it still leaves hanging more specific questions of empirically documenting, or even theorising, black masculinity.

It was to take well over another decade before a black male theorist would address the question of black masculinity more empirically as an object of study *per se*. Robert Staples' book *Black Masculinity* remains a seminal analysis of the significance of race in understanding masculinity (Staples, 1982). Staples starts with the assertion that: 'It is difficult to think of a more controversial role in American society than that of the black male' (Staples, 1982: 1). He sets up, and to a limited extent also explicates, a primarily structural functional account of black masculinity in the United States. Consequent within this are three somewhat implicit points: first, that black men are emasculated; second, that the causes of both black men's oppression and their sexism are essentially structural and relate to the history of colonialism, slavery and the rise of monopoly capitalism; and third, that second-wave feminism, whether black or white, fails to acknowledge black men's suffering and the causes of their sexism. There are five thematic parts to his analysis, focused on a consideration of the social system, the problems of crime and violence, issues of sex and sexuality, male/female relationships, and masculinity and sexism. Though some of Staples' ideas are perhaps now excused as simply products of their time, his analysis remains flawed and problematic on several counts. First and foremost, in adopting an overly simplistic structural functional model of sex roles, Staples consistently elides questions of black male responsibility for practices of violence, sexism and homophobia, rendering such factors as problems endemic to 'the system'. More theoretically he also sets up a contradiction between his explication of black male powerlessness and the now well known difficulties of any form of sex role analysis in dealing with questions of power (see Introduction, Chapter 1, Chapter 2). What is often linked to this is his thesis of emasculation, which raises a second set of unanswered questions within the context of his work. Staples asserts, with some force, that he sees 'the black male as being in conflict with the normative definition of masculinity' as this 'has always implied a certain autonomy over and mastery of one's environment' which black men do not have by virtue of the slavery (Staples, 1982: 2). However, he then repeatedly notes the importance of black male hyper-sexuality both as media invention and to some extent reality as it is 'motivated by the fear of his sexual power' (Staples, 1982: 76). While this could potentially be explained through recourse to psychoanalytic theory, this may well still be at odds with his wider structural functional analysis and the sense of contradiction here is neither explicated nor unpacked. Yet, perhaps ironically, it is Staples' politics which are his greatest weakness. In particular he sets up an unhelpful and polarised conflict with second-wave feminism, asserting that 'it is the man who needs attending to' (Staples, 1982: 3). He then criticises second-wave white feminists for taking a perspective that is insufficiently global and 'visceral and racially nationalistic' (Staples, 1982: 160). Though there is some credence to this point, also asserted in work by black feminists, Staples' repeated absolution of black male responsibility and blaming of monopoly capitalism is unhelpful in setting up an opposition *against* feminism rather than making an attempt to work *with* it. What is even more telling here is Staples' unease concerning the decline of marriage and the rise of what he calls 'interracial dating', coupled with his discomfort in discussing homosexuality. Following a detour into the difficulties of conducting empirical studies into sexuality, he concludes that the morality of homosexuality is 'not a judgement for this writer' and then asserts that:

> Recognizing the rights of homosexuals to lead their lives in peace, however, does not preclude the speculation that men indulge in it for a variety of motives, not all of them positive, and that problems exist in the internal structure of the homosexual community.
>
> (Staples, 1982: 97)

In sum, it is indeed a pity that Staples, in providing one of the few fully focused investigations into black masculinity, often fails to elevate the subject beyond a flawed complaint against the United States and second-wave feminism.

A more contemporary, and indeed more radical, direction is taken by David Marriott whose book *On Black Men* clearly extends the legacy of Fanon (Marriott, 2000). In his foreword, Marriott points out that his work is an 'exploration of the symbolic role of black men in the psychic life of culture' (Marriott, 2000: vii). This leads him to consider the wider and more cultural significance of the representation of black men within film, literature and photography, drawing heavily on psychoanalytic theory and the work of Fanon more particularly. His most fundamental assertion is that such (mis)representation has devastating psychological consequences for black male identity, leading to black men's internalisation of loathing and lack of self-esteem as a culturally marginalised 'other' within wider patterns of white male fantasy and projection. He writes:

> In particular, it is, I think impossible to separate black men's angry-anxious concern about being reduced to type – black types: imbecilic, oversexed, criminal, murderous, feckless, rapacious – from the many, and conflicting, ways in which black men were and continue to be stereotyped in European and American cultural life.
>
> (Marriott, 2000: viii)

And:

> From the public spectacle of lynching to the private dramas of erotic consumption, lynching scenes to 'art' images of black male nudes, what

is revealed is a vicious pantomime of unvarying reification and com-
pulsive fascination, of whites taking a look at themselves through images
of black desolation, of blacks intimately dispossessed by that self-same
looking.

(Marriott, 2000: xiv)

These are powerful words indeed and Marriott's anger is nearly visceral
on occasion. In covering such diverse topics as the work of photographers
such as Cameron and Mapplethorpe, the nineteenth-century black intellectual Alexander Crummell, and the work of Freud and Fanon, Marriott
produces a blistering polemic against the premising of white culture on the
subordination and near annihilation of black culture, focusing heavily
on images of mutilation and death, dying and violence. However, his analysis shows some marked weaknesses: first, while Marriott's selection of
imagery and sources is as diverse as it is graphic, it is hardly exhaustive and
his over-emphasis on factors such as lynching, and the often over-cited work
of Mapplethorpe is arguably as extreme as it is limited. Second, despite
his location within literary analysis, Marriott ignores an entire canon of
studies concerning the complexities and polysemy of textual interpretations
and their relationship to cultural meaning (Barthes, 1977; De Man, 1979;
Derrida, 1982). More importantly, Marriott's repeated and unequivocal
statements of interpretation of such imagery are set up without contestation
either theoretically or empirically. For example, his Epilogue uses the highly
inflammatory example of the Stephen Lawrence inquiry yet, in focusing
on a unilateral reading of the images of Stephen, Marriott elides the wider
questions the trial raised concerning more insidious forms of institutional
racism. Thirdly, and most fundamentally, Marriott's arguments would benefit enormously from the utilisation of some kind of wider empirical evidence.
His repetitive assertion that racist imagery is 'endemic' to white Western
culture and, what is more, that this is catastrophic psychologically for the
entire black population, ends up as little more than an unproven *assumption*
when potentially it could have formed an effective *demonstration* of racial
imagery and prejudice.

Beyond such extensions of Fanon's legacy, there appear to be two
different, yet not entirely opposed, directions to the analysis of black
masculinity by black male theorists. These are encapsulated and exemplified
in two fairly recent collections, one taking a primarily more theoretical and
culturally informed point of view and the other centring more on questions
of experience and the ongoing struggles within black politics, particularly
in the United States. Attacking the question of the connections of race
and masculinity from the former perspective is Harry Stecopoulos and
Michael Uebel's work *Race and the Subject of Masculinities* (Stecopoulos
and Uebel, 1997). This is a collection of essays from leading academics
mostly located in the fields of literature and cultural studies, including
coverage of icons ranging from Jean Genet to Malcolm X and from Elvis

Presley to Eddie Murphy, as well as subjects as diverse as Negro blues and body-building. Not surprisingly for a collection this eclectic, it is left to the editors in the introduction to try to pull things together. Starting with the theme of identity politics, Uebel asserts that 'throughout this volume racial male subjectivity is read insistently in the context of the historical and cultural forces of which identity is both the result *and* the potential agent' (Uebel, 1997: 2). Consequently, race and masculinity are seen as socially constructed, interdependent and, what is more, *dialectical* concepts that are mutually constitutive within a framework that attempts to break down the opposition between what Uebel, drawing on Cornel West, calls 'identity from above', or hegemonic and imposed notions of self and subjectivity and 'identity from below', or the subordinated subjectivities and experiences of oppressed groups (West, 1992). Thus, the rather more implicit thrust of the analysis is that the notion of a (white) hegemonic masculinity or race is as illusory as it is real and is indeed premised on those concepts and practices that are supposedly subordinated to it. Thus the collection also forms something of a veiled critique of the work of Connell (Connell, 1987).

More overtly, the collection draws heavily on the legacy of queer theory and the work of Butler on performativity with very varied results. Consequently, Uebel – drawing on Dollimore – asserts that 'transgressive desire for the other displaces and potentially dismantles racism, colonialism, and imperialism' and critiques the concept and practice of relativism in support of an alternative notion of 'radical proximation' (Uebel, 1997: 8). Dollimore himself critiques traditional theories of sexual difference that claim homosexuality is merely a rejection of sexual difference, and invokes the work of Fanon and Said, plus Genet in particular, to illustrate the intersection of racial difference with wider questions of gender and sexuality (Dollimore, 1997). Elsewhere in the collection, other authors consider a variety of primarily literary sources while Dyer, McDowell, and Muñoz in different ways demonstrate the historical and indeed racial importance of the body (Dyer, 1997b; McDowell, 1997; Muñoz, 1997). Though many of these essays are erudite and insightful, several profound difficulties would seem to remain. (Theories of the body are critiqued fully in Chapter 8 and the concepts of performativity and queer theory are considered more directly in Chapter 5 and Chapter 6.) First, no amount of textual, performative or other deconstructive theorising of the 'unreality' of race and masculinity as concepts can truly undo the 'reality' of ongoing legacies and practices of racial subordination and oppression, nor address the experiences and daily discrimination that many men and women from racial and ethnic minorities face. Second, though much of this work is politically motivated, it is ultimately self-referential due to its heavy reliance on psychoanalytic and similar terminology that is rarely explicated, if at all. Finally, and far more simply, many of these culturalist studies fall on deaf ears if any reader, even if academically informed, has not read the given texts, seen or witnessed the given artefacts, or engaged with the given cultural arenas (see also Chapter 7).

A very different collection and indeed perspective is formed by Devon Carbado in *Black Men on Race* (Carbado, 1999). In the foreword to the volume Kimberlé Williams Crenshaw asks the question: 'I wonder what it would take to fully integrate gender and sexuality into Black political consciousness' (Crenshaw, 1999: xii). It is this question of the potential integration of gendered and sexual awareness into anti-racist politics in relation to black masculinity *per se* that informs the entire volume. The volume is also clearly influenced by a series of contemporaneous events including the controversial Million Man March in Washington, DC when many black men protested for greater awareness of black men's rights in 1995, and the trials and media spectacles of Mike Tyson and O. J. Simpson. There are more specifically four thematic questions that in turn tend to inform the four parts to the volume. These are: first, the gendered construction of black racial victimhood as a primarily male phenomenon that tends to exclude or undermine attention to black women; second, with the exception of at least some forms of black feminism, the tendency towards heterosexual and heterosexist normativity in most anti-racist politics and studies; third, the normalisation of heterosexual masculinity within most forms of anti-racist protest or analysis; and fourth, the linguistic limits of identity politics *per se* in setting up discrete categories of identity that tend to obscure wider underlying connections between them. This last point is a particularly interesting one, yet it is often undeveloped elsewhere in the volume. These themes inform the four parts of the volume, which investigate first, the Million Man March and issues of racial division and solidarity; second, the engendering of black racial victimhood and the significance of sexual abuse and objectification exemplified in the trials of Tyson and Simpson; third, the exposure of homophobia within black politics; and fourth, the importance and problematics of black male feminism. Though some of the essays are academically informed this is, for the most part, a descriptive collection. Carbado concludes in the Epilogue that 'A Black male feminist collection remains to be published' and prescribes the need for men to increasingly recognise themselves *as* men and to resist their privileges as male or white or heterosexual, a point made much earlier by many white theorists in the then burgeoning growth of critical men's studies of masculinity but often wholly obscured within this collection (Farrell, 1974; Hoch, 1979; Tolson, 1977). Though such work is well intentioned and often provocative, the lack of theorisation of most, if not all, of the issues returns us to many of the problems encountered when looking at the work of Robert Staples.

Black macho: black feminism

Given the weaknesses often found in the perspectives of black male theorists in relation to questions of black masculinity, it would seem necessary to consider the work of black feminists. Nevertheless, as is the case with many forms of feminism, black feminists are often not concerned to inter-rogate black masculinity *per se*, but rather its effects and consequences for black women and black sexual politics more widely. With this in mind, their conclusions are often negative, highlighting the profound sexism seen to be inherent in both black politics and black men themselves, if not forming an outright condemnation of black male avoidance, negation and undermining of the emancipation of black women. This point is put most emphatically by Michelle Wallace in her extended essay *Black Macho and the Myth of the Superwoman* (Wallace, 1990). Her polemic has two key – and gendered – dimensions, neatly summarised in the introduction to the second edition:

> The resulting mythology was really an extension and reversal of the white stereotype about black inferiority. It dictated that black men would define their masculinity (and thus their 'liberation') in terms of superficial masculine characteristics – demonstrable sexuality; physical prowess; the capacity for warlike behavior. Black women would define their femininity (or their 'liberation' – which was not, however, a movement) in terms of their lack of these same superficial masculine characteristics – precisely because the myth of their inferiority, the black female stereotype, had always portrayed them as oversexed, physically strong and warlike. One of these myths I called 'Black Macho' and the other I called 'The Superwoman'.
>
> (Wallace, 1990: xix–xx)

The main thrust of Wallace's analysis is to critique the thesis of black male emasculation, arguing that black politics have become premised on the reclamation of black manhood to the exclusion and detriment of black women. In conjunction with this, Wallace makes a severe critique of the matriarchal stereotypes and prejudices surrounding the role of black women in relation to the family, infamously argued by the authors of the Moynihan Report to be the pathological root of all black oppression in the United States (Moynihan, 1965). In sum, for Wallace, the black movement quite literally became black macho: she argues that the black movement 'was nothing more or less than the black man's struggle to attain his presumably lost "man-hood"' and 'that the black man risked everything – all the traditional goals of revolution: money, security, the overthrow of government – in the pursuit of an immediate sense of his own power' (Wallace, 1990: 32 and 48). Wallace mixes her own autobiography with savage critiques of various literary sources, including the work of Mailer and Baldwin, emphasising the 'growing distrust, even hatred, between black men and black women' that is in turn premised on the hatred of black men and black women by white men and white women (Wallace, 1990: 13). It is in many ways a convincing and cogent analysis, yet it leaves little room for manoeuvre or indeed ways forward.

This angry and discouraging diagnosis has been echoed and critiqued repeatedly by other black feminists since, particularly in the work of bell hooks and Patricia Hill Collins (Collins, 1991; hooks, 1982). In the introduction to her influential work *Ain't I a Woman*, hooks critiques Wallace's essay as 'neither an important feminist work nor an important work about black women' (hooks, 1982: 11). She also tends to disregard Wallace's autobiography and argues that a more rigorous *prima facie* attack on black male sexism is required. Underlying this is hooks's concern with black male sexism as a thing distinct, if not necessarily a thing apart, from wider patterns of racial oppression and subordination. Consequently she asserts: 'Black male sexism existed long before American slavery' (hooks, 1982: 88). Yet, like Wallace, she critiques the emasculation thesis as 'a reaction against the fact that they [black men] have not been allowed full participation in the power game' with white men (hooks, 1982: 94).

A prolific writer, hooks' later work has increasingly focused on questions of representation (hooks 1992, 1994). In *Black Looks*, she writes:

> There is a direct and abiding connection between the maintenance of white supremacist patriarchy in this society and the institutionalization via mass media of specific images, representations of race, of blackness that support and maintain the oppression, exploitation, and overall domination of black people.
>
> (hooks, 1992: 2)

Her more recent works tend to rework this point repeatedly and constitute collections of essays on an increasing array of topics ranging from Malcolm X to Madonna and from pornography to Whitney Houston's role in the film *The Bodyguard*. hooks's work is often a heady mixture of the history of black politics in the US, critiques of popular culture, polemic and injections of autobiography. However, her political agenda is consistently inclusive, arguing that black women's emancipation links in with, and must work with, the wider feminist project and black men. That said, however, little of her work focuses more specifically on questions of black masculinity until the publication of *We Real Cool* in 2004 (hooks, 2004). Here hooks attempts to provide a politically informed analysis of black masculinity that is at once critical and supportive of black men. Structured partly chronologically and partly according to developmental stages, hooks covers a typically diverse range of topics from plantation masculinity to the trauma of black men's childhoods and from Mohammed Ali to spiritual redemption and recovery. However, though hooks' analysis begins to break down the antipathy between black feminism and black masculinity, it moves remarkably little forward from the studies provided by Fanon and Staples decades earlier (Fanon, 1970; Staples, 1982). While not absolving them from responsibility, she repeatedly sees black men as victims of white supremacist culture and misrepresentation in being feared and objectified but not loved.

The anger this invokes in black men is then seen to infect their sense of self, their low self-esteem and their negative relations with women. Thus we are returned to the territory of the emasculation thesis once again. Second, some of her more specific considerations are questionable politically. Her discussion of Ali as a more positive role model for black men and the O. J. Simpson trial as a contemporary form of lynching are – to say the least – controversial. Lastly, her analysis by increasingly drifting towards a notion of spiritual redemption tends to elide wider academic discussion or critique, and chapters titled 'Doing the Work of Love' and 'Healing the Hurt' are more suited to a self-help manual or a lay sermon than an academic essay.

Patricia Hill Collins makes a more directly feminist critique of black male writing *en masse* in *Black Feminist Thought* (Collins, 1991). This work forms a major and wide-ranging documentation of the subordination of black women, considering such issues as colonial history and stereotyping, the role of black women within work and the family, slavery and the necessity for political activism. Crucial to this is her exposure of the 'prominent masculinist bias' of work on racism and ethnicity and the interdependence of both experience and consciousness and sexism and racism for black women (Collins, 1991: 8). Thus she begins to set up a black women's standpoint in coalition with other oppressed minorities. A key issue is the question of black women finding voice, raising consciousness and becoming increasingly self-defined and self-reliant within the wider 'matrix of domination' (Collins, 1991: 225). This implicitly raises questions of culture and ideology that Collins rarely addresses directly other than through her rather under-theorised discussion of relations of domination and resistance. Cogent as much of this argument is in exposing the problems faced by many black women, particularly within the United States, it has very little purchase on questions of black masculinity, other than to provide a critique of it.

One exception, perhaps ironically, comes from a white feminist, namely Lynne Segal, who devotes a chapter to the subject of black masculinities in her now somewhat dated book *Slow Motion* (Segal, 1990). Taking a primarily historical approach, Segal starts from the premise that from the start of the slave trade in the 1560s through to its abolition in 1833 and beyond, black men have been the racialised object of white men. She writes: 'White men created the image of Black men as yet another contrast necessary for their own self-image' (Segal, 1990: 169). Moving through a diverse range of literary and media sources, from Social Darwinism to the novels of Ryder Haggard, Segal draws on and endorses the ideas of James Baldwin and Frantz Fanon concerning the projection of white male fears and fantasies onto black male bodies and moreover black men's lives. However, Segal is more critical of the work of Staples for its construction of black men as victims and its failure to recognise the internal 'contradictions' of masculinity, though she never quite spells out what these actually are. The recurrent thesis of emasculation espoused by Baldwin, Fanon and Staples does, however, for Segal lead to the failure of black men to critique the significance of their own masculinity for women, a point put forcibly by a range of black feminists from writers such as Alice Walker and Maya Angelou through to more revolutionary polemicists such as Michelle Wallace and bell hooks. The often gloomy prognosis offered by these women leads Segal to conclude that 'despite two decades of Black feminist criticism, it is unclear whether Black men have been listening' (Segal, 1990: 200). In a rather strange sleight of hand, though, Segal then sees more potential in, and progress made by, openly gay black writers such as Isaac Julien and Kobena Mercer in high-lighting the construction and artifice of masculinity itself, and her final paragraph is optimistic:

> In challenging the images of Black masculinity, Black men threaten the centrality of white masculinity. As Black people, like women and gay men, dissect and reject the conceptual hierarchies which construct them as subordinate, and struggle to transform the power relations they express and maintain, the mantle of white manhood, its preeminence once so seemingly obvious, looks increasingly frayed and threadbare.
>
> (Segal, 1990: 204)

What is lacking in Segal's analysis, as is the case with so much work – black and white – on the relationship between masculinity and race, is any real interrogation of the more theoretical underpinnings of such assertions. The first of these assertions concerns the emasculation thesis itself. While this is to some extent evidenced in historical sources and rather more strongly through the documentation of black men's experiences, past and present, it remains a mostly untested and unproven assumption that rests on the – for the most part implicit – invocation of Freudian psychoanalytic theory concerning the role of repression and displacement as potential resolutions to the conflicts of the id and ego and, in particular, the often distorted and populist importance attached to Freud's assertions concerning homophobia as a form of repressed homosexuality. Consequently, this is to say the least a sticky wicket. The second problem concerns the role of the media and indeed all forms of representation more widely in relation to attitudes, practices and patterns of discrimination. To say that such a relationship is complex would be an understatement, yet the ease with which such cause and effect arguments are set up between the (mis)representations of black men in any form and the multitude of their oppressions from an intensely personal lack of self-esteem through to structures of subordination operating in relation to such factors as employment, remains both notable and unquestioned. Of greater concern still is the obverse argument here, that questioning the representation of black men will lead to their emancipation more widely. Though I do not doubt that misrepresentation has a significant – and indeed often profoundly negative – impact on black men themselves and wider patterns of racial discrimination, this remains a set of connections in need of far greater explication and, moreover, demonstration.

The colour white

Despite the often profound limits to much of the work by black theorists concerning masculinity, this pales into insignificance when compared with the complete neglect – indeed the overwhelming *whitewash* – of the subject of the issue of black masculinities by most white academics working in the area of masculinities. With very few exceptions, if any, none of the major works within this arena, past or present, makes any significant inroad into understanding the relationship between masculinity and race or ethnicity and though such theorists as Connell repeatedly raise race as a key aspect of the interplay of hegemonic and subordinated masculinities, attention to race *per se* often remains both abstract and cursory (Connell, 1987, 1995).

One significant and growing – yet often neglected – dimension of the study of race and masculinity is the analysis of whiteness. It is necessary, however, to point out that this work is in its infancy and premised almost entirely on a wider platform of cultural and textual analysis, if not poststructural theory and politics. One starting point here is Ruth Frankenberg's edited collection of essays titled *Displacing Whiteness* (Frankenberg, 1997). In her substantial introduction to the volume, Frankenberg asserts: 'Whiteness emerges as a process, not a "thing", as plural rather than singular in nature' (Frankenberg, 1997: 1). She then goes on to document four key dimensions to the analysis of whiteness, namely: first, its historical dimensions and formations; second, its role in relation to the body politic; third, its links to questions of performativity and subjectivity; and last, its political dimensions and connections with wider movements towards reform. This then leads towards a wide-ranging set of analyses of theoretical subjects as diverse as Roland Barthes and Kate Chopin, places as far apart as Detroit and London's Docklands, and cultural texts ranging from *Gandhi* to Minstrel Shows. However, despite Frankenberg's invocation of a 'cast' of racialised 'characters' including 'White Man', attention to questions of masculinity throughout the volume is scant. Even Cohen's discussion of the obviously masculinised London skinhead culture of the late 1980s in its attempt to develop a more racialised understanding of Bourdieu's rather ungendered concept of habitus does remarkably little to enlighten the whiteness of Western masculinities (Cohen, 1997). Similar problems also seem to beset Alastair Bennett's book *White Identities* which, in ranging even more widely than Frankenberg's, still includes little discussion of the question of the relationship of whiteness to masculinity (Bennett, 2000). Bennett's chapter on the landscapes of masculinity in relation to the mythopoetic men's movement, for example, manages to reduce discussion of the mythopoetic men's movement into a mere return to primitivism and colonialist fantasy. It would seem that grasping the nettle of the masculinity of whiteness and the whiteness of masculinities is indeed difficult.

Far more extensive in its analysis of the relationship between whiteness and masculinity is Richard Dyer's work *White*, which tends to follow on from much of his earlier work concerning questions of representation and their links with sexuality and gender, and homosexuality and masculinity more particularly (Dyer, 1997a). Dyer's most fundamental premise is that racialised forms of representation are 'central to the organization of the modern world' (Dyer, 1997a: 1). Whilst this is a point often made in studies of racial identity more widely, Dyer is at significant pains to point out that whiteness is as much, if not more, a part of this as blackness. The problematisation of race as a problem for racial and ethnic minorities is, for Dyer, part of both their objectification and their subordination:

> As long as race is something only applied to non-white peoples, as long as white people are not racially seen and named, they/we function as a human norm. Other people are race, we are just people.
>
> (Dyer, 1997a: 1)

This draws Dyer into making a series of parallels between whiteness, masculinity and heterosexuality as the defining norms of race, gender and sexuality respectively, while whiteness, femininity and homosexuality are constructed both as other and as problematic. In the series of chapters that follow, Dyer seeks to expose whiteness as a social and historical construction and the outcome of centuries of Western colonialism and imperialism, covering such topics as the rise of Christianity, the development of photography, body-building and neo-classicism, *The Jewel in the Crown*, and – most luridly of all – the whiteness of death in the form of the Holocaust, pale sickliness, the vampire myth and AIDS. Dyer's work is often as impassioned as it is wide-ranging in its use of representational sources, concluding:

> The combination of extreme whiteness with plain, unwhite whiteness means that white people can both lay claim to the spirit that aspires to the heights of humanity and yet supposedly speak and act disinterestedly as humanity's most average and unremarkable representatives.
>
> (Dyer, 1997a: 223)

Though there are clear links between Dyer's work and other, more specifically focused works such as McClintock's (1995) historical study of the racialisation of early advertising for Pear's soap in *Imperial Leather*, any such eclectic and textually focused study of representation inevitably starts to groan under the weight of such grandiose assertions. In addition, the cogency of an otherwise more than convincing argument tends to be undermined by the lack of interrogation of more theoretical parallels with wider studies of gender.

Of greater concern is the direction of such textual analyses towards cultural solipsism. One example is the collection *Whiteness* edited by John Tercier and written by the London Consortium in conjunction with the ICA and Birkbeck College, University of London (London Consortium, 2000).

Tercier asserts that the essays 'make the claim that within certain bounds, and at certain levels of function, arbitrary choice ceases and whiteness itself, what it is and what is has become, inscribes on its own blank surface the reality of the ideal of the "immaculately white"' (London Consortium, 2000: 17). How exactly can whiteness, as a quality or concept and not an active entity, 'inscribe' itself on anything, let alone do so according to certain 'functions'? This reification of whiteness continues in the idea that it 'not only challenges, it threatens' (London Consortium, 2000: 19). How? While it is perhaps inappropriate to expect such self-proclaimed 'ruminations' to develop a full degree of academic coherence, it is ironic to say the least that the study of whiteness as a social construct should lead to its reification into essentialism.

As stated at the outset, the study of whiteness is as yet a tentative step in the direction of understanding black masculinities. Though it shows much potential for opening up the social construction of white Western hegemonic masculinities to scrutiny, and indeed for beginning to destabilise their certainties, the tendency towards cultural or textual solipsism rather than empiricism undermines many of its more grandiose assertions and claims. Similarly, while there clearly *is* a role for such textual interrogation as undertaken by critics such as Dollimore and Dyer, this needs welding to wider and more social investigation (Dollimore, 1997; Dyer, 1997a).

Conclusions: in black and white

> There is, first, the task of filling in the picture on a worldwide scale.
> (Kimmel, Hearn and Connell, 2004: 9)

Throughout this chapter, I have been severely critical of much of the prevailing work, past and present, on black masculinities. While I accept that this is clearly and intentionally provocative, I make no apology for it. Consideration of black masculinities within black literatures is often thin and still premised primarily on the thesis of emasculation which remains, for the most part at least, left at the level of an unproven claim or assumption rather than either an empirically demonstrated statement of fact or a theoretically interrogated and argued case. None of this of course excuses the overwhelming whitewashing of the entire issue of race and ethnicity within most, if not all, critical or pro-feminist white men's studies of men and masculinities. To be clear, the study of masculinities remains in black or white and not in colour. The lack of consideration of masculinity and ethnicity more widely is more than pertinent. The study of black masculinities, such as it is, is mostly dominated by a specifically black North American cultural and political agenda that makes remarkably few inroads into the wider study of gender and ethnicity or, more specifically, the analysis of Asian, Catholic, Chinese, Eastern, Hispanic, Indian, Irish, Islamic, Japanese, Jewish, Latin or Oriental masculinities. The incipient and indeed still somewhat *separate* literature developing on this dazzling array of 'other' masculinities has yet to truly inform a wider analysis of ethnicity, race and masculinity (see Kimmel, Hearn and Connell, 2004). In sum, then, the task of colouring in questions of masculinity or, in short, rendering them something other than black and white, remains a job to be done.

5   Identity and desire
Gay male sexuality and masculinity

There can be little doubt that gay liberation has scored some notable victories in recent decades in undermining prejudice and applying constant pressure towards greater and greater legal equality, developing a thriving commercial subculture and, above all, achieving unprecedented visibility for sexual minorities. Yet unease remains both in terms of the progress made and the problems that remain and, moreover, the sense that these achievements remain perilous. If the AIDS epidemic proved anything it was how easily prejudices could resurface, and the rise of both Islamic and Christian fundamentalism, now increasingly powerful factors in the political landscape in the United States and the West more widely, is – to say the least – worrying. While TV programmes gurgle and giggle in celebration of all things gay – gay style, gay comedy, gay life – real gay people by their millions take risks every day when they come out, have sex, or even walk home. In sum, it is all too easy to become complacent. It is the purpose of this chapter to assess this situation and indeed consider the extent to which this relates to the question of masculinity and the ongoing connections of gender and sexuality.

The relationship between gay sexuality and masculinity appears, at first glance, quite simple: gay sexuality negates masculinity. The litany of terminology associated with homosexuality over the past century provides ample demonstration of the never-ending association of the homosexual with the effeminate: limp-wristed, shirt-lifting poofs, pansies and queens. Nevertheless, the defining feature of the gay man is that he loves or simply eroticises men as opposed to women and therefore, in some sense, the masculine as opposed to the feminine. This factor was strongly reinforced in the 1970s when, in the wake of gay liberation, many gay men rejected the effeminate in favour of the hyper-masculine, sexually driven world of clone culture. All of this leaves us with something of a conundrum, for if gay men are not real men at all, or gender deviants whose relationship to masculinity is essentially one of *lack*, then how does this square with their attempts to reclaim the masculine, if only through desire?

It would seem that at the crux of this contradiction, and without necessarily invoking any specific psychoanalytic connotation, is the wider playing out of the relationship of identity and desire. Within the traditional Freudian heterosexual frame at least, this is, stereotypically, quite simple: the male, in identifying as masculine, learns to desire what he is not, on some level at least, namely the female and the feminine. Yet in relation to homosexuality this relationship is far more complex: the homosexual male, in possibly still identifying as masculine, but strongly undermined by stereotypes and attitudes to the contrary, desires what he perhaps still is or wants to be, which is also masculine. Or, to put it more simply, in relation to homosexuality desire and identification become, if not the same, then certainly less distinct.

The sense of contradiction surrounding male homosexuality and masculinity would also seem to work on several strongly interrelated levels: first, and most personally, in relation to homosexual men themselves who are caught up in still being men but also desiring them, which renders them somehow not men at all; secondly, more socially, in relation to questions of representation and attitudes which often see gay men as either promiscuous perverts of some monstrous masculine sexuality or as effeminate queens whose only relationship to the masculine is one of negation; and thirdly, discursively and historically, in relation to possessing a sexuality which is somehow never simply just a matter of preference but always a matter of gender and definitions of normalcy and deviancy.

It is my primary intention in this chapter to expose, explore and perhaps resolve some these contradictions concerning homosexuality and masculinity which, when connected, constitute the complex phenomenon that is contemporary gay masculinity. As frequently noted, this invokes a focus on the politics as well as the theory of gender and sexuality, as the one has constantly informed the other and vice versa (Weeks, 1985). There are three key sections: first, a consideration of the history of homosexuality; second, a discussion of various academic and political perspectives taken on the successes and failures of gay liberation; and third, an evaluation of more recent theoretical attempts to resolve, or at least understand, the contradictions of masculinity and homosexuality.

The homosexual triumphant: his story of homosexuality

It is now well known, within more academic circles at least, that homosexuality is a culturally specific, modern and Western phenomenon (Caplan, 1987; Greenberg, 1988; Katz, 1976; Plummer, 1981; Weeks, 1977). Though same-sex desire is in all likelihood universal throughout time and space, the homosexual as a type of person is only a century or so old and only fully exists in a similar form within parts of the United States, Australasia and Northern Europe, with variant forms elsewhere within the developed world. What this assertion crucially rests on is the distinction of sexual acts and sexual identities or, to put it more directly, same-sex alone does not a gay man make. This accounts among other things for the routine ability of a large number of men who have sex with men, in public toilets or elsewhere, not to regard themselves as 'gay' at all. It is also borne out in studies of sexual behaviour that report discrepancies between the very large numbers of men who have had sexual experience with other men and the much smaller numbers of men who identify themselves as homosexual or gay, most famously in the Kinsey Report of the 1940s and reinforced in later research (Kinsey *et al.*, 1948; Spada, 1979; Wellings *et al.*, 1994).

What this assertion also rests on is the logic of social construction. Social constructionist theory in a variety of ways seeks to demonstrate that sexuality, far from being biological, constant or inevitable, is socially variable, contingent and ambiguous. Fundamental in this is the now legendary work of anthropologist Margaret Mead in Samoa as well as the wider sociological concern with the social rather than biological nature of human society (Cooley, 1902; Durkheim, 1951; Mead, 1977). More recently, social constructionist accounts of sexuality have come to depend, quite fundamentally, on the work of Michel Foucault. Foucault, in his pioneering *History of Sexuality*, saw the homosexual as a specific type of person 'invented' as it were through the work of a series of Northern European scientists of sex, or sexologists, in the late nineteenth century including Karoly Maria Kertbeny, who coined the term homosexual, Krafft-Ebing and Magnus Hirschfeld amongst others (Foucault, 1978, 1984a, 1984b). The assertion that the homosexual identity is a culturally specific phenomenon that varies in perception, practice and outcome from time to time and place to place also strongly undermined the notion that the homosexual identity at least, if not same-sexual activity, is simply the result of some kind of behavioural, biological or psychological essence.

That said, this particular history of homosexuality is not without critique, perhaps most tiresomely from variant forms of populist essentialism that never-endingly try to claim that homosexuality is the result of some abnormality in hormones, the brain, or parental upbringing (see, for example, Le Vay, 1993). The problems of essentialism are now well established and based on three central points: first, that the claims made are of dubious reliability or validity in scientific terms, often being based on small samples, animals or identical twins from which wider generalisations are necessarily limited; second, that in reiterating the significance of the aetiology of homosexuality they have had the consequence, intended or not, of both marginalising and pathologising homosexuality through the lack of any comparable attention to heterosexuality; and third, that such claims undermine the capacity for change and absolve responsibility both personally and socially leading to an 'I/they can't help it' model of homosexuality.

The ambiguity of these claims more politically has not gone unnoticed, where attempts have not only been made to pathologise homosexuality through aversion therapy for example, but also to establish the rights of those with a gay biology through an appeal to Civil Liberties or a similar platform. Similarly, constructionist claims often both champion homosexuality as an alternative lifestyle choice yet can also lead to fears of contagion, or gay sexuality 'rubbing off', which often underpins much resistance to gay and lesbian parenting (Epstein, 1987, 1988; Evans, 1993). It is not my intention here, however, to evaluate these claims in detail or to fuel an already very old and tired debate between essentialists and constructionists.

I do, however, wish to raise several concerns in relation to the Foucauldian history of homosexuality as it is most commonly perceived, played out and perpetuated within predominantly sexual-political understandings of sexuality. It is of critical importance here to note that I am not attempting to provide a critique of Foucault's work *per se*, but rather questioning some of the ways in which it has been adopted and applied elsewhere. I am thinking particularly of the work of various gay historians and its adoption within some forms of socialist feminism as well as some of its more contemporary and eclectic variants (Bristow and Wilson, 1993; Harwood *et al.*, 1993; Patton, 1985; Segal, 1987; Weeks, 1985). Although varying significantly, all of these theorists cite Foucault as a major influence in adopting a politically informed perspective that is at pains to point out both that homosexuality is socially constructed and that gay liberation represented a high water mark in wider movements towards greater social acceptance of sexual diversity. As I have already documented and critiqued these perspectives in detail elsewhere, it is not my wish to do so again here (Edwards, 1994, 1998). However, it remains necessary to summarise some of the key problems: first, they fail to fully problematise gay liberation both theoretically and politically; second, to varying degrees, they present a view of sexual history that is insufficiently racialised or gendered; and third, they tend to lead to a form of triumphalism, or a kind of 'we've made it' perspective that offers few solutions to current problems other than to reiterate the joys of diversity and pluralism *ad nauseam*. The rest of this section will document some of these difficulties more fully, particularly as they pertain to the relationship of homosexuality and masculinity

First, the history of homosexuality remains profoundly gendered. As I have argued elsewhere, gender and sexuality as practices, discourses and indeed constructs are intricately linked and it is often far more accurate to talk in terms of gendered sexualities and sexualised genders rather than gender and sexuality, as if they were two distinct categories (Edwards, 1990). In addition, the stigmatisation of male homosexuality also has much to do with gender. Gay men are often castigated as the wrong sort of men: too masculine, too promiscuous, too phallic or too lacking in masculinity, somehow incompetent at it, or simply effeminate. Similar themes also emerge in relation to female homosexuality, where lesbians become butch diesel dykes and illustrate masculinity in the wrong body or some kind of feminine hormonal sexuality gone wild, or lipstick lesbians who just can't help themselves to 'a bit of the other'. In sum, the gay man is often oppressed for being the wrong sort of man and the lesbian is subordinated for being the wrong sort of woman.

What also comes into play here, however, is a sense that the commonly played out history of homosexuality as socially constructed fails to recognise the significance of gender *even within in its own terms*. Some feminists have highlighted this gender absence as indicative of a deliberate attempt to suppress the importance of feminism, depoliticise academia, and indeed exclude women (Stanley, 1984). However, the issue here is perhaps wider and indeed more historical. Women's sexuality, particularly in any form autonomous from men's, has had a long history of struggling to find voice in the face of often concerted attempts to silence it or even deny its existence. The comparative invisibility, even now, of lesbianism compared with the public spectacle, if not pariah-like, status of gay male sexuality, is testimony to this, as is the frequent de-sexualisation of female homosexuality into mere 'romantic friendship' (Faderman, 1981). Recent attempts to reclaim some sense of the sexuality of lesbianism either discursively through reinventing the connotations of the identity of the dyke or through representations of women as promiscuous sexual predators, for example in the work of Della Grace, have often succeeded more in openly parodying gay male sexuality and less in finding an alternative voice for the women who simply wish to express their sexual desires for other women (Grace, 1993). It is, I think, clear that this contemporary constructionist story of sexuality is indeed *his* story of *his* homosexuality and it is not satisfactory as an explanation of, or even as an engagement with, its female equivalent. Strictly within that caveat, it *may* remain satisfactory as an understanding of the history of male homosexuality alone. However, as we shall see, several difficulties remain.

The gendering of this history of homosexuality does not end with the simple differentiation of its male and female variations. Far more significantly, the history of male homosexuality remains gendered *per se*. The most cursory glance through past forms of male same-sex sexuality reveals a very significantly varying, yet equally profoundly unending, connection with gender. Greco-Roman culture may show no appropriate parallel with contemporary understandings of gay male sexuality, yet equally demonstrates its connection with questions of maleness and masculinity. Spartan sexual relations were hardly formations of gay identity, yet they were importantly connected with initiations into socially prescribed patterns of manhood (Eglinton, 1971). Similarly, the molly houses of the Renaissance were in no way simple equivalents to contemporary gay male clubs, bars or ghettos, yet they did perform the function of providing meeting places for perceived gender as well as sexual deviants (Bray, 1982). In addition, the sexology of the nineteenth century made repeated reference to the connection between male same-sex desire and gender, whether as a third alternative or as an inversion (Carpenter, 1908). Equally, the clone culture of the 1970s was much concerned to prove that gay men were men and not simply gay and, in attempting to reformulate the relationship between sexuality and masculinity, the connection remained. None of these historical moments is remotely the same or even easily comparable, but they do in very different ways repeatedly allude to the continued connection and not separation of 'the love that dare not speak its name' (Douglas, 1983: 262–264) with questions of masculinity. To assert, then, that sexuality is a thing apart from gender for anything other than heuristic purposes is not only theoretically inadequate but empirically inaccurate and politically naïve. However, this potentially raises a further problem, namely the tendency to subsume an analysis of sexuality within that of gender. This is the perspective taken in some forms of radical feminism, severely critiqued by Gayle Rubin among others and whose work I will return to shortly (Rubin, 1984).

It is perhaps, however, the politics of this history of homosexuality that are its weakest link. I have already noted its feminist limitations and one could equally highlight its wholesale whitewashing of the issue of race, colour or ethnicity, as have Isaac Julien and Kobena Mercer (Mercer and Julien, 1988). What is perhaps most insidious here is the sense in which it fails to meet the needs or expectations of even privileged white gay men themselves. Though, as we shall see, sexism, racism and ageism are but some of the 'isms' thrown at gay male culture, it is gay men themselves who often seem to lose out most and suffer most directly. As one disillusioned writer in the gay press recently pointed out:

> It was the politics of visibility, but rather than create an image that was drawn from our inner selves, we appropriated a macho stance. For the first time, we congregated in defined gay spaces, but because our struggle was based on sexuality, the meeting points were based around sex. Despite gathering under the 'gay' banner, our ghetto was very much homosexual. By looking like 'real men' we made gay sex more acceptable but lost an opportunity to create a gay identity beyond the active sex object.
>
> (Miles, 2003: 34)

This may seem pessimistic, but Miles is far from alone in his complaint that gay culture is often a shallow, youth-dominated, image-, sex- and body-obsessed world predicated on self-loathing, leaving profoundly little room for any alternative but to conform, pump iron and deny one's emotional dissatisfactions, a feeling that arguably remains largely unchanged and undiminished since gay liberation. In addition, given the media's increasing fuelling of gay, and perhaps all, culture as merely a matter of fashion, looks and entertainment, the pressures are probably becoming worse. Moreover, those who question or confront their dissatisfactions with this situation often opt out of commercial gay culture completely, retreating to coupledom, private social networks, or only occasional encounters with either 'the scene' or politics. The commonly played out constructionist history of homosexuality has no answer to this. Within this perspective, the homosexual is not only triumphant academically as a socially constructed category, but also victorious socially, politically and personally as an alternative way of life.

In its never-ending emphasis on the power of coming out, in its championing of the hard-won benefits of gay liberation, and in its promotion of the politics of pluralism for sexual minorities, all that remains is to metaphorically, and perhaps literally, throw one's legs in the air and enjoy it. Such an account never even conceives of the question 'and then what?', let alone offers any solution. It is to this question of the failings and problems of gay liberation that we now turn.

From camp defences to macho pretences: the problems of gay liberation

Gay liberation is problematic not least because liberation *per se* is problematic, both theoretically and politically. In theoretical terms, the notion of liberation tends to imply essentialism and, in relation to sexuality, this is compounded by its conflation with the concept of repression and the assertion of some otherwise contained or constrained sexual desire. The difficulty here is not so much the charge of essentialism, which must remain in some senses merely a descriptive term, but rather the sense of confusion invoked concerning what exactly is being liberated: a sexual desire, a sexual identity, a sexual community, or all three? This is not to deny in the least that gay men still constitute a marginalised, stigmatised and, on occasions, even *demonised* group, yet such an experience is perhaps more accurately understood as a problem of subordination, emancipation or indeed oppression. The term liberation therefore remains rather inadequate in theoretical terms.

This sense of ambiguity or even ambivalence concerning gay liberation was, however, also illustrated more academically. Some of the earliest works on gay politics, particularly those of Hocquenghem and Mieli, attributed a liberatory force to gay desire in celebrating promiscuity, pushing the boundaries of decency and more generally going against the mores of mainstream heterosexual society; while others, particularly those of Altman and Weeks, saw gay politics as a culturally specific phenomenon contingent on histories of movements towards reform and slowly shifting morals and values (Altman, 1971; Hocquenghem, 1972; Mieli, 1980; Weeks, 1977). It was perhaps not surprising, then, that much of this ambivalence should also be played out through a series of academic debates that followed the onset of gay liberation. These more theoretical debates were in themselves often founded on the political involvements of young writers and academics making their careers in colleges and universities. Most of these controversies centred on various, and often violently opposed, perspectives of the development of commercial gay culture and the practices and attitudes of gay men, most notoriously those of the overtly sexualised and hyper-masculine clone.

The gay clone has now become something of pariah, both within academic circles and more popular culture, pumped and inflated into near mythic status as *the* iconic symbol of gay liberation. With his sexuality blatantly displayed, literally bulging out of his plaid shirts, leather jackets and button-fly jeans, and publicly paraded down the streets of many of the world's major cities in celebration of his unconstrained promiscuous desire for more and more of precisely the same thing, namely those like himself, he became the emblem of the 'sex' in homosexuality, or what Michael Bronski once called 'sex incarnate' (Bronski, 1984: 191). Proclaimed by some as the epitome of the guilt-free lifestyle of sexual liberation and castigated by others as the nadir of misogynist self-loathing, the cruising gay clone came, perhaps mistakenly, to represent gay sexuality in its entirety and to divide politically motivated academia like an axe through an apple. More precisely, as I have demonstrated elsewhere, what this entire uproar often centred on was the perceived relationship of the homosexual to the masculine (Edwards, 1994, 1998).

It is perhaps proper to start with gay men's own perspectives on their liberation and indeed the clone that some of them helped create. One of the earliest and most influential of these was a chapter by Gregg Blachford in Ken Plummer's path-breaking collection *The Making of the Modern Homosexual*, titled 'Male Dominance and the Gay World' (Blachford, 1981). Relying heavily on an Althusserian understanding of the role of subculture, Blachford perceived both reproduction and resistance to male domination in post-liberation gay culture. To put it more simply, macho gay male culture neither fully resisted nor purely reproduced male domination by virtue of its strict containment *within* a subculture. A linked yet less academically informed argument was made by Jamie Gough who, while acknowledging the sexist implications of some contemporary gay culture, saw macho gay men as merely aping 'real' masculinity (Gough, 1989). Joseph Bristow, in a powerful polemic against lesbian accusations of homosexual misogyny, pushed this argument further, seeing the gay clone as contrived and playful, theatrical and fake, quite literally unreal (Bristow, 1989). The comic effect of this was not lost on gay men themselves, who joked that any illusion of the clone's masculinity was lost as soon as he opened his mouth, while society at large bore witness to disco group The Village People doing a number of decidedly camp dance routines dressed as gay cowboys, cops and construction workers. Consequently, gay masculinity was often quite literally only skin deep. From this perspective, then, masculinity and homosexuality were exposed as increasingly playful social constructions that had no *intrinsic* interaction or relationship.

At the same time others still felt that gay male promiscuity could, or even should, be celebrated, a point put most forcibly in John Allen Lee's *Getting Sex: New Approach – More Fun, Less Guilt* (Lee, 1978). Lee argued that gay men were quite simply better at 'getting sex', having developed a highly sophisticated system of dress codes and visual cues to indicate sexual preference as well as adapting a variety of formal and informal public contexts in which to practise sex and indeed enjoy it. Evidence for this was provided in the literary but often autobiographical accounts of John Rechy and Edmund White as well as in various surveys of sexual behaviour at the time (Jay and Young, 1979; Rechy, 1977; Spada, 1979; White, 1986). Similarly, in *The Silent Community*, Edward Delph conducted an ethnographic study of men's sexual behaviour with other men in public and semi-public places, such as parks, toilets and saunas and, in doing so, emphasised both its sophistication and indeed its silence (Delph, 1978)

What these studies also illustrated, however, was the connection of gay men's sexual practices with questions of masculinity, not only in reinforcing the stereotype that men are simply more promiscuous than women, but also in the sense that the clone not only donned a masculine appearance but practised a stereotypically masculine sexuality that was divorced from emotional commitment and intimacy, a form of sexual expression so minimal that even conversation could destroy it. This was of course precisely its appeal, the emotionally risk-free, pared-down and butt-naked excitement: pure, exposed and throbbing – the cock stripped bare – all of which opened up another problem, namely the charge of phallocentrism, particularly from lesbian feminists (Dworkin, 1981; Jeffreys, 1990; Stanley, 1982).

Others, however, were less convinced. In 'Two Steps Forward, One Step Back', John Shiers sounded a personal note of painful concern (Shiers, 1980). In particular, this centred on his perception that gay men were still caught in the double bind and indeed double standards of heterosexual society so, in trying to maintain more socialist or feminist convictions, gay men ran the risk of losing sight of their own, primarily sexual, cause. Consequently, when copying more traditional patterns of monogamous sexual practices with long-term partners in private, gay men risked little social opprobrium, but in publicly displaying a promiscuous desire for the masculine they often felt the full wrath of their stigma and heterosexual society's homophobia. Ultimately, then, gay men were in a no-win situation of being forced into a closet not of their own making or made into public pariahs when they broke its bounds. Rumbling under the surface here were increasing concerns relating to the potential pitfalls of the newly sexualised, and indeed masculinised, dimensions of gay liberation.

Similarly, others complained that development of an increasingly body-conscious commercial scene and networks founded on the promotion of sex without love was not for all and ultimately was yet another lesson in the continued internalised alienation of homosexuality (Adam, 1987). Of fundamental importance in this was the articulation, or reworking, of the relationship of homosexuality and masculinity. Gay culture, in asserting that gay men could be real men too, while divorcing homosexuality from its more negative relationship to masculinity, also forced them together into a form of matrimony that was not altogether happy. In particular, Michael Pollak saw the promiscuous cruising of the clone as a form of 'internalised maximisation of profits' or a performance-driven masculine sexuality in which gay men notched up partners like cars off a production line (Pollak,

1985). In short, the constraints of the closet were often swapped for the pressures of performance. Of importance in this was Pollak's historically focused analysis of the development of gay male culture alongside emergent forms of masculinity within industrial capitalism, which were in turn perceived as founded on a form of self-alienation. In addition, and often rather under the surface here, was an increasing concern with the relationship of gay sexuality to questions of masculinity, and Pollak's work shows distinct parallels with Seidler's wider emphasis on masculinity as being premised on rationality and emotional repression (Seidler, 1989).

In more romantic vein, some also complained that the commercial gay world provided little emotional rather than sexual sustenance, a point made most strongly in the historically nuanced and erudite work of Barry Adam and echoed elsewhere (Adam, 1987; Dowsett, 1987). This reached its most extreme form in the novels and plays of Larry Kramer, an AIDS activist in New York who once infamously accused gay men of quite literally 'thinking with their cocks' and 'fucking themselves to death' (Kramer, 1978, 1983, 1986).

The mention of AIDS at this juncture is not coincidental and the conjunction of the rise of the epidemic with the critique of clone culture is not insignificant. When AIDS was first recognised in the early 1980s, predominantly in the gay communities of the United States and as a sexually transmitted disease that continued to affect disproportionately the gay male population in Western societies, it was quickly perceived as a symbolic phenomenon as much as, if not more than, a medical condition. To put it more simply, AIDS was rapidly presented and understood as a morally loaded disease of *lifestyle*. At the epicentre of this once again were the sexual activities of the promiscuous gay clone, and indeed 1970s gay culture more generally. The moral outrage, homophobic vitriol and backlash that took place against the gay community, particularly through the tabloid media who often presented AIDS as the 'gay plague', is now well documented, particularly in the work of Simon Watney in the UK and Randy Shilts in the US (Shilts, 1987; Watney, 1987). It was perhaps not surprising, then, that gay studies often went on the defensive and further invoked the logic of constructionism and the discursive legacy of Foucault to prove that AIDS had no intrinsic connection with gay sexuality other than one of creating illness and stigmatisation (see, for example, Altman, 1986; Crimp, 1988; Patton, 1985, 1990).

However, this also had the effect, intended or not, of overriding an intriguing dimension of the connection of masculinity with sexuality, particularly in relation to gay male sexuality, that the epidemic raised. To put it directly, AIDS in threatening the very life, let alone style, of promiscuous gay male sexuality in the 1970s opened up the question of just what having lots of sex meant to gay men and quite where their identities might end up without it. The fundamental dependence of gay male identity, and indeed masculinity more widely, on sexuality and particularly sex *per se* was raised primarily in more social psychological circles, particularly in the work of Person and Kimmel as well as my own, yet it was never fully raised in gay studies and quickly turned into an often media-driven and pejorative question of 'sex addiction' (Edwards, 1992, 1994; Kimmel, 1994; Person, 1980). In a sense, then, AIDS triangulated the relationship of gender, sexuality and identity more strongly, though often the issue was forced onto the agenda only through an individual, and indeed collective, experience of grief.

This important, if rather painful, line of argument was pursued to some extent by Leo Bersani who sought to connect a personal question of mourning, particularly in the wake of the AIDS epidemic, to a political question of militancy (Bersani, 1988, 1995). The overall thrust of his analysis was to seek to marry, rather than divorce, the intensely individual, psychological and sexual with the social, external and pedagogic. At the centre of this logic was, once again, the promiscuous sexuality of the cruising gay clone. In the first instance Bersani rejected the argument that the rise of a gay hyper-masculinity was necessarily about subversive play or parody, arguing that sexual desire remained, in essence, a serious business that could potentially reinforce patriarchal or conservative politics as much as it could undermine them. Thus, a homosexual, or simply sexual, love of rough trade and uniforms did not make it radical. As a result, gay men were, and are, in the uneasy situation of potentially desiring, and perhaps even sleeping with, their enemies. This is an argument which could easily be used to bolster some more simplistic and homophobic arguments, yet precisely because Bersani, like Butler considered later, invokes psychoanalytic theory, the issue becomes inverted and gay men's desire for the masculine remains not only problematised, but also *celebrated*, precisely for its constant invoking of the disavowed, male, sexual object.

What begins to emerge here is a bi-polarised debate in which the post-gay liberation gay man is seen as *either* the emblem of a celebration of uninhibited sexual expression *or* simply the latest incarnation of sexual oppression. While both perspectives *in extremis* remain problematic, it is the liberal or perhaps liberationist approach that is most questionable. In denying that the development and form of gay culture had *any* connection with wider society other than to challenge it, or indeed with masculinity other than to celebrate it, gay liberationists also ran the risk of disowning all political responsibility, a problem highlighted by the feminist critique of gay sexuality to which I now turn.

Of most direct significance here are the conflicts that soon developed between gay men and lesbians. In the first instance, gay liberation included gay men and gay women, yet within a very few years the two groups had suffered a very acrimonious divorce and many lesbians found their interests better served within the women's movement. Most fundamentally, this centred on a profoundly differing set of needs and wants, or what Annabel Faraday once called the 'polar experiences' of gay men and lesbians (Faraday,

1981). While gay men were often primarily concerned with sexual liberation in the face of continued public hostility and actually rising, rather
than falling, criminal prosecutions, lesbians were finding that much of their
own liberation depended on their gender rather than their sexuality. The
women's movement in highlighting the role of heterosexuality in women's
oppression also often offered very clear and direct support for lesbians with
more feminist or gender-oriented concerns. More problematically, gay men's
comparative economic power was increasingly overt and being channelled
into the rapid expansion of a commercial gay scene of shops, bars, clubs,
saunas, restaurants, and a host of other services from which lesbians felt
increasingly excluded, a factor that rapidly turned into fierce accusations of
sexism and misogyny. Liz Stanley, for example, experienced considerable
disillusionment in working with gay men politically and Sheila Jeffreys argued
similarly that gay liberation was merely another aspect of *men's* sexual liberation of *men's* sexual needs masquerading as the permissive society (Jeffreys,
1990; Stanley, 1982). Conversely, some gay men increasingly complained
that lesbians were often aggressive and moralising in their lack of support
for gay men's concerns and some lesbians could themselves perhaps be
accused of being complicit in heterosexual homophobia. Joseph Bristow,
Craig Owens and others argued strongly that misogyny and homophobia
were not opposed but were two sides of the same coin of patriarchal and
heterosexual dominance (Bristow, 1989; Owens, 1987). This conflict rapidly
became both overly polarised and problematic in itself, often diverting wider
political energies into infighting.

Nevertheless, such conflict exposed a deeper divide within feminism in
relation to questions of gender and sexuality, and feminist accounts of gay
liberation were often confused and conflicting. Perhaps most influentially,
Gayle Rubin in her article 'Thinking Sex', argued strongly for an analysis
of sexuality as a separate mechanism, or what she called a 'vector of oppression', not simply dependent on, but indeed distinct from, the analysis of
gender (Rubin, 1984). She documented 'hierarchies of sexuality' through
which heterosexuality, whether male or female, and particularly if marital,
was still privileged over homosexuality and was in turn less stigmatised
if monogamous, while promiscuity and prostitution, sadomasochism and
paedophilia, were deemed the lowest or worst of all. This in many ways
revolutionised, or at least counteracted, an increasingly vociferous North
American radical feminist view of sexuality as solely an extension of gender
domination, theorised most fully in the work of Andrea Dworkin and
Catharine MacKinnon (Dworkin, 1981; MacKinnon, 1987). The most
fundamental thrust of this perspective was to perceive sexuality primarily as
a form of power, most notoriously in relation to rape and pornography.

Without wishing to stir up an already overly whipped debate, the conflict that developed within feminism concerning sexuality also exposed a
profoundly different, if not competing, set of feminist perspectives on gay
liberation. For Rubin, and indeed a variety of other feminist writers including

Pat Califia, Mary McIntosh, Lynne Segal and Carole Vance, gay men constituted a marginalised group with their own agenda and gay liberation
that, though far from unproblematic *for* women, was not necessarily *about*
women, the latter of which remained primarily the responsibility of feminism
(Califia, 1994; Segal and McIntosh, 1992; Vance, 1984). For Dworkin and
MacKinnon, as well as for Sheila Jeffreys and others, however, this separation was false (Dworkin, 1981; Jeffreys, 1990; MacKinnon, 1987; Stanley,
1982). For them, gay liberation was indeed about gender oppression and gay
men were deeply bound up with the degradation of women and the feminine.
The macho gay clone in celebrating the male and masculine sexuality was
then engaged precisely in the annihilation of the female and feminine
sexuality more widely.

What opened up rapidly here was the sense that it was the relationship of
gender and sexuality, here homosexuality and masculinity, that was at issue.
The more liberal feminist approach in successfully exposing the complexities
of sexuality also ran the risk of separating it entirely from gender; while more
radical or revolutionary feminists in asserting its very connectedness to
gender could lose sight of its specific significance. One potential solution
to an often escalating and entrenched sense of conflict emerged in the form
of a more poststructural feminism concerned precisely to undermine the
binaries of gender and sexuality *per se*, which I consider in the next section.

However, given the ongoing concern here with the connection and not
separation of homosexuality and masculinity, the development of men's
critical studies of masculinity remains significant if rather overshadowed. We
are presented with something of a problem here, though, namely the heterosexist bias of men's studies, a point put most forcibly by Tim Carrigan and
his colleagues in 'Toward a New Sociology of Masculinity' (Carrigan,
Connell and Lee, 1985). They argued that the emergent men's studies, particularly in the late 1970s, recognised neither the significance of gay liberation
in attempting to undermine traditional masculinity nor the importance of
heterosexuality in maintaining male domination, but paid mere lip service to
gay men in token chapters and short passages in otherwise overwhelmingly
white, middle-class and heterosexual works and perspectives. This was more
than partially explained as a result of the development of a new men's studies
of masculinity *as a response to* second-wave feminism both personally and
politically, and partly as a necessary outcome to the limits of the functionalist
sex role theory that informed these studies and which could only adapt to
seeing masculinity as a singular rather than pluralist concept and practice
(see Chapter 2).

However, where did this leave the new critical studies of men and
masculinity in relation to gay liberation? The answer is in some senses
frustratingly not very far forward. Following the arguments of radical
feminism, some made a blistering assault on the failures of gay liberation and
made gay men out to be near traitors to the cause of gender politics, while
at the opposite extreme the New Men's Movement promoted a return to a

traditional patriarchal order that was often implicitly if not explicitly homophobic (Stoltenberg, 2000). Although less problematic politically, the vast majority of more contemporary men's studies of masculinity still remains overwhelmingly generalist in focus, often merely making fairly fleeting or very specific mention of gay masculinities.

One exception to this, and perhaps a significant development in overcoming it, came in the work of Connell. In *Gender and Power*, Connell (1987) challenged the idea of a singular male sex role, arguing for a pluralistic and hierarchical notion of masculinities in which some forms were hegemonic and others subordinate. Thus, most obviously, black, gay and working-class masculinities were seen as subordinate to and indeed oppressed by white, heterosexual and middle-class masculinities that remained mostly dominant or hegemonic, although this was still contingent on changing social and political contexts. This took on a more empirical dimension in *Masculinities* (Connell, 1995). Following interviews with a small sample of gay men, Connell remains ambivalent concerning the impact of gay liberation on wider gender or masculinity politics. While acknowledging the fundamental subversion of heterosexual object choice in the formation of gay identities, Connell reiterates the sense that men's bodies also incorporate masculinity and so, in desiring them, gay men remain in a sense 'very straight'. The often overplayed watering-down of gay politics and its co-option into consumer culture also adds to the sense that the position of gay men for Connell remains contradictory in terms of gender politics. Here, then, gay men's identification as men may problematise masculinity but their desire for men limits their commitment to sexual politics. More particularly, such judgements on gay male sexuality also problematise the role of critical studies of masculinity that, like some forms of second-wave feminism, can be accused of kicking a minority when it's down rather than addressing their own heterosexism. We are, then, back to where we started, or the relationship between desire and identification in relation to homosexuality and masculinity. The question then is how to go forward.

From homosexual to homosocial: the poststructural solution

In this next section, I focus initially on the work of Eve Kosofsky Sedgwick and Judith Butler as two of the most eminent and influential poststructural theorists in relation to gender and sexuality. In addition, I will then consider more recent attempts to apply their work more directly to the question of gay masculinities.

In *Between Men*, Sedgwick started to forge a major reconsideration of the role and nature of homosexuality through an analysis of its representation across a range of North American, British and some other European literature (Sedgwick, 1985). In particular, she constructed a new concept of homosociality to describe the range of affective relationships between men that exist on a continuum from the unemotional to the fully homosexual.

As a result, though perhaps inadvertently, she drew a parallel with Adrienne Rich's influential notion of the lesbian continuum used to describe relationships between women (Rich, 1984). The main thrust of her analysis was, however, to interrogate the relationship of the homosexual and the masculine and, in particular, to expose the extent to which the two concepts are interdependent. Her discussion was also historically focused, seeing the homosexual identity as interdependent with emergent forms of masculinity throughout the nineteenth century. This then led to a series of highly sophisticated textual analyses of a selection of literary works from the mid-eighteenth century through to the mid-nineteenth century, from which Sedgwick extrapolated a complex map of developments in the gendered nature of male relationships. As an analysis within the discipline of literary criticism *per se* this was sophisticated, and indeed often quite dazzling, yet it remained problematic not least because of the exposition of a series of social and political developments from an analysis of primarily elite cultural texts.

Sedgwick then extended her analysis of the role of the homosexual in *Epistemology of the Closet* (Sedgwick, 1990). Following on from Foucault, she sought to deconstruct the category of the homosexual and, more importantly, the entire divisive system of sexual categorisation. The initial aim of her analysis was to undermine the persistence of 'the homosexual' as a defining category that simultaneously created the closet from which the homosexual had to endlessly 'come out'. The difficulty here was, and is, that the closet remains not merely a semantic construction, but also an institutionally supported social reality premised on wider processes of stigma and ostracism. To put it more simply, the discursive closet would not matter were it not for the negative consequences that may, and often do, ensue in coming out from the more social closet. However, the cut of Sedgwick's work was as much to address the semiotic question of the relationship of reader and text, as exemplified in her final chapter on Proust, as it was to address the question of homosexual oppression

Sedgwick's work also echoed that of Dennis Altman in *Homosexual: Oppression and Liberation* in which he foretold that the end of homosexual oppression would also entail the end of the homosexual identity (Altman, 1971). What was also implicit in Altman's predicament was, however, the perceived *necessity* of the homosexual identity in order to oppose the social, and indeed ontological, assumption of heterosexuality. Ironically, though recent decades have witnessed an ever-strengthening 'discourse of homosexuality', centred on increasing visibility and opposition to older negative definitions and stereotypes, discussion of heterosexuality has, for the most part, tended to remain overshadowed and it is difficult to see how Sedgwick's reverse policy of '*un*speaking' the homosexual can undermine this discursive privileging of the heterosexual, let alone make the quantum jump into its social and political dominance. The end of the homosexual, then, does not necessarily entail the end of the heterosexual and the project remains, perhaps ironically, to remove heterosexuality from the sanctity of its discursive closet.

In later work, Sedgwick (1995) forges a further disjuncture between sex and gender, here masculinity and homosexuality, as two concepts she perceived as not *necessarily* in any way directly related. In sum, masculinity does not necessarily relate to men, or men only, and Sedgwick returns to an understanding of gender centred on androgyny, as explored previously by Sandra Bem, whereby some men, and women, have more, or less, masculinity and indeed femininity (Bem, 1974). This would seem not only to implode gender dualisms but also to throw up another question entirely, namely the extent to which masculinity has anything to do with men, gay or straight, at all – a point I considered more fully in Chapter 1.

A similar problematic underpinned Judith Butler's attempt to implode the dualisms of gendered identity in *Gender Trouble* (Butler, 1990). Butler sought, in the first instance, to undermine the fundamental necessity of the category of 'woman' and asserted instead that a feminist politics must produce a radical critique of the politics of identity *per se*. Thus, the main thrust of her analysis was that gender exists primarily at the level of discourse. In addition, at least by implication, the bottom line of Butler's argument would seem, like Sedgwick's, to be that the feminine has little to do with the female and femininity little to do with women. However, as outlined in Chapter 6, Butler's ideas quickly became as controversial as they were influential, particularly in relation to the perception that there was an implicit attempt in Butler's work to shift emphasis away from more institutional practices of power towards more semantic concepts of discourse. Nevertheless, the concept of performance remained an important one that opened up potentially radical political solutions to overly entrenched understandings, and indeed practices.

How, though, does such a perspective work in relation to questions of masculinity and homosexuality? Butler, in following Freud, argues that masculine identification depends on a prior formation of sexual orientation and, in particular, a rejection of homosexuality (Butler, 1995). As a result, masculinity fundamentally and psychologically depends on the disavowal not only of femininity but of homosexuality and, in doing so, is predicated on a lack, or absence, rather than a given or a presence. The problem then becomes a near algebraic one: masculinity as a positive identification depends on a double, not single, negative dissociation. The additional, and profoundly psychological, difficulty here is that the loss of homosexuality is never avowed and therefore cannot be mourned. Butler's argument here draws on Freud's analysis of polymorphous perversity, whereby the infant experiences – and indeed gains from – both homosexual and heterosexual attachment but in order to successfully form a gender identity must suffer a loss, a loss moreover that cannot be affirmed. The double problem that then ensues for the male infant is that neither the attachment to another male, nor its loss, can be recognised, leading to the impossibility of *either* affirming *or* mourning homosexuality. This also has wider social implications reflected in the lack of recognition of gay male relationships and the intensity of difficulties involved in their loss for whatever reason. Thus, more particularly, the AIDS epidemic is seen to expose the anguish of gay men's grief as a difficulty in mourning *per se* and not only in relation to the epidemic more specifically. In sum, male homosexual attachment is put onto the never-never: never having lost and never having loved.

Where, though, does this leave our analysis of the relationship of homosexuality and masculinity? By way of concluding this section I consider the work of Bech as perhaps the most complete attempt to document the more contemporary nature of the relationship of masculinity and homosexuality in terms of more poststructural theory (Bech, 1997). In *When Men Meet*, Bech starts by critiquing social constructionism for its lack of explanatory power and then moves on to examine, pivotally, what he calls absent homosexuality. This is in essence a reworking of Sedgwick's notion of the homosocial, where masculinity is seen quite literally to depend on both the permanent presence and indeed absence of homosexuality. To put it more simply, relations between men, both past and present, are characterised by the constant possibility of, and quite simultaneously the equally continuous prohibition of, homosexuality. Thus homosexuality *per se* works as a primarily invisible mechanism in the maintenance of masculinity. For example, the homosexuality of many films is demonstrated through the explicit lack or absence of portrayals of homosexuality, a point echoed elsewhere (Kirkham and Thumin, 1993; Simpson, 1994). Bech starts to demonstrate the crucial extent to which homosexual identity depends even more fundamentally on masculinity than heterosexuality.

This is intriguing but it leads Bech into a constant over-playing of the significance of certain stereotypes of homosexuality, namely that homosexuality is all about furtive glances and even more furtive sexual practices usually conducted in cities. Quite where this leaves the monogamous practices of the suburban and rural homosexual is anyone's guess. His reworking of the relationship of homosexuality and masculinity also retains an untapped potential. In particular, it starts to tip into an analysis of visual culture and the ways in which the male, and the masculine, have increasingly become both the object as well as the subject of the gaze, for example in relation to contemporary patterns of sexual objectification, advertising and the world of fashion. This forms what he calls a 'telemediated' society, or visual and media culture that simultaneously emphasises processes of aestheticisation as well as sexualisation, by which relations between men become, almost by quirk, absent of absent homosexuality. Importantly, this would seem to extend Sedgwick's more historical and textual analysis of the homosocial towards an understanding of more contemporary and empirical developments concerning masculinity, yet Bech's analysis in the final instance is left hanging and inconclusive. Also implicit and problematic here is Bech's invocation of the increasing globalisation of gay sexuality, given the rising significance of the Internet and international travel and of sexual practices generally that not only inform the development of the AIDS epidemic and sex trafficking but also, according to Dennis Altman at least, begins to scramble the very certainties of gay identity, both theoretically and politically, as gay identity becomes at once both globalised and localised (Altman, 2001).

To summarise, these applications of poststructural theory have reworked understandings of the relationship of homosexuality and masculinity, in terms of sexuality and gender, as follows: successful heterosexual and masculine identification psychologically and socially depends on the repudiation of *both* femininity and homosexuality. In so doing, gay male sexuality offers a *potentially* radical challenge to both a psychological and social sexual and gender order. In addition, this poses a series of difficulties for gay men themselves, whose relationships and even losses are not avowed or recognised and whose desires have the potential to work against them as much as with them. In sum, the relationship between desire and identification, which I have argued to be at the core of the problematic raised by identity politics, is both explored and explicated beyond a sense of simple contradiction to become something which, in a sense, cuts both ways. In this scheme of things, then, gay men are neither more nor less 'masculine' or misogynist than straight men, but located in an awkward, and perhaps even dialectical, relation to gender both psychologically and socially.

Having said this, a number of significant difficulties remain both theoretically and politically. Perhaps the most fundamental of these is the relationship of such psychoanalytically or textually centred theory to social or even cultural practice. While some extrapolation of social and cultural implications from such work is perhaps easily accepted as simply commonsense, wider aspects and questions, including the issue of social and cultural change, are in no way straightforwardly 'read off' from the use of psychoanalytic, literary or textual analysis. Without wishing to imply any form of return to positivism, the sense of distance involved is often further reinforced through the lack of any more empirically centred research or evidence that might otherwise help to fill the gap exposed between theory and practice.

A second and equally difficult problematic concerns the question of value. Identity politics, for all its faults in setting up overly polarised and often divisive contests, not only used but rather developed, intentionally or not, a system of values. In relation to our discussion here, masculinity became problematised in value terms as something which was not neutral and which also had an impact on such phenomena as institutional power relations and violent crime. Some of this impact at least is potentially lost in overemphasising the analysis of masculinity at the expense of understanding men (see also Chapter 1).

Thirdly, as pointed out in Chapter 1, though masculinity remains a social construct that has no *necessary*, in the intrinsic sense, connection with men, it is clearly incorrect to state that is has *no* relationship to men *at all* or that this is not qualitatively different from its relationship to women. Furthermore, this also potentially undermines the sense in which masculinity itself can become problematised for both men and women. To put it more simply, if men and masculinity are not one and the same then they may still remain related and in separating them one should not disconnect them entirely.

More importantly, the tendency to separate analysis and theory from questions of practice and politics tends to neglect the fundamental ways in which patriarchy and indeed masculinity are reinforced and perpetuated through institutions both formal and informal and, perhaps most importantly of all, the resistance to change that may also come from individual men and women themselves. What this also begins to expose in more directly political terms is a problem of both relativism and liberalism. Masculinity, though clearly a lot more 'open' than once conceived is, quite clearly, not an entirely mutable phenomenon that is 'up for grabs', and some forms of 'performing' and 'doing' masculinity remain more, or less, problematic than others.

Where does this leave us in relation to gay men and indeed gay masculinities? Poststructural theory would seem to offer some more theoretical solutions to the conundrums and deadlocks often posed by identity politics, yet it equally tends to elide discussion of its applications and implications in practice. In sum, the difficulty remains more political. Despite all of this, there seems little reason to presume that these questions cannot be addressed more fully. More significantly, and perhaps ironically, this also seems to depend on undermining rather than reinforcing the sense of separation that has developed between so-called 'old guard' identity politics and 'avant garde' poststructural or queer theory and politics (Seidman, 1995). The continuing logic of social constructionism is critical here and the questions and the problems involved, if not necessarily the answers, would seem to remain the same.

Conclusions: identity and desire

At the risk of stating the obvious, the problem posed by gay masculinity is essentially one of sex. Gay men, by definition, desire other men yet also, to some extent at least, identify as men. To return to where I started, the current – and apparently increasing – acceptance of gay male sexuality is predicated far more on the question of identity than it is on desire, for if all the frightfully pretty, and perhaps even prissy, queens that occupy our TV screens today actually started having sex, in the sense of actually doing it in all the ways that gay men do, they would be off the air in seconds. In addition, the dual marketing of nearly all forms of visual culture from the endless parade of drop-dead gorgeous male flesh to the homosexual titivation of many story lines shows just how far gay desire has to go in coming out of the closet. Historically, of course, male same-sex desire has usually tended to undermine masculinity or to be socially acceptable only within strictly proscribed limits, for example in the initiation rights of ancient Greco-Roman culture. The contemporary attempts of gay liberation to celebrate a more unbridled form of gay male sexuality are therefore understandable. Yet it remains gay male desire rather than gay male identity that is most problematic in terms of gender politics. In often desiring casual, or promiscuous, sex with men frequently defined as somehow 'masculine' through reference to their physique, self-presentation, style of dress or quite simply penis size, gay male desire often remains chained to limited models of masculinity. Yet what does this matter unless it impacts on attitudes or practices more widely? In short, desire matters not unless it relates to identity. To be absolutely clear here, my point is emphatically not to moralise against gay male sexuality or, less still, to demonise an already stigmatised minority for its lack of feminist conviction, but to urge gay men and indeed gay politics more widely, to consider their own desires and preferences more critically *for themselves*. When gay male culture celebrates youth over age, sex over love and even style over substance, then where does this leave the older, more loving, men of substance that they inevitably become? It seems, then, that contemporary gay male culture, itself now reaching middle age, has developed its own self-portrait and even, like Dorian Gray, made its own Faustian deal with the devil with all that implies for its identities and desires (Wilde, 2000).

6 What are you looking at?

Masculinity, performativity and fashion

Despite the increasing popularity of performativity as theory and concept, and indeed the profusion of its uses, its definitions are often diffuse and its application to questions of masculinity, particularly outside cultural studies or queer politics, is often distinctly scarce. The purpose of this chapter is threefold: first, to attempt to document, delineate and define performativity theory and to open it up to sociological critique; second, to consider its applications to questions of masculinity; and third, more particularly, to provide a critique of performativity theory through a study of men's fashion. In this last instance, it is my assertion that if performativity theory is ineffective in relation to the world of fashion, which is often perceived as artificial and free-floating, if not necessarily superficial and postmodern, then it won't work anywhere and its application to questions of masculinity, and indeed gender identity more widely, is decidedly limited. As a result of these three intentions there are three sections: first, a discussion of performativity theory *per se*, its definitions, applications and critique; secondly, a consideration of performativity theory in relation to questions of masculinity; and thirdly, an analysis of men's fashion that attempts to evaluate, and perhaps synthesise, performativity theory more widely in the light of an empirically as well as theoretically informed study.

Dragging it up: the problems, limits and applications of performativity

What is performativity? In the first instance, it is necessary to differentiate, if only perhaps artificially, an understanding of performativity from the more common parlance sense of performance, from which it differs in two key senses. First, the concept of performance, whether in an artistic or theatrical form such as a play, a movie or an opera or in terms of 'putting on a show' more widely, clearly implies a sense of separation from the 'real' person so that, for example, an actor takes on a role that lives only as long as the play in which he or she acts, or a pop star has a media-driven *persona* that is often perceived as separate from the more private *person*, perhaps quite necessarily. Performativity theory refutes any such separation, as this implies the existence of an underlying and natural, or true and essential person that is not acted or performed. Second, performativity theory, in its attempt to demonstrate the artifice of human social interactions and identities in their entirety, argues that *all* acts, including those that are rendered entirely normative, are a form of performance or are 'performative'. In sum, there is no distinction between the performer and the performance for all is performative.

This second point clearly illustrates the extent to which performativity theory extends the anti-essentialist logic of social constructionist theory to imply that, at every level, identity is socially constructed, dynamic and open rather than natural, inevitable and fixed. To consider this in more detail, I will posit that one needs to recognise a second level of differentiation, between *doing* and *being* in relation to identity, and some of the fundamentals, and indeed history, of social constructionist theory. This distinction will also recur in later sections.

Although often unacknowledged, social constructionist theory can be seen to originate within the founding tenets of sociology that, in more general terms, sought to assert the social rather than the natural bases of human behaviour. Moreover, there was often a clear connection with the wider context, indeed legacy, of the Enlightenment and the rise of more scientific understandings of individual and social practices. For example, Emile Durkheim studied the way suicide, a phenomenon usually perceived solely within either individual or psychological limits, was often also strongly related to levels and patterns of social integration more widely (Durkheim, 1951 [1897]). In addition, some years later, George Herbert Mead, in criticising both what he saw as sociology's undervaluing of individual subjectivity and Cooley's over-emphasis on psychology, developed the concept of the 'I' and the 'Me' to explain precisely the more social development of the individual (Cooley, 1902; Mead, 1934). Mead argued that an internal sense of self, or the 'I', developed primarily in interaction with external social interactions and processes, or the 'Me'. Ultimately this meant that no sense of self, thought, or human action could exist in isolation from its more social context, a point explored in depth in the fields of interactionism and phenomenology.

Nevertheless, this still left the exact nature of the relationship of self and society open to further interpretation and indeed politicisation. The rise of identity politics in the 1960s and 1970s, itself following in the wake of new social movements such as feminism and gay liberation, often politicised the social construction of identities as part of an overall strategy of challenging what were frequently perceived as the natural or inevitable bases of human behaviour in relation to such issues as gender, sexuality and race. For example, the maternal instinct, sexual aggression in men, and racial differences in intelligence were all seen as being socially constructed rather than biologically determined (Woodward, 1997). However, though social constructionist theory in a variety of forms asserted that identities were socially constructed in an *external* sense, a more *internal* sense of self was often not specified or perhaps even perceived as being in conflict with the external one. Primary examples of this were feminist, anti-racist and gay ideas centred on the notion of liberation (see Chapter 2). These asserted that though patterns of oppression were often socially constructed, it remained the task of identity politics to emancipate, free or liberate a true, or more essential, individual or collective self. In addition, this was clearly also fuelled greatly by the rise and expansion of psychoanalytic theory throughout the twentieth century which, in different ways, consistently asserted the significance of a fragmented subjectivity often at odds with a more ordered external identity. Thus, while identities were increasingly recognised as being socially constructed in a more objective sense, the more subjective experience of gender, race and sexuality, or even the very categories themselves, often remained unchallenged (Wittig, 1997). For example, while femininity was increasingly recognised as a socially constructed identity, the category, and indeed experience, of being female was left unquestioned. To put it more simply, while social constructionist theory often questioned identity at the level of *doing*, it frequently failed to problematise identity at the level of *being* or, to return to Mead, it tended to emphasise the 'Me' rather than the 'I' in identity, and in turn tended to politicise rather than theorise the relationship between the two.

The problem of subjectivity in relation to identity, and indeed the construction of the human subject *per se*, were taken up in the work of Foucault as well as other French philosophers including Lacan and Derrida (Derrida, 1982; Foucault, 1984b; Lacan, 1977). It is not within the scope of my study here to document their ideas in detail, but, in more general terms and in varying ways, all these theorists sought to destabilise any essential notion of self, and human subjectivity was increasingly perceived as fragmented, multiple or simply contingent on social, historical or ideological contexts. All of this in turn can be seen to inform the theory of performativity. As I have illustrated previously, performativity theory expanded the logic of social constructionism to include such questions of subjectivity yet, to paraphrase Mead, it took this further still in rejecting the distinction between the 'I' and the 'Me' almost completely (Mead, 1934). Consequently, identities were perceived increasingly as matters of doing rather than being and a state of being only existed quite temporarily through repeated doing. The legacy of French existentialism, particularly the work of de Beauvoir and Sartre, was also present here, as what was often implicit in such analyses was the sense that the self was seen to have no *a priori* existence (De Beauvoir, 1952; Sartre, 1969).

With the possible exception of Simone de Beauvoir, none of this, though, tells us much about the relationship of performativity to gender, for which we need to consider the work of Judith Butler. Despite an often opaque writing style, Butler's work has been elevated to become the benchmark in understandings of gendered performativity and her name has now become synonymous with the invention and development of the concept (Butler, 1990, 1993). As I have already started to illustrate, this is something of an overstatement for the concept, if it has a particular fixed point at all, originates in the work of J. L. Austin (Austin, 1962). Austin's speech act theory attempted to show how discourse, or acts of speech, writing and naming can alone and in isolation produce, and indeed fix, meaning. For example, to say at the moment of birth 'It's a girl' gives an otherwise genderless infant the meanings, and indeed the subjective and objective position, of being a girl. Where Butler departed from Austin was in her attempt to incorporate this into a wider feminist project, starting in *Gender Trouble* (Butler, 1990). Here she sought to deconstruct the very category of 'woman' and argued that a feminist politics must produce a radical critique of identity *per se*. Also, in following French feminist and existentialist philosophy more widely, Butler then attempted to weld a Foucauldian notion of discourse to a primarily Lacanian form of psychoanalysis. Consequently, she argued that subject positions, in the Foucauldian sense, could not be understood without reference to the unconscious, as defined in Lacanian terms or, to put it more simply, that what they were was part and parcel of what they were not. For example, a masculine subject position was perceived as a rejection of a feminine subject position in unconscious terms. In addition, via a series of often dense and psychoanalytically driven investigations, she also attempted to demonstrate the mutual dependence and contradictions of the categories of sex and gender as wholly artificial and unnatural con-structions that exist primarily at the level of repeated performance. As a result, she saw gender as, quite literally, only truly existing through a contin-uous process of acting, speaking, and doing. There was, however, an added dimension here, for she also argued that gender was performed according to social sanctions and mores that could, and did, lead to what she called 'punishments' on a number of levels that varied from social ostracism to legal control. Nevertheless, the thrust of her analysis was that gender primarily existed at the level of discursive formations in the Foucauldian sense.

Butler later attempted to demonstrate this further through an analysis of drag, or female impersonation, in order to illustrate the imitative and contingent nature of gender itself. These issues were addressed most fully in *Bodies That Matter*, where she tried to define and unpack performative theory in more detail (Butler, 1993). In particular, she sought to separate understandings of performativity from simpler notions of theatricality and, furthermore, argued that performative acts were not necessarily subversive, or rather that this depended on the wider political context. Thus, though drag performances of gender could be contained within a wider heterosexual frame, for example within the historical legacy of camp comedy, other forms of their expression may be more subversive, as in the case of queer politics that attempts to subvert, and indeed invert, the very history and notion of the term 'queer'.

Butler's work has been embraced with considerable enthusiasm by queer theory and some aspects of lesbian and gay studies more widely (Bristow and Wilson, 1993; Harwood *et al.*, 1993; Nicholson and Seidman, 1995). Perhaps most famously, Judith Halberstam attempts to employ similar processes of discursive deconstruction in her work on female masculinity, attempting ultimately to rupture *any* connection between sex and gender in her discussion of cultural texts and practices ranging from Radclyffe Hall's *The Well of Loneliness* and lesbianism to queer activism and more contemporary drag king performances (Halberstam, 1998; Radclyffe Hall, 1982). Perhaps not surprisingly, however, both Butler's and Halberstam's discussions of drag more specifically led to considerable debate and controversy, primarily at a more political level, within the feminist movement, and their ideas are viewed with an increasing sense of scepticism, a situation well summarised in the recent work of Lynne Segal (Segal, 1999). Segal locates Butler's work within a wider tradition of queer politics which she in turn perceives as emerging from the study of sexuality as a category in its own right. This movement itself was spearheaded by the work of Gayle Rubin who, in the 1980s, challenged the then growing North American radical feminist attempt to subsume the analysis of sexuality within the study of gender (see Chapter 5). For Segal this also led, perhaps quite positively, to a *de*-marginalising of minorities and a celebration of perversion but also, more negatively, to the collapse of a more radical feminist politics based on the woman-identified woman. However, Segal then questions this, arguing that 'an awareness that gender is "socially", "performatively" or "discursively"constructed, is very far from a dismantling of gender' and she notes how easily performative theory sits alongside wider consumer capitalist politics of commodified individualism and free choice (Segal, 1999: 63). Thus, for Segal at least, while importantly documenting the *power relations* of gendered discourse, Butler's work runs the risk of missing an analysis of gendered *power per se* as an institutionally coercive, politically sanctioned and socially practised series of mechanisms of oppression. In addition, what this also illustrates more widely is the tendency of performativity theory to undermine or neglect the more material, in the sense of economic and physical, foundations of identity and identity politics and indeed power itself. More specifically, one more controversial development here has been the way in which considerations of performativity have also begun to feed into debates about the body (see Chapter 8). Despite its potential and pitfalls in relation to feminism, where does performativity theory lead us in relation to questions of masculinity?

The great pretender: masculinity and performativity

In common with and following on from the feminist critique of femininity, the critical – if not necessarily sociological – analysis of masculinity starts from the premise that masculinity is a social construct. Thus, neither men's position of power, nor the problematic aspects and effects of masculinity varying from emotional repression to sexual violence, are seen as inevitable and fixed or the result of biology and destiny. Consequently, masculinity is seen to vary from time to time and place to place and, more importantly, to have the capacity to change and develop towards more positive ends. Thus, in crude terms, it was argued that if masculinity was simply the result of testosterone one might as well give up on any progress in sexual politics or alternatively castrate the entire male gender, something that, though perhaps appealing to some, one suspected might not solve the problem (Connell, 1987). This then became precisely the conundrum on which critical men's studies of masculinity were founded or, in short, the emancipation of women was seen to depend increasingly on the unpacking of masculinity and perhaps even the liberation of men, the problematic and political implications of which did not go unnoticed within feminism (see Chapter 2). More specifically, it also opened up the potential to relate masculinity to questions of performativity, both more academically in terms of social construction and more politically in terms of men's own experiences and capacity to change.

In more theoretical terms critical men's studies of masculinity originated in primarily functionalist and often North American sex role theory that argued that any gender identity, and this included masculinity, was the result of socialisation or more simply social learning. Early studies in this area, particularly in the 1970s, were also at pains to point out that the male sex role was also limiting and indeed negative, for men as well as women (David and Brannon, 1976; Farrell, 1974; Goldberg, 1976; Hoch, 1979; Tolson, 1977). The most common complaint here was that men were chained to a model of masculinity that was fundamentally one-dimensional, emotionally limiting and, interestingly for our analysis here, centred on models of performance, whether in the boardroom or the bedroom, that were as outmoded as they were unattainable. Recognisable as this image of big boys not crying, growing into men grunting and groaning through the rest of their lives, soon became, two difficulties arose: first, socialisation did not take place on a level playing field and, while similarly socially constructed, masculinity remained socially privileged over femininity; and second, if masculinity was socially constructed then who or what constructed the constructors (Connell, 1987; Edley and Wetherell, 1995; Kimmel, 1987b)? I will return to these questions shortly. What these early studies did raise was the sense that masculinity, rather than femininity, was the more immediately and perhaps more directly 'performed' gender. It is the purpose of the rest of this section, to interrogate further the question of just what masculinity has to do with performativity, and indeed vice versa, through an analysis of men's critical studies of masculinity.

As previously outlined in the Introduction, the study of masculinity can be perceived to have developed in three stages or 'waves'. The first wave, as I have already started to outline, saw masculinity as a socially constructed identity into which boys were socialised to become socially acceptable men. This identity was primarily defined in terms of sex role theory, which argued that masculinity was simply the consequence, effect or outcome of the male sex role. The elements of this role, and indeed its emphasis, centred on the key institutions of family, work and education through which boys became men and, in particular, by which strong values of competitiveness, careerism and success were instilled. Consequently, many studies sought to demonstrate how boys were encouraged to participate in sports and other outdoor or competitive activities while their emotional sensitivities were otherwise actively repressed through the withdrawal of physical affection and the increasing stigmatisation of expressions of vulnerability such as crying (Maccoby and Jacklin, 1974). These processes were then reproduced, and indeed reinforced, through the competitive aspects of schooling, which in turn fed directly into the expectations of the workplace. Furthermore, most authors in the area were at pains to point out that these processes had negative consequences for men themselves, who were perceived as increasingly trapped within a position not of their own making and chained to a series of hopelessly unrealistic expectations that undermined both their physical health and psychological happiness, as well as having a negative impact on the women with whom they worked and lived (Goldberg, 1976).

However, various and increasingly virulent criticisms were levelled at these perspectives and developments, including the sense that such complaints were clearly at odds with men's positions of power and indeed their opportunities to change the situation and that this was a predominantly white, middle-class and heterosexual perspective that took insufficient account of the varying experiences of working-class, black, and gay men (Carrigan, Connell and Lee, 1985). Nevertheless, what remains interesting for our analysis here was the sense in which the concepts and practices of masculinity alike were increasingly perceived as centred on a model of performance. Men were seen to essentially 'perform' their masculinity through success at sports, in their careers, or through their sexual conquests. Consequently, this then became an historic moment in which masculinity rather than femininity was perceived as the greater pretender. The difficulty for our analysis here, however, is twofold. First, this model of performance was limited to one form of masculinity, namely a predominantly white, Western, heterosexual and, on occasions, middle-class masculinity. Thus, the performative aspects of other forms of masculinity whether black, gay or working-class were often left unexplored. Second, and moreover, these early studies of masculinity offered little theorisation of performativity in relation to masculinity and tended to utilise mostly commonsense understandings of the concept. In addition, more politically, any analysis of the performative dimensions of masculinity opened up the potential for change. To put it more simply, if men were perceived to perform masculinity one way, then it was argued they could perform it another way or not perform it at all. However, the growing recognition of the significance, and indeed persistence, of gendered inequalities and men's often profound unwillingness to change at all, did much to undermine the development of the concept, whether academically or politically, and men's studies of masculinity rapidly started to turn their attention elsewhere.

Heavily influenced by developments in feminism during the 1980s, the second wave of men's studies of masculinity was significantly more critical of the male sex role, men's complaints and indeed any discussion of masculinity as a performance. The work of Connell in particular sought to undermine such one-dimensional understanding of masculinity and to open it up to a wider consideration of social structures and their relationship to a plurality of masculinities and indeed a complexity of outcomes (Connell, 1987). Thus, some forms of masculinity were perceived as hegemonic and indeed oppressive to others that were subordinate so that affluent, white and heterosexual men had a part to play in the oppression of poorer men or those occupying positions across a varied spectrum of ethnicities and sexualities. More significantly still, men's practices of masculinity were open to scrutiny as actively challenging, passively complying with, or simply negatively reinforcing the status quo. The study of masculinity was also increasingly exposed to a wider variety of theoretical influences, including more philosophical enquiry in the work of Vic Seidler, radical feminist interrogation around questions of violence in the work of Jeff Hearn, and the role of autobiography in the work of David Morgan, to mention only some (Hearn, 1998; Morgan, 1992; Seidler, 1989). Similarly, the institutions of education and work were increasingly investigated and the problems of masculinity's links with crime and violence uncovered (Hearn and Parkin, 1987; Messerschmidt, 1993; Pollard, 1985). Progressive and expansive as much of this work was in opening up new lines of enquiry and advancing more theoretical understandings of masculinity, it often came up with few answers to such real and persistent problems as discrimination in the workplace and sexual expression. More particularly for our analysis here, despite some potentially clear applications, it did little to advance understanding of performativity, as either a concept or practice, in relation to masculinity.

Perhaps partly due to some of these frustrations, the third wave or development in men's critical studies of masculinity has often sought to completely overhaul the entire concept of masculinity and has tended to shift attention away from the practices of masculinity to their theorisation. Much of this theorisation has in turn been informed by the rise of poststructural theory, including some queer theory and, perhaps not coincidentally, it has also refocused attention once again on questions of performativity, particularly in the work of Mark Simpson whose book *Male Impersonators* highlights this dimension (Simpson, 1994). Simpson analyses a series of contemporary topics relating to questions of masculinity, including the rise of male narcissism, changes in men's shopping practices, and shifts in representations of masculinity either in advertising, for example in relation Levi's jeans and Calvin Klein underwear, or the media more widely, as in the case of the career of film star Tom Cruise. The thrust of Simpson's analysis is that traditional understandings of masculinity centred on work and formal public life have begun to break down and are being replaced by more media- and image-driven notions of masculinity that centre on matters of how men look and, more particularly, lead to an undermining and indeed blurring of boundaries concerning sexuality. The rise of gay culture is seen as being critical here, as is the inevitable emphasis placed on men simply looking at other men within an increasingly visual culture, a point picked up on in recent discussions of the rise of men's fashion and the New Man that I will consider in detail shortly (Edwards, 1997; Mort, 1996; Nixon, 1996). Simpson's work is heavily informed by his reading of Freudian psychoanalytic theory, particularly as it relates to the formation of masculine identity and its dependency on repressed, yet often unresolved, polymorphous perversity if not homosexuality. His sense and use of the concept of performance is, however, rather under-theorised while his work otherwise tends to remain located within journalism.

Poststructural theory has been applied with more rigour to the question of sexual politics in the work of Alan Petersen (Petersen, 1998). Petersen criticises, with some severity, the second wave of men's studies of masculinity for their under-theorisation of sexuality and gender as well as their neglect of poststructural theory and more postmodern forms of feminism, including the work of Foucault and Butler, as well as the theory of performativity *per se*. The underlying thrust of his critique is that men's studies of masculinity have traditionally lacked an awareness of their own epistemological foundations within modern Western philosophy and therefore possess a strong tendency towards an essentialism of sexuality and gendered identity, a reinforcement of various dichotomies including those of sex/gender, mind/body, and heterosexual/homosexual, plus a distinct propensity towards the reification of masculinity *per se*. Consequently, for example, the work of Connell is criticised for reinforcing the sense in which 'sex' as a fixed biology is separate from 'gender' as a socially constructed culture, while the male body is not problematised as an historical category but seen to be a fixed entity that is merely reflexively acted on by an autonomous and rational self. Similarly, Connell's influential conception of hegemonic and subordinate masculinities is seen to unquestioningly reify its own categories and to insufficiently critique their construction and indeed variation. Moreover, in common with many other Anglo-American authors, Connell is seen to neglect many more contemporary developments within feminism and questions of ethnic variation. As I have already discussed in Chapter 2, there is much salience in Petersen's critique yet there remains a difficulty in moving forward from such criticisms towards new directions or applications in the study of masculinity. More specifically, his discussion of performativity remains primarily prescriptive and under-developed. Whatever the theoretical merits of more poststructural theorisations of masculinity, they have yet to demonstrate many more empirical applications.

Where poststructural theorisations of masculinity have often been applied more directly is in media studies. David Buchbinder in particular applies performance theory in some detail to a variety of media formats, from which he extrapolates some wider generalisations (Buchbinder, 1998). Like Mark Simpson, Buchbinder draws heavily on psychoanalytic theory to assert that successful masculine identification fundamentally depends on a negation of both the feminine and the homosexual. Consequently, gay masculinity is seen to disrupt both the essentialism and the stability of masculine identity, as in the case of gay men 'straight acting' and therefore highlighting masculinity precisely as an act or performance. Evidence for these assertions is found in textual representations of masculinities varying from advertising for men's underwear to Hollywood movies and from *The Tempest* to *Dracula*, all of which, when successfully deconstructed, are seen to expose the anxieties and contradictions of masculine identity. Erudite as his analysis often is, the difficulty remains in making the rather quantum jump from textual representation to social practice. Pfeil's *White Guys: Studies in Postmodern Domination and Difference* similarly plunders a wide range of primarily cinematic texts in relation to masculinity yet tends to end up doing little more than assuming a connection with wider societal developments (Pfeil, 1995). Evidence of the effectiveness of performativity theory in analysing textual representations of masculinity does not necessarily constitute evidence of wider social change outside of those representations. This is of course a point explored more fully elsewhere (see Chapter 1).

The most radical conjunction of masculinity and poststructural theory is, however, found in the work of MacInnes, who predicts the end of masculinity as a result of the increasing instability of the very categories of gender and an assault on the values of masculinity in particular (MacInnes, 1998). MacInnes's assertion rests on a partly philosophical and partly historical foundation. He argues that masculinity is not only an historical construction but one which is entirely historically contingent and, in particular, was set up as a defence of patriarchy in the wake of modernity. Consequently, he also sees it as increasingly irrelevant as the gender identities of both masculinity and femininity are now perceived to be rapidly imploding under the weight of contemporary developments including changing employment patterns and feminism. In sum, masculinity is perceived to have come unstuck as it was poorly stuck together in the first place. MacInnes's argument is partly supported through an analysis of some more empirical dimensions such as the feminisation of employment, yet is far more rigorously defended in relation to his re-evaluation of the work of political philosophers such as Hobbes, his reconsideration of the legacy of psychoanalysis and more particularly Freud, and his use of the work of some key feminists such as Pateman and Rubin on the sex/gender system (Pateman, 1988; Rubin, 1975). Fundamental in all of this is the idea that sexual genesis is falsely confused with sexual difference, or 'what results from us all being born *of* a man *and* a woman with what results from being born *as* a man *or* a woman' (MacInnes, 1998: 17). More elementally, MacInnes seeks to separate masculinity from men and to see it simply as a quality or set of attributes applicable to men or women. Implicit within this analysis, then, is the sense that masculinity does not exist, other than through historically constructed performance. Though in some ways both appealing and relevant to our investigation here, this perspective is not without its problems *per se*, as I have outlined in Chapter 1. Nonetheless, what is still significant here is the sense that MacInnes's analysis, while extending the logic of perceiving masculinity in terms of performative theory, remains primarily philosophically rather than empirically driven.

In conclusion to this section, I have repeatedly explored and, I hope, also illustrated the often unresolved relationship between studies of masculinity and the theory of performativity, or indeed more commonsense understandings of performance. Though there is a very clear and apparent sense in which contemporary Western masculinities are often centred on models of performance, whether on the sports field, at work or in sexual relationships, this remains often poorly developed and under-theorised in earlier studies of masculinity. Later studies have gone some way towards developing a more sophisticated theoretical understanding of performativity yet have equally often failed to demonstrate many more direct or empirical applications. Moreover, then, can performativity theory enlighten a more empirical analysis of masculinity in relation to men's fashion?

Dandies, idols and lads: men's fashion

Men's fashion is perhaps something of a contradiction in terms: women are fashionable, men are not. Evidence for this assertion rests primarily on two interlinked factors: first, the separation and indeed gendering of production and consumption that is now commonly perceived to have taken place following the rise of industrial capitalism; and second, a canon of work on fashion, and costume history in particular, that has tended to follow Flügel's notion of the Great Masculine Renunciation where he argued that men and masculinity became divorced from issues of fashion and decoration during the nineteenth century (see, for example, Craik, 1994; Flügel, 1930; Lury, 1996; Nava, 1992; Wilson, 1985). Recent literature has, however, gone some way to overturn this assumption. In particular, Chris Breward has provided a far more detailed and nuanced history of men's fashion which suggests that men's fashion is as multiple and complex as the formations and constructions of masculinities to which it clearly relates, a point echoed in my own work as well as elsewhere (Breward, 1999; Cole, 2000; Edwards, 1997). More specifically, discussions of the New Man within sociology and gender studies have also tended to question any rigid polarising of gender and fashion (Chapman and Rutherford, 1988; Mort, 1996; Nixon, 1996). The purpose of this section is to reassess the relationship of masculinity and fashion and, more particularly, to evaluate the extent to which the theory of performativity provides a tool for understanding more contemporary developments in relation to masculinity.

When studying fashion, however, one is faced with an immediate question of definition in the first instance. Most fundamentally, one may understand fashion as *dress*, or adornment more generally, yet this is distinct from, though equally clearly related to, fashion as *style*, or a wider phenomenon of taste which can potentially apply to more or less anything. For example, it is important to distinguish discussion of men's fashion as a range of clothes on or off the catwalk (fashion as dress) from men's fashion as a series of codings of what is 'in' or 'out' (fashion as style). The question is compounded further by realising the distinction between fashion as a matter of *production or design*, epitomised in its purest form in haute couture, and fashion as a matter of *consumption or use*, most clearly evoked through patterns of customisation and street style. This question of definition has major ramifications more academically as different notions of fashion are studied and analysed in different ways and indeed in different locations or disciplines. For example, haute couture has traditionally been studied under the auspices of art history while street style has usually been analysed by theorists of subculture. Similarly, this affects the sociological discussion of fashion, which focuses primarily on fashion as a phenomenon rather than fashion as dress while, interestingly, the study of fashion *per se* still remains located within the domains of art and design (see Edwards, 2000).

Significantly, most of the more sociological literature on men's fashion seeks to understand its significance as a phenomenon rather than as a matter of dress and, in addition, is often theoretically led rather than research-driven. Moreover, most of this work tends to postulate a series of fairly grandiose points related to the sexual politics of the 1980s and 1990s, often focused strongly on the iconography of the New Man as the organising factor in the analysis, with varying outcomes. For example, Chapman and Rutherford's ground-breaking collection *Male Order: Unwrapping Masculinity* framed its analysis of the New Man primarily in terms of responses to feminism, yet ended up mostly admitting that this development was more the result of ploys in marketing than progress in sexual politics, while the journalist Jon Savage similarly wrote that the New Man was simply the same old wolf in designer clothes (Chapman and Rutherford, 1988; Savage, 1996). Frank Mort's *Cultures of Consumption* provided an analysis of the phenomenon as a form of cultural history, in which the rise of the New Man was seen as the result of a series of shifts within commercial culture itself since the Second World War, including the rise of tailoring *en masse* for men and the development of various entrepreneurial initiatives in the 1980s, as well as the reinvention of the flâneur in areas such as Soho in London (Mort, 1996). Sean Nixon's somewhat linked analysis centred more on developments in visual culture, and the New Man was seen precisely as a figure of spectatorship constructed at the level of advertising itself, as well as in retailing, marketing and the media more widely, which were in turn supported through the expansion of flexible specialisation in mass production (Nixon, 1996). Mort and Nixon remained tentatively positive concerning these developments in terms of their capacity to reconstruct new forms of masculinity within consumer culture along less traditional and less divisive lines. My own work challenged some of these points, particularly in relation to the pluralism of some of the imagery, yet also remained primarily an analysis of men's fashion in relation to a much wider set of developments in consumer culture and masculinity (Edwards, 1997). One of my key concerns here was the extent to which the contemporary expansion of men's fashion was potentially socially divisive through its often heavy emphasis on a form of consumer culture that tended to target the young, white and affluent or city man, which often had the effect, intended or not, of excluding many older, rural or simply poorer men (Edwards, 2000). As explored in Chapter 2, a similar literature has also started to develop to investigate the significance of men's style magazines such as *GQ* and *Arena* (Benwell, 2003; Jackson *et al.*, 2001)

Arguably underlying all of these analyses, however, is an often unacknowledged concern with understanding or perceiving masculinity as increasingly a matter of performance. Consequently, all of these studies in differing ways seek to demonstrate the significance of changes in masculinities, whether in terms of sexual politics or wider developments in visual and commercial culture and, in particular, relate to ways in which masculinity is seen to increasingly depend on matters of style, self-presentation and consumption as opposed to more traditional models of masculinity centred on work and production or, to put it more simply, masculinity is perceived to be increasingly predicated on matters of how men *look* rather than what men *do*. In the aforementioned studies, concern is raised as to the wider significance of increased attention to men's appearances, male vanity or even patterns of exhibitionism and voyeurism, which are then perceived, implicitly at least, as 'performances' of masculinity. Consequently, one *could*, though I am not saying one *should*, see these analyses as evidence for, or perhaps against, understanding masculinity in terms of performativity.

This perception is premised in turn on a series of assumptions concerning the meanings of men's fashion or indeed fashion in general. These include: first, the notion that fashion is a primarily ephemeral if not superficial phenomenon that gains much of its significance through its connection to questions of identity; second, that this further illustrates the socially constructed and contingent nature of identities and indeed masculinities; and third, that this relates, perhaps quite directly, to questions of identity politics, and sexual politics more specifically, as fashion is perceived to have the potential to disrupt commonly perceived understandings of gender, race or sexuality. It is, I think, clear that the recent sociological analysis of men's fashion, primarily operating through the organising principle of the New Man, is strongly linked to the wider analysis of masculinity and performativity outlined earlier, or is at least on the same terrain with it. However, I wish to assert that this connection is in turn premised on an understanding of men's fashion that is partial and incomplete, if not inadequate. These limits are in particular exposed through taking a more empirical and less theoretical approach to the subject of men's fashion.

The expansion of interest in matters of men's fashion and appearances arguably remains an empirical fact demonstrated in the following ways: first, the rise of men's designer fashion and catwalk collections, a phenomenon first introduced in the 1980s; second, the rise of cultural intermediaries in relation to men's fashion and, more specifically, the developing crop of style and fashion magazines used to disseminate, dissect and direct matters of men's fashion and grooming; third, the exponential growth of various markets related to men's style and appearances including cosmetics and grooming products, plus the rise of spas, treatments and similar services including cosmetic surgery; fourth, the growth of interest in men's fitness and sports, particularly as pertaining to gym culture, personal training and health and fitness magazine titles; and fifth, an overall rise in media interest in such issues coupled with the clear promotion of an interest in men's appearances *per se*, whether in the form of direct advertising, for example for jeans or moisturisers, or the wider promotional culture surrounding male models, sports stars and celebrities (Edwards, 1997).

None of these developments are without limits, though, both in terms of their scope and their wider significance. In the first instance, it is important to realise that men's fashion and indeed all fashion is as much a matter of production as it is consumption. More particularly, as various commentators have noticed, the production of fashion has become increasingly globalised, racialised and based on flexible, if not necessarily small-scale and batch, production methods (McRobbie, 1998; Nixon, 1996; Phizacklea, 1990). Importantly, this tends to undermine any simplistic or one-sided understanding of the wider significance of fashion in terms of its consumption alone. To put it more simply, fashion is as much a commercial phenomenon as it is a sexual and political one. As a result, its wider importance in terms of contemporary identities primarily rests on what is a partial understanding of it as a matter of consumption. Secondly, the expansion of interest in matters of men's fashion and style is perhaps more media-fuelled than real, as the market for women's fashion, let alone related markets in cosmetics and accessories, still remains several-fold larger than the market for men's fashion. Thirdly, the significance of men's fashion is more demographically specific and often focused strongly on younger men, more affluent men or, most importantly, those living and working in a metropolitan environment. Moreover, rates of growth across the sector remain relatively even, so there is little reason to predict any incipient change in outcome. In sum, then, in assessing the significance of men's fashion we are considering the more specific importance of fashion consumption within particular economic, demographic and geographic limits.

However, having said this, shifts in men's fashion and patterns of consumption remain significant more academically in ways that clearly relate to matters of masculinity and performativity. First, the increased attention to questions of men's fashion and appearances can be seen to undermine previously rigid boundaries concerning the social acceptability of men's consumption. It is clearly now more socially acceptable for at least some men to indulge in what have previously been defined as feminine forms of consumption, including shopping for fashion, using moisturisers, colognes and similar cosmetic products, or taking an interest in improving their appearance more generally. There are of course still limits to this as men's use of make-up, skirts and high heels tends to remain both unacceptable and untenable. Second, these developments can also be perceived to lead to some blurring of the boundaries concerning both gender and sexuality as the consumption patterns of both men and women, whether heterosexual or homosexual, are argued to have become more similar and encoded more according to other geographic or demographic factors. This is in turn potentially a reflection of the wider significance of lifestyle marketing and consumption patterns in which *psycho-graphic* matters of styles, attitudes and personality are increasingly seen to override previously *demographic* matters of age, gender or class (Edwards, 2000). A third factor here is the way in which changes in men's fashion can be seen to illustrate wider processes within visual and media culture including, in particular, the role of celebrity cultures and the influence of media icons such as David Beckham, whose feminised form of masculinity, including his considerable interest in fashion and grooming, is a near permanent feature of media interest (Cashmore, 2002).

So where does this leave us in relation to our understanding of masculinity and performativity? On the face of it, fashion has much to do with matters of performance, often demonstrating the artifice and contingency as well as the fluidity of appearances and identities that are in turn strongly related to questions of race, sexuality and indeed gender. In addition, one could also argue that an increased emphasis on men's fashion *per se* undermines many more essentialist understandings of masculinity and indeed gender divisions more widely. More fundamentally, fashionable, image-conscious or simply 'dressy' men are often seen to arouse anxieties in gendered as well as sexual terms, being perceived not only as potentially gay or sexually ambiguous but as somehow not fitting in, particularly in terms of rumbling any wider belief in masculinity as a form of profoundly 'un-self-conscious being-ness' or in undermining the notion that 'real' men just throw things on or just *are* men. All of this would seem to bolster the claims of performative theory to understand, and indeed undermine, more traditional notions of masculinity. The problem here, however, is that one can equally argue that such displays of the artifice and performance of masculinity precisely reinforce the distinction between 'real' and 'unreal' masculinity or, more specifically, between acting or *doing* masculine and *being* masculine as outlined earlier.

In this sense, then, an analysis of men's fashion backfires on any performative perspective that seeks to undermine such boundaries. More problematically, such performative understandings of men's fashion are limited on two counts: first, empirically in relation to the fact that, as I have previously documented elsewhere, fashionable men are a fairly demographically specific group; and second more academically as any increase or developments in it may well not mean anything very much in terms of sexual politics or gendered identities and a lot more in terms of wider commercial and visual cultures (Edwards, 1997). In short, the contemporary rise of men's fashion and male vanity may have little to do with the supposed increasing significance of performative aspects of gendered identity, or indeed have much to do with masculinity at all.

Conclusions: What are you looking at?

Commonsense would seem to indicate that contemporary Western forms of masculinity may have much to do with matters of performance. From the boardroom to the bedroom and from the bar counter to the bar bell, masculinity would seem to be all about performing, showing off or, more particularly, to be about being competitive. Coupled with this, the superficial, fickle or just plain vain world of fashion, now perhaps perceived as turning its attention to questions of men and masculinity as much as women and femininity, would appear to add credence to the idea that masculinity is increasingly all about artifice, appearance and dressing up or, in short, performance.

It is perhaps surprising, then, that literatures on masculinity, fashion and performativity alike have tended to lack much articulation, or even consideration, of such questions. In the first instance, this is perhaps explained in relation to the rise of performative theory as an extension of the logic of social construction on the one hand and as an engagement with the legacy of existential philosophy on the other. The impact of performative theory has, however, primarily remained limited to the fields of feminism and queer theory. Yet we are faced with a curious return to where we started. When Ann Oakley wrote *Sex, Gender and Society* and Sandra Bem carried out her famous studies of androgyny, the world – at least academically – seemed to acknowledge that sex does indeed have little, if anything, to do with gender and masculinity is simply a set of culturally constructed qualities that men, or women, may or may not possess when assessed (Bem, 1974; Oakley, 1972). However, well over thirty years later, it seems we have gone backwards as the recurrent postmodern attempt to prove the artifice of masculinity through performativity seems to only reinforce the sense that real masculinity might still exist somewhere else. Just as the drag queen consistently reveals the cock beneath the skirt, so performativity reveals the body beneath the performance. Similarly, when Simon Watney wrote that when Western governments started producing campaigns telling people that AIDS was not a homosexual disease, they ended up telling them most emphatically that it *was*, he revealed the discursive logic of any binary (Watney, 1987). Thus, essentialism proves constructionism; male proves female; black shows white; and so on, and vice versa, *ad infinitum* . . . Of course, performativity is supposedly all about breaking down binaries yet, in its near existential battering of biological realities, it ends up reconstructing the loop and reinforcing the dualisms all over again.

The adoption of performativity theory within studies of masculinity more specifically has tended to remain restricted to early sex role theory, itself often rejected by later studies and more contemporary analyses of masculinity influenced by poststructuralist theory (Buchbinder, 1998; David and Brannon, 1976; Farrell, 1974; Hoch, 1979; Petersen, 1998; Pfeil, 1995; Simpson, 1994). In either case, more empirical applications have often been lacking. More sociological studies of masculinity and fashion, particularly in the guise of the analysis of the New Man, have often raised questions concerning performativity yet have often also failed to acknowledge these more explicitly or to provide much empirical support for their often equally implicitly assumed answers (Chapman and Rutherford, 1988; Mort, 1996; Nixon, 1996). A more empirical analysis of fashion *per se* provides *some* support for understanding masculinity as an increasingly performative phenomenon, yet this remains strictly limited within specific and primarily consumption-driven economic, demographic and geographic parameters (Edwards, 1997). It is ironic, then, that what one is looking at here is a phenomenon that is often ill explored, poorly documented, and a good deal more limited than it might at first appear.

7 The spectacle of the male
Masculinity and the cinema

We look at men all the time and in all contexts from the home to the class-room and from the workplace to the street, yet the paradox or conundrum here is that we are often unaware of quite *what* we are looking at or that we are indeed looking at it. The unconsciousness of this gazing *per se* is perhaps significant or worthy of investigation in itself and is most recently studied in relation to the rise of men's fashion (Edwards, 1997; Mort, 1996; Nixon, 1996). Conversely, cinematic images of men and indeed masculinity are perhaps some of the most conspicuous and, moreover, most *conscious* forms of looking at men that we engage in. It is the intention of this chapter to explore and unpack exactly how and what we are looking at when we look at men, particularly when considering masculinity as it is presented through the medium of cinema.

There is now a vast literature covering representations of men and mas-culinity within the worlds of film and cinema and, more importantly, an equally copious academic concern with the mechanisms of how we look at men and the gender relations involved in viewing (Cohan and Hark, 1993; Jeffords, 1994; Kirkham and Thumin, 1993; Mackinnon, 1997; Mulvey, 1975; Neale, 1982; Silverman, 1992). In sum, *how* we look is often perceived as impacting on *what* we are looking at and vice versa. More significantly, the most fundamental axiom or linchpin around which these looking rela-tions are perceived to revolve is gender. Gender is in turn seen as a signifier of difference or a matter of fundamental bi-polar division that in turn forms and underlines an entire understanding of cinema and indeed representation *per se* (Mulvey, 1975, 1981)

Attempting to explore, unpack and assess what exactly is going on in such an analysis involves a discussion of the following concerns: first, the nature and analysis of viewing relations and how these are connected with questions of gendered difference; second, a discussion of how such an analysis is then applied to the cinema, masculinity or society more widely; and third, a direct attempt to put such an analysis into practice through a consideration of some recently released films. My ultimate concern here, however, is to critique the limits of a culturalist and media-driven analysis of questions that remain, quite fundamentally, social and sociological yet simultaneously almost entirely neglected within social science and sociology more widely.

Interrogating the gaze: masculinity and looking relations

Laura Mulvey's article 'Visual Pleasure and Narrative Cinema', first published in 1975, has arguably been one of the most influential pieces of
feminist writing in recent history and has, more particularly, defined an
entire field of study ever since (Mulvey, 1975). That field of study is perhaps
most aptly called the feminist analysis of viewing relations, given its *prima
facie* concern with the gaze as gendered and indeed sexualised. Mulvey's
starting point is political and the use of psychoanalytic theory to feminist
ends more particularly. Thus she openly asserts: 'Psychoanalytic theory is
thus appropriated here as a political weapon, demonstrating the way the
unconscious of patriarchal society has structured film form' (Mulvey, 1975:
6). In common with more existentialist feminist writers previously, Mulvey's
task is to try to open up, and indeed disrupt, the patriarchal unconscious that
otherwise marginalises and undermines the female and the feminine into an
abject castrated 'other' (De Beauvoir, 1953). The sense of negation or
negativity is further underlined in her explicit attempt to destroy such forms
of visual pleasure as a part of a wider political agenda. This rather grandiose
set of intentions rests more theoretically on the two key strands of psychoanalytic theory most commonly appropriated within feminism, namely
the work of Freud on sexuality and Jacques Lacan's analysis of the mirror
phase in identity formation or identification (Freud, 1977; Lacan, 1977).
Consequently, the visual pleasures offered through narrative cinema for
Mulvey are essentially two-fold: first, scopophilia or the voyeuristic pleasure
derived through looking; and second, narcissism, or the pleasure developed
from recognition and identification. So far, Mulvey's analysis is relatively
uncontroversial yet the true cut and thrust of her perspective appears when
these concepts are overlaid in gendered terms according to the following,
rather fixed, axiom:

> In a world ordered by sexual imbalance, pleasure in looking has been
> split between active/male and passive/female. The determining male gaze
> projects its phantasy on to the female figure which is styled accordingly.
> In their traditional exhibitionist role women are simultaneously looked
> at and displayed, with their appearance coded for strong visual and
> erotic impact so that they can be said to connote *to-be-looked-at-ness*.
> (Mulvey, 1975: 11)

Clearly such a perspective correlates strongly with the parallel development
of a broader feminist imperative to expose the sexual objectification of the
female and women more widely (see, for example: Brownmiller, 1984; Greer,
1971; Millett, 1971). In addition, it also resonates strongly with the more
widely theorised gender dynamic that equates the male and the masculine
with the active subject and the female and the feminine with the passive
object. The more particular problematic that then ensues is the idea that the

male and the masculine 'cannot bear the burden of sexual objectification' (Mulvey, 1975: 12). Similarly, narrative plotlines are themselves also seen to reinforce the activity of the male subject, often conceived as heroic or powerful, and the passivity of the female object who mostly serves the purpose of providing erotic interest alone, while the narrative itself enhances wider processes of sadistic pleasure. However, Mulvey then goes on to analyse the ways in which the female and the feminine still retain the potential to threaten the male and masculine through their constant evocation of the threat of castration and therefore their capacity to inject anxiety or displeasure into narrative cinema and patterns of representation more widely. She attempts to demonstrate these processes through an analysis of the Alfred Hitchcock films *Vertigo*, *Rear Window* and *Marnie*, each of which play heavily on the look itself as well as wider patterns of voyeurism, desire and identification. Consequently, the (male) viewer ends up disorientated despite numerous: 'pure examples of fetishistic scopophilia' (Mulvey, 1975: 14).

Perhaps not surprisingly, Mulvey's work has since received a veritable barrage of reworking and criticism. It is worth considering a few key examples in more detail prior to providing some wider commentary. Steve Neale in 'Masculinity as Spectacle' takes Mulvey's work as a starting point for an analysis of masculinity and cinematic representation (Neale, 1982). In particular, he highlights the comparative neglect of masculinity within media studies as emblematic of the wider sense in which heterosexual masculinity has tended to remain unproblematised precisely because of its function as the structuring norm around which the rest of gendered and sexualised representations are defined. Following this he draws on the work of John Ellis to investigate the extent to which narcissistic identification as opposed to scopophilic desire is central to understanding the relationship of masculinity and cinematic representation (J. Ellis, 1982). Underpinning this discussion is the sense that processes of desire and identification are fragmented and fluid, multiple and dynamic, and even contradictory rather than fixed, unitary and uniform. Mulvey's analysis is criticised, implicitly at least, for its overly simplistic and one-dimensional understanding of such dynamics. In particular, Neale points to the legacy of omnipresent all-powerful male heroes in films ranging from the classic roles of Clint Eastwood and Charlton Heston in *A Fistful of Dollars* and *El Cid* to the *Mad Max* and *Superman* films more recently. Neale's point here more particularly is that these heroes are characterised through their silence and emotional reticence to the point of masochism. Similarly, Willemen's work on Anthony Mann's films is used to illustrate the sense in which male heroism is premised on the repression of the homosexual and homosexuality (Willemen, 1981). Mulvey herself addresses some of these points in 'Afterthoughts' where she considers the film *Duel in the Sun* as representative of a dual process of what Neale calls 'narcissistic authority' symbolised by nostalgia and idealism on the one hand and 'social authority' symbolised by marriage and the family on the other (Mulvey, 1981). Furthermore, Neale points to the sense in which the eroticism surrounding film stars such as Rock Hudson or John Travolta in *Saturday Night Fever* also tends to somehow feminise them, which adds further testimony to the idea that the sexual objectification of the male in cinema invokes homosexual desire that is in turn often repressed or disavowed. In sum:

> While mainstream cinema, in its assumption of a male norm, perspective and look, can constantly take women and the female image as its object of investigation, it has rarely investigated men and the male image in the same kind of way: women are a problem, a source of anxiety, of obsessive enquiry; men are not.
>
> (Neale, 1983: 15–16)

Ultimately, Neale reworks and redirects Mulvey's thesis rather than confronts it, highlighting in particular the significance of the disavowal of homosexuality that is also involved in patriarchal looking relations. Interestingly, Ian Green in an article titled 'Malefunction' argues precisely this, and furthermore, argues that Steve Neale does not go far enough in arguing against Mulvey and the terminology she employs. Importantly, Green is critical of the employment of psychoanalytic theory within media studies more widely, seeing them as 'reading off' meanings of scenes rather than making an attempt to problematise matters of fractured and multiple interpretations. To put it more simply, he asserts that media studies tend to over-simplify psychoanalytic theory *per se*. Green is particularly intrigued by the fractures and contradictions in looking relations that are perceived as being present in the examples of Hitchcock films that Mulvey and Neale employ and he starts to provide a more complex analysis of male desire and identification. In particular, he seeks to separate directly 'gay' forms of identification and their disavowal from more implicitly *homosexual* patterns of voyeurism that he argues emphatically are, as it were, 'there' (Green, 1984: 48).

Rodowick, however, is rather more directly critical of Mulvey's work (Rodowick, 1982). In particular, he highlights Mulvey's over-simplification of certain contradictions and complexities within Freud's theory and, most importantly, her eliding of masochism as part of masculinity. This point is also discussed at length in Kaja Silverman's influential work *Male Subjectivity at the Margins* (Silverman, 1992). Rodowick argues that 'Mulvey discusses the male star as an object of the look but denies him the function of an erotic object', and asks: 'So where is the place of the feminine subject in this scenario?' (Rodowick, 1982: 8). In short, Mulvey is seen as locked into an overly polarised schema necessitated though her political position as a feminist and furthermore ends up 'falling back on biological essentialism' (Rodowick, 1982: 9). Mulvey's essentialism is premised on her overly polarised view of gender or, in short, where are the variations *within* gender viewing relations? Following this, Rodowick reconsiders some aspects of Freud's work and comes to the following conclusions: first, that desire, for Freud at least, may potentially disrupt the set positions of 'masculine' and 'feminine' that are in turn more accurately perceived as overlaying what he calls the 'sedimentary structure' of desire (Rodowick, 1982: 13); second, that psychoanalytic structures are in a sense treated in a reductionist fashion as simply equivalent to various cinematic forms when they are not; third, that there is an overemphasis on form *per se* at the expense of a textual analysis; fourth, that the psychoanalytic appropriation of the concept of patriarchal authority more specifically requires further study; and finally, that the role of memory is almost entirely neglected in considering looking relations and cinema. In sum, Mulvey's appropriation of psychoanalytic theory is crude and overly simplistic.

Kenneth MacKinnon takes such matters further still (MacKinnon, 1997). In *Uneasy Pleasures*, MacKinnon is concerned with the perceived rise of the sexualisation, and indeed objectification, of men since the 1980s in a variety of contexts including advertising and video, photography and pornography, as well as cinema. Not surprisingly, his starting point is a critique of Mulvey's theories for a series of essentially false assumptions: first, that the spectator is always male or masculinised; second, that the spectacle conversely is always female or feminised; third, that the spectator's pleasure is essentially powerful; and fourth, that this pleasure is sadistic rather than masochistic. More importantly, Mulvey is seen to omit both the *possibility* of a feminised male object and the role of masochism as a form of pleasure for *both* men and women. Interestingly, MacKinnon's critique is most stinging when considering Mulvey's neglect of female or feminine spectatorship:

> The question, put extremely simply, arises: Do women never look? [. . .] Thus, the female spectator of narrative cinema is either temporarily a transvestite, enjoying masculine power in fantasy in order to stay under the spell of the film, or else uneasily oscillating between her sense of her femininity and a nostalgia for the masculinity of pre-Oedipal life.
>
> (MacKinnon, 1997: 12)

Here MacKinnon draws on Mulvey's later work in 'Afterthoughts' where she attempts to incorporate female as well as male spectatorship into her analysis through the application of the concept of transvestism as a form of female identification (Mulvey, 1981). However, this analysis is still clearly locked into the fixed axiom of male activity and female passivity and MacKinnon then proceeds to analyse a plethora of examples that are perceived to undermine Mulvey's analysis. These range from male nudity and body building, seen as exemplifying male rather than female exhibitionism, to the importance of women's scopophilia in the role of flâneuse and shopper; and from the wider sexual objectification of men in visual cultures as diverse as Take That videos and Mapplethorpe's photography, to the Nick

Kamen adverts for Levi's 501 jeans and the rise of pornography for women and gay politics. Consequently, MacKinnon demonstrates the sheer diversity and plurality of sites within which gendered looking relations are rendered far more complex than Mulvey could foresee: 'The present study is an attempt to affirm that the male object has been there, for an awfully long time, and is now much more evident and in far less need of outing than he was when Mulvey wrote her accounts of visual pleasure' (MacKinnon, 1997: 14).

However, perhaps the most severe critique of Mulvey's work, and indeed of the thesis of looking relations more widely, comes from another woman, namely Jane Gaines. Writing from a Marxist perspective in 'White Privilege and Looking Relations', Gaines savages Mulvey and her followers alike for the development of what she calls 'textual detachment' that 'has special implications', namely creating 'the impression that developments in an ideological realm are unrelated to developments elsewhere in social life' (Gaines, 1986: 60). The main thrust of Gaines's argument is to critique the uncritical appropriation of psychoanalytic theory and its concepts into cultural studies and sexual politics as it were *in lieu of*, or in tandem with the neglect of, a continued wider engagement with Althusserian Marxism. Ultimately this leads towards an analysis of the often heated controversy surrounding the perceived relationship of culture and ideology that is well outside the scope of this chapter. Despite this, however, Gaines exposes a series of important neglects within Mulvey's thesis and its later variants: first, the implicit heterosexual assumptions underpinning the study of looking relations that do little to engage fully with gay sexuality and, most problematically of all, ignore lesbian looking completely; second, the sense in which any feminist analysis that privileges gender relations over all others also 'functions ideologically' to 'reinforce white middle-class values' (Gaines, 1986: 61); and third, that this therefore obliterates an analysis of the historical and cultural specificity of the experiences of black women and more widely the sense that those experiences are precisely *not* reducible to a transhistorical or transcultural concept of patriarchy such as that employed by Mulvey. From this Gaines then provides an analysis of the myths, and indeed racialised looking relations, involved in the film *Mahogany* whereby black male looking is disavowed through a not dissimilar mechanism to that of gay looking and black female sexuality is subject to what Spillers calls the 'paradox of non-being' or being rendered all-powerful object within the white gaze yet devoid of any active subjective ownership (Spillers, 1984). Gaines concludes that Mulvey's analysis, and also those studies similarly informed through the uncritical appropriation of psychoanalytic concepts, 'may not comprehend the category of the real historical subject, but [their] use will always have implications *for* that subject' (Gaines, 1986: 79).

Gaines's analysis eventually leads us to question the entire premise of the theory of looking relations, or at least its more uncritical psychoanalytic variants, if not the field of cultural studies and gender more widely. These are very important points indeed, yet it is fair and appropriate in the first instance to suspend further investigation of these claims until we have considered the applications and potential of such studies in more detail.

Celluloid males: masculinity and media studies

Following Mulvey's work on the interrogation of gendered looking relations, recent decades have witnessed a significant expansion of interest in the matter of cinematic representations of masculinity. Importantly, many of these studies have attempted to apply some of the main tenets of feminist theory, or the analysis of gender and representation more widely, to the understanding of masculinities. More particularly, rather than continue to theorise such factors as gendered looking relations, many authors have attempted to apply such theoretical tools more specifically or, as it were, put them into practice within film and media studies (see, for example: Cohan and Hark, 1993; Jeffords, 1994; Kirkham and Thumin, 1993). It is not within the scope of this chapter to discuss all of these studies in detail, but rather to discuss more generally some of their key themes and elements and to question the potential and limits of such studies. The literature on cinematic depictions of masculinities, let alone other forms of media representations of masculinity, including those in magazines and advertising, is now vast to say the least, and attempting to cover this is well outside the aims of the current project. The following section aims to draw out the main themes of such studies more generally rather than analyse them in detail more specifically.

In the first instance, it is worth considering the foundations of contemporary media studies of masculinities. Media studies of any sort are, in essence, an analysis of representation. Thus, movies, advertisements and television programmes are, most fundamentally, cultural texts and this then opens up the question of the connection of text and context or the wider relationship of representation and reality. Underpinning this in turn are two developments within the social sciences. The first relates to the study of language and more specifically semiotics, discussed more fully in Chapter 4, and the second relates to the rise of new social movements and more particularly identity politics in the 1960s and 1970s considered most directly in Chapter 2 and Chapter 5. As previously outlined, the study of language and semiotics has, over the process of time, tended to make the following points: first, all forms of representation from linguistic codes to Hollywood films, do not merely reflect a fixed or uniform reality, rather they often construct varying and dynamic *realities* according to time, space and a miscellany of contextual conventions; secondly, there is no singular or unidirectional 'reading off' of meanings from texts, rather these are matters of interpretation and consumption as much as intention and production; and thirdly, all matters of representation are tied up with questions of historical, social and political context, which in turn invoke vectors of power and inequality (see Hall, 1997).

It is precisely this more political dimension of representation that is picked up on in identity politics and the rise of new social movements including feminism, gay and lesbian liberation, and black protest (see, for example, hooks, 1992; Russo, 1987; Wolf, 1991). The point here, put simply, is that many prevailing representations are perceived not only to not reflect reality but, more profoundly, to fracture, distort or quite literally *misrepresent* reality and the experiences of minorities or more oppressed groups and the issues they face. From this, one might safely conjecture that media studies of masculinity are premised on the following foundations: first, that representations of masculinity like masculinities *per se* are perceived as social constructs that vary from time to time and place to place; second, that there is then no direct connection of representations of masculinity with the realities of masculinities as lived acts, practices or identities; and third, that there *is*, conversely, a likely connection with wider prevailing motivations and ideologies concerning sexual, racial and gendered identities.

Having articulated some of the underlying foundations and tenets of media studies of masculinity more widely, it is worth spelling out some of their more specific points or claims. As Cohan and Hark argue, most of these in one way or another return to the question of looking relations:

> Rather than examine the paradox of a masculinity that derives considerable social and sexual – not to say spectatorial – power from being castrated, wounded, and lacking, film theory has for the most part confidently equated the masculinity of the male subject with activity, voyeurism, sadism, fetishism, and story, and the femininity of the female subject with passivity, exhibitionism, masochism, narcissism, and spectacle.
>
> (Cohan and Hark, 1993: 2)

Consequently, Cohan and Hark argue, at least implicitly, that Mulvey's analysis tends to essentialise masculinity and render it as an, or even *the*, unproblematised norm of patriarchal society. In challenging this, the essays in their edited collection are then seen to 'take pains to establish that masculinity is an effect of culture – a construction, a performance, a masquerade – rather than a universal and unchanging essence' (Cohan and Hark, 1993: 7). Thus one of the most common, yet also least explicit, points of many recent media studies of masculinity is that most mainstream cinematic representations of masculinity have the effect, intended or not, of exposing its contradictory and indeed constructed qualities. For example, Hark sees the heroics of *Spartacus* as exposing 'a dilemma of masculine subjectivity [. . .] between two unsatisfactory models of male power' (Hark, 1993: 153), while Holmlund sees Stallone's rampaging in the *Rambo* series as a form of masquerade and sees him quite literally as a clone of 'real' masculinity (Holmlund, 1993). Similarly, Yvonne Tasker sees many male-oriented action movies of the 1980s including *Die Hard*, *Lethal Weapon* and

Tango and Cash as for the most part performative enactments of masculinity that offer no hard and fast distinction of parodic versus oppressive forms of masculine performance (Tasker, 1993). The question here then centres on the extent to which such representations are self-consciously ironic or alternatively reinforce prevailing patriarchal structures.

A similar point of contradiction concerns the extent to which many films are seen to invoke homoerotic desire or identification and yet to simultaneously set up a series of defences against it. An early example of this is Steve Neale's analysis of *Chariots of Fire*, which he sees as exemplifying the playing out of the Oedipus complex and, in particular, the relationship of father and son that in turn depends on the repression of homosexual desire (Neale, 1982). The role of homosexual desire in representation is also a recurrent theme in the work of Richard Dyer. In 'Don't Look Now' Dyer examines the male pin-up and indeed the male object *per se* as a form of representation (Dyer, 1989). In following Mulvey's interrogation of looking relations in the first instance, he argues that a series of contradictions ensue when looking at men. The first of these relates to the implied passivity of being looked at that of itself tends to undermine the masculinity of the object. A second problematic is invoked in relation to the viewer who, given the aforementioned repression of homosexuality, is usually coded as female, but the gender inversion involved in an 'active' female subject observing a 'passive' male object often backfires, thus explaining the failings of much pornography aimed at women. Third, further contradictions ensue in the undermining of the passivity of the male object through a variety of mechanisms including the deflecting of the gaze so that the model, or indeed actor, looks aloft or through the camera, the implied activity of models as doing things or at least as ready to do things through the tautness of their pose or more simply their muscularity, and most directly the use of the accoutrements and implied roles of masculinity from work and sports to uniforms and the outdoors.

In later studies, Dyer is equally incisive concerning the cinematic representations of homosexuals as sad suicidal cripples or sexualised villains in film noir and the various inflections of homosexuality surrounding the queen and the dyke in Hollywood more widely, including the sad yet fastidious young man of the 1950s and 1960s, and the development of macho and lesbian feminist imagery in the 1970s and 1980s (Dyer, 1993). Dyer routinely recognises the patterns of stereotyping and misrepresentation involved, yet in his analysis of Dirk Bogarde in *Victim*, for example, refrains from making any one-dimensional or simplistic judgement (Dyer, 1993). Conversely, Vito Russo's very thorough-going analysis of cinematic representations of homosexuality in *The Celluloid Closet* is scathing in its attack on the systematic misrepresentation of lesbians and gay men as at best a bit suspect or weird and at worst murderous or deranged, concluding: 'It has become clear [. . .] that what we need is no more films about homosexuality' (Russo, 1987: 325).

What is interesting for our analysis here, however, is the repeated sense that such misrepresentations of homosexuality centre on the *gendered* as well as sexualised contradictions invoked. Consequently gay men are represented in primarily gender deviant forms as effeminate, or at least over-fastidious in their dress, while lesbians are commonly portrayed as butch or mannish. Examples cover the full range of Hollywood films from *Irene* in the 1920s to *Car Wash* in the 1970s and from Hitchcock's *Rope* in 1948 to *The Killing of Sister George* in 1969. Given Hollywood's continued struggle to deal with more overt forms of gay sexuality, including the ongoing rumours concerning actors and stars still 'in the closet', Dyer's point concerning the contradictory sense of the necessity to represent homosexuality on occasion while somehow still managing to hide or distort it remains a more than pertinent one.

It is also one which resonates in the study of the buddy movie, in which Fuchs as well as Tasker outlined earlier in different ways equally assert the significance of the repression of homosexual desire within the frame of male bonding that goes on in films such as *Lethal Weapon* and *Tango and Cash* (Fuchs, 1993: Tasker, 1993). Fuchs employs Sedgwick's concept of the homosocial, considered in detail in Chapter 5, in order to understand the development and dynamics of the contemporary North American buddy movie. More particularly, she argues that the relationship between the two male lead characters in such buddy films is, in essence, 'heterosexualised' and represses homosexuality. Thus: 'As the interracial cop-buddy film sustains its extralegal, politically progressive viewer, it also represses and recuperates the most threatening, invisible (non)difference of homosexuality' (Fuchs, 1993: 197).

A third theme of media studies of masculinity centres on the wider relationship of gender and genre or, more specifically, the connection of typologies of cinema with certain forms of maleness. Commonly considered genres include epics, Westerns, war films, horror movies, and extreme action movies. Consideration of Westerns and other classic epics such as *El Cid* and *Spartacus* tend to highlight the following points: first, that they are concerned with various forms of heroism, in turn premised on ritualised notions of self-sacrifice; second, that the body is a critical site of both spectacle and (repressed) homoeroticism; and third, that the violence in such films is often conceived as a form of endurance within the wider formation of a successful masculine identity (Kirkham and Thumin, 1993).

To consider some of these genres in turn, war films are often similarly violent yet open up an additional range of issues, studied in the work of Donald (Donald, 1992). Donald highlights the following: first, the role of rites of passage or inductions of masculinity through which the hero emerges as successfully tested in his manhood and stripped of femininity; second, the fact that women and indeed the feminine are side-lined, under-valued or somehow symbolically annihilated as either eternally forgiving or sexually voracious; and third, despite the all-male world that ensues, the fact that homosexuality remains fiercely repressed and rejected, often as part of the wider repudiation of the feminine; fourth, following this, that toughness, sufferance and standing up for ideals become essential signifiers of manliness; and lastly, that successful masculine identification depends on the repression of any emotional expression, a point picked up previously in Neale's analysis of male masochism (Neale, 1982).

The interpretation of horror films is for the most part almost entirely psychoanalytic. For example, Barbara Creed argues that the horror movie represents another form of male masochism as the monsters involved are often feminised. She invokes the work of Kristeva to see the frequent use of monstrous food and waste, gorging and fasting as a form of psychic abjection (Kristeva, 1982). Similarly, Dracula is perceived to play on the fears of the *vagina dentata* and menstruation while the werewolf is seen as a further signifier of feminine monstrosity given its lunar connections (Creed, 1993). Hutchings tends to argue against an overly one-dimensional understanding of the more contemporary horror film as simply misogynist, a charge easily substantiated given the tendency of the vast majority of slasher films to involve seamless and graphic depictions of screaming female victims savaged by predominantly male or masculine predators, and argues that the pleasures involved for male spectators are as masochistic as they are sadistic. Consequently, the often teenage male desire for horror depends on their essentially contradictory need for power and affirmation as 'masculine' young men otherwise insecure in their identities (Hutchings, 1993). A similar point is made in Wells' analysis of 1950s science fiction horror such as *The Incredible Shrinking Man* and *The Invasion of the Body Snatchers* where, as it were, size clearly matters and is perceived as a key measure of successful masculinity (Wells, 1993). Furthermore, Wells also argues that the anxiety invoked in such films clearly relates to wider concerns surrounding the security of masculine identity following the Second World War. What tends to underpin much of this discussion is the use of psychoanalytic theorising to open up connections of cinematic representations of masculinity with wider historical and social developments, a point I will explore more shortly.

The action film is one of the most commonly considered genres in the field of media studies of masculinity, particularly in the wake of the development of more extreme 'all action' films in the 1980s, including the *Rambo* and *Terminator* series and the rise to stardom of actors such as Sylvester Stallone and Arnold Schwarzenegger. A leading exponent of such studies is Susan Jeffords whose work *Hard Bodies: Hollywood Masculinity in the Reagan Era* develops a strong critique of the action genre (Jeffords, 1994). Jeffords argues that Ronald Reagan's own Hollywood career and rise to the presidency were not entirely coincidental but rather, given his role in reshaping economic and foreign policy, 'One of the reasons that Reagan was able to carry out these social, economic and cultural changes was his link to one of the most pervasive and influential features of American culture, the Hollywood film industry' (Jeffords, 1994: 3). Key to Jeffords' analysis is her triangulation of an analysis of cinematic representation with the deconstruction of ideal types of North American masculinity together with a critique of the politics of the 1980s. Consequently, she argues that Reagan came to symbolise, and indeed galvanise, a perceived crisis of nationality with a crisis of masculinity, a theme also picked up on in the work of Robert Bly and played out in the extreme action film (Bly, 1991). Of more specific concern for Jeffords is the role of the male body as a symbolic spectacle of both personal and national invincibility. In sum, the *Rambo* and *Terminator* films became metaphors for the symbolic resolution of wider social and political conflicts and crises.

Such themes are also picked up on the work of Holmlund and Tasker outlined earlier and developed to wider and different ends in the work of Fred Pfeil (Holmlund, 1993; Pfeil, 1995; Tasker, 1993). Pfeil's work *White Guys: Studies in Postmodern Domination and Difference* analyses representations of masculinity in a variety of media formats including what he calls the male rampage film, of which he writes:

> The *Lethal Weapon* and *Die Hard* films are at once a sign of opportunity – an indication that the sign white-straight-working-man is in flux and open to renegotiation – and a warning sign reminding us that if, as activists and theorists, we find ourselves uninterested in the task of seeking to manage, mine and refine that white-straight-working-man sign, other groups and forces will certainly be more than willing to shoulder the task for us, and in ways in which we are unlikely to approve.
>
> (Pfeil, 1994: 33)

It is clear that Pfeil's terrain here is shared with wider political projects that seek to analyse more postmodern forms of masculinity, including Kaja Silverman's influential analysis of masochism and male subjectivity, to form what he calls a 'libidinal politics', as well as using performative and queer theory more widely as considered in Chapter 6 (Silverman, 1992). Pfeil's concern more particularly is with a one-dimensional representation of masculinity that is seen to endorse a politically reactionary view of masculinity, as a purely white and heterosexual phenomenon. He sees this as exemplified in the macho posturing and all-male heroics of the action film, yet is positive that 'the normative definitions and regulative images of white straight masculinity have indeed been changing' (Pfeil, 1994: 260). It is more than significant at this point that these media studies of masculinity are perceived not only to try to extrapolate connections of cinema with wider culture but, moreover, to seek to *politicise* that relationship.

This sense of making – what seem to me to be increasingly grandiose – claims premised on media studies and similar analyses of cinematic representation of masculinities alone leads me to raise a series of wider, and indeed more serious, concerns. Underlying this is an unease concerning the increasing emphasis placed on the wider social and political dimensions of such analysis. Consequently, and without wishing to undermine media and cinematic studies of masculinity out of hand or to regard the claims made as simply invalid, I wish to question the extent to which the foundations of such studies can actually support the structures of analysis and assertions resting on them. In the first instance, film and media studies of masculinity are, quite strictly, limited to the examples they invoke or, in short, matter not one jot nor pertain to any standard of validity if the audience or reader has not seen the film in question. To put it most simply, how can one assess the validity of a media studies interpretation of any cultural 'text' unless one has already 'read' that text in some way? Though I myself, for example, have seen hundreds of films, I am at a complete loss to know whether many of the aforementioned authors are right or wrong in their interpretation of numerous films that I have not seen.

Secondly, and perhaps slightly more seriously, it is also of some concern that, despite the ongoing legacies of interpretivist analysis in social science, the questioning of language and the problematising of the position of meaning within artistic and sociological analysis alike, the authorial voice in almost all of these studies remains loud, clear and unconditional (see Chapter 2). Thus, most of these authors state what lines of text, actors' gestures, film-maker's directions and even the films themselves 'mean' without question. Worse still, many not only 'read off' the meanings of such cultural texts as unproblematic but furthermore imply that their interpretations of the underlying 'truths' of many films are somehow *more* valid than any lay interpretation, and this in turn would seem to invoke, rather ironically, a charge of essentialism. More widely, it perhaps exposes a wider tension between the dual legacies of Marxist realism and more phenomenological social science that underpins the development of media studies *per se*.

A third problematic here depends precisely on the role and intention of such studies and their proposed relationship with wider society. A particular difficulty here is the tendency of such studies to collapse into a kind of textual solipsism, or in-depth analysis of a very few examples, that often fails to make any wider connection or comparison across the genre or indeed across different media forms. The mileage in making more historical comparisons of the representations of John Wayne with Sylvester Stallone, let alone with a TV programme such as *The A Team* or perhaps the media coverage of baseball or similar sports, is, one suspects, potentially immense yet almost totally neglected.

A fourth more specific difficulty here is the dependency of many media studies of masculinity on psychoanalytic theory. This is itself often contentious and potentially at odds with many of the wider and more culturalist claims made. Though recent decades have witnessed the attempt to reclaim psychoanalysis towards more political ends, there is far from any uniform consensus concerning either its role or its importance for sexual politics more widely. Gaines's stinging analysis of the implicit racism and heterosexism of many of these analyses, and indeed their foundations, coupled with the by no means unproblematic relationship of psychoanalysis and Marxism, is more than germane here (Gaines, 1986).

Following on from this, lastly and most fundamentally, there is no easy or straightforward relationship of any form of representation to the realities it may, or may not, attempt to represent. Though many interpretations of such representations may make sense or appear valid due to their 'fit' with other wider or more prevailing interpretations of given phenomena, this does not necessarily make them right or true in any sense. Consequently, while many would agree that the extreme action movies of the 1980s were reactionary, or perhaps now comical, others may take them at face value. One of the most fundamental difficulties here is the lack of empirical work on the consumption of such cultural texts to support the claims made, and while it would be both practicable and advisable to study multiple, and indeed lay as well as academic, readings more empirically, this is rarely done. The additional irony here is that many film and media studies of masculinity rely on historical rather than contemporary examples, making them in some senses slightly dated and even less easily verified. With these points in mind, in the final section I wish to produce an analysis of some contemporary media examples as they pertain to matters of masculinity, with a view to considering whether such an analysis is indeed properly located within media studies or the social sciences more widely.

Touching the void: contemporary cinema and North American masculinity

In this final section, I wish to analyse three more contemporary films that have, in one way or another, at least some *overt* connection to questions of masculinity, particularly as they pertain to contemporary North American culture. These are *American Beauty* (dir. Mendes, 2000), *American Psycho* (dir. Hannon, 2000) and *Fight Club* (dir. Fincher, 1999). This is of course both a subjective and an arbitrary selection yet I hope also recognisable to both an academic and a lay audience. A key question here is the extent to which a strictly media or film studies analysis of such movies is entirely satisfactory in understanding their connection with, or implications for, understanding contemporary masculinities.

When Bret Easton Ellis wrote his third novel *American Psycho* it caused a storm of controversy, particularly in the United States, where radical feminist groups denounced it as a misogynist's guide to cutting up women and Simon & Schuster, who had offered him an initial advance of $300,000 to write it, then refused to publish it. The book was eventually published by Vintage in 1991 (Ellis, 1991). His first two novels *Less Than Zero* published in 1985 and *The Rules of Attraction* published in 1987 were dark and satirical tales of affluent Californian youth in the 1980s that often opened up a near existential terrain of adolescent alienation and nihilism centred on drug-taking, sexual promiscuity and, often implicitly, extreme violence (Ellis,

1985, 1987). Given Ellis's youth and upbringing in Los Angeles, questions were raised concerning the degree of autobiography involved, although in interviews Ellis has always denied any direct association. Yet despite the darkness and potential controversy invoked throughout such work, nothing and no-one could quite predict either the outrage or sheer shock caused by *American Psycho*. It tells the tale of Patrick Bateman, an extremely wealthy and good-looking Wall Street dealer. Told in the first person, it opens up, as in the dilation of the eye's pupil, an ever more graphic insight into his sexual predilections and his use of increasingly extreme forms of violence and torture. He is, in short, the ultimate seductive and successful serial killer whom no-one suspects. The novel is written in the same deadpan style throughout, whether Bateman is discussing – often at great length – the details of his grooming routines, designer suits and competitive games-playing with other dealers or, as the novel progresses, the increasingly graphic and horrific descriptions of his torture, mutilation and murder of a miscellany of victims, from the homeless and rival dealers to prostitutes and even his ex-girlfriend. Given the level of controversy and graphic violence involved, one could wonder how a movie of such a work could be made at all, let alone by a female director. Conversely, one could also argue, given the previously very strong feminist critique, that a proposal for such a movie might not have succeeded at all with a male director.

Hannon's film necessarily differs from the novel in several respects (dir. Hannon, 2000). First, much of the violence of the novel is either cut completely or rendered significantly less graphic. In fact, of the twenty-four murders in the novel, only around a fifth or less are included in the film and one of the most fully developed scenes in the film, namely involving Bateman's luring of his adoring secretary to his apartment to murder her with a nail gun, is also one of the few, yet telling, occasions on which he feels a sense of guilt and lets his victim go. A second, and linked, factor here is Hannon's increasing use of satire and comedy within the film version and, while this is certainly present within the novel, Ellis's overly dry writing style tends to undermine any more direct or overt sense of comedy. Thirdly, the film – through virtue of a greater sense of playing on visual irony – heightens the audience's sense of the absurdity of the story and indeed the absurd *per se*. Particularly crucial here is the climactic scene of extended and extreme violence concerning two prostitutes. In an earlier scene Bateman allows the two women to escape with sexual injuries only and this is, in essence, presented seriously, yet when the two women are lured once again one is murdered and the other tries to escape. At this point, the film quite clearly tips from the serious into something nearer to parody or comedy as Bateman is then seen running after her and round his apartment building completely naked, covered in blood and waving a circular saw. Though the scene is of course horrific it is also quite simultaneously rather incredible and ridiculous. Shortly after this, Bateman makes a mock confession at great length into a police answer phone in the early hours of the morning and then, when investigated, no evidence is found suggesting that Bateman is not only a psychopath but increasingly unstable. The film ends leaving unanswered the question of whether Bateman did indeed do the killings or just imagined doing them. Though the same question is raised in the novel, Ellis's relentlessly emotionless writing style, combined with his much more graphic depiction of the violence, tends to lead one to query whether this is the true or real question at all. The implication, and I would argue intention, of the novel, and to a lesser extent the film, is that the visual commodification of culture more widely is linked to the question of violence more specifically. To put it more simply, the human and the social – in parallel with the theses of Baudrillard – are collapsed into the visual and the material so that sex, bodies and relationships are as indistinguishable, disposable and meaningless, or meaningful, as clothes, CDs and interior design (Baudrillard, 1983). Thus the more significant question is not 'Did he or didn't he?' but rather whether Bateman or American culture *per se* is the American Psycho. The title of the novel and the film itself would seem to imply a dual meaning here.

Having said this, a number of difficulties still remain in interpreting the film's meaning. The first of these concerns the role of Bateman as sexual object. Though the novel makes it clear that he epitomises the handsome glamour of a young Wall Street dealer and that he quite knowingly uses his sex appeal to lure his victims, the film perhaps inevitably invests far more in presenting him as a sexual object. Played by the good-looking and undeniably well muscled Christian Bale, Bateman is imbued with a powerful sex appeal that is blatantly displayed from the start. One of the earliest scenes from the film makes this particularly explicit as the camera lingers extensively over Bale's body, paying particular attention to his buttocks as he urinates, and showing him full length if not full frontal and either nude or near nude throughout an entire scene of him exercising, showering and cleansing, while his monologue concerning his fitness and grooming regime is simultaneously interspersed with a distinctly lyrical piano score. The implication here is that Patrick Bateman/Christian Bale is about as near to an Adonis or sex god as contemporary masculinity can get. Thus Bale, more overtly and more extremely than in the novel, presents Bateman as the epitome of contemporary muscular and virile sex appeal, in turn coded within the frame of the North American yuppie, perfectly coiffed and exquisitely suited, with his tie knot jutting under his chiselled jaw like a permanent erection. However, his muscularity and grooming, if not his dress sense specifically, are equally if more implicitly also recognisable as gay. Though the novel tends to elide such discussion through its presentation of Bateman in the first person, the film cannot escape the inevitable ambiguity concerning his sexuality. Another scene is significant here. This is where Bateman attempts to video his sexual exploits with two female prostitutes. Surprisingly little is made of the objectification of the two women here. However, considerably more attention is paid to Bateman's adoration of his own oiled and gleaming, pumped and pumping physique on the video screen. Thus, the film locates, and perhaps even inverts, narcissism into the heterosexual rather than homosexual gaze.

A second problematic relating to the film is its reworking of the elements of satire, nihilism, horror and comedy that make up the story in total. As I have already illustrated, the film tends to play up the elements of satire and comedy while playing down the elements of horror and nihilism. This tends to have the impact, intended or not, of rendering the film less serious and perhaps more significantly less far-reaching in its meaning and implications for its audiences. Though it remains possible to read the novel as a comedy, the controversy concerning the novel rather than the film indicates that this is not an entirely convincing interpretation of its meaning. Moreover, Ellis's novel is long and his writing style is tedious and turgid to read if one does not, as it were, read more into it. Conversely, the film is relatively short and more easily consumed satisfactorily as a comedy or more straightforward satire – for example, many audiences may snigger at the clumsily out of date and unsophisticated mobile phones used in the film, while readers of the novel may well unconsciously apply more contemporary mental images of mobile phones.

This leads me to the third and final problematic of *American Psycho*, namely the extent to which it works at the level of irony. Consequently, what is invoked here is a wider political concern with its potential uses and indeed abuses. The original feminist critique of the novel was premised on the idea that it could be read, by men, as a manual for the mutilation and murder of women. This claim is undermined on a variety of fronts: first, by the equal number of male and female victims involved, although it has to be said that the violence against the women is often presented in more detail; second, by the sheer implausibility if not impossibility of many of the murders; and third by the alternative or deeper readings of Bateman's behaviour to which I have already alluded, including – it should be noted – the readings that may be made by gay men or women. However, the unease concerning the graphic depiction of female mutilation, torture and murder remains. This is, I think, due to the way in which the violence featured in the film, or even the novel, may still, at least potentially, be *enjoyed*. Consequently though *American Psycho* may, in many ways, be seen to undermine Mulvey's thesis, a tension remains concerning the potential visual pleasures surrounding (mostly) female mutilation and murder (Mulvey, 1975, 1981). Hannon's film, in extensively cutting much of the violence as well as its graphic description, and in invoking a far greater sense of comedy and satire, avoids some of that unease – yet not entirely. Having said this, the film also loses much of the novel's ultimate power in exposing the dark underside of American culture, a theme often explored more fully and more successfully in the work of directors such as David Lynch among others.

So how does this relate to questions of masculinity more widely? The key here I think resides in the opening interior monologue of the film:

There is an idea of a Patrick Bateman, some kind of abstraction. But there is no real me, only an entity, something illusory. And though I can hide my cold gaze and you can shake my hand and feel flesh gripping yours and maybe you can even sense our lifestyles are probably comparable, I simply am not there.

What this would seem to imply is a sense of existential crisis or a sense that the masculine identity that Bateman inhabits is not only illusory but empty, a hollow shell. This is added to further by the visual content of the film, which shows, simultaneously, Bateman removing a clear face mask. The trick here is that removing the mask reveals nothing that was not there already and the same cold and impassive gaze confronts the camera, implying that, in a sense, nothing more is underneath. One can further suggest here that Bateman's psychosis is induced through precisely this sense of existential crisis and resolved, temporarily, through practices of extreme violence that are otherwise an attempt to reclaim some meaning to his masculinity.

A similar theme is invoked more explicitly and directly in *Fight Club* (dir. Fincher, 1999). Also based on a novel by a young American, Chuck Palahnuik, Fincher's film tells the tale of Jack's encounter with Tyler Durden and his initiation into the world of underground fight clubs where disillusioned men in office jobs and similar mundane occupations ditch their collars and ties for bare-fisted fighting in attempt to reclaim the meaning of their manhood (Palahnuik, 1996). Two factors are of immediate importance here: first, the sense in which the film's fictional story was perceived and has since gained greater credence as 'real', given numerous if rarely researched rumours of the existence of such fight clubs across many Western societies; and second, its semi-overt linking to the politics of the men's movement in the United States and the ideas of Robert Bly in particular, explored more fully in Chapter 2 (Bly, 1991). The film also gained a significant degree of media attention due to the directorship of Fincher, who had already achieved much success with the dark thriller *Seven* and his pairing once again with the über body and stardom of Brad Pitt, whose intensive working-out and lean muscularity was widely reported prior to the film and borders on being a subject itself within the film given the constant camera attention to his bare – and often greased and glistening – torso, heightened still further by his adoption of low-rise trousers that expose the muscles across his pelvis. Jack himself is played by Edward Norton, a young actor also in ascendance since his role in *Primal Fear* (dir. Hoblit, 1996).

The film starts with an inexplicable plot by Durden to blow up a block of buildings while pointing a gun at Jack and then continues to be told through the internal monologue of Jack, who works as an insurance clerk and suffers from insomnia. To alleviate his suffering he falls 'slave to the IKEA nesting instinct' and, it is implied, other consumerist or shopping addictions. Furthermore, he also starts to trawl around a wide range of support groups including one for men's testicular cancer. The satire on support groups, men's consciousness-raising, yogic meditation and other forms of slightly hippie-inspired or similar 1970s-esque developments is clear and cynical. It is also enhanced through Jack's association with Marla Singer, a woman whom he meets playing the same game of faking entrance to support groups. Playing very much against her prior Merchant Ivory type, Helena Bonham Carter plays her character as a kind of proto-feminist, neo-punk. She is, though, little more than a mysterious and sexually alluring female hologram of shades and cigarette smoking who, under Fincher's direction, clearly takes significant reference from the *femme fatale* roles of film noir while exerting a hefty degree of late 1990s cynicism at the same time. Far more significant is Jack's encounter and ensuing relationship with Tyler Durden, who introduces him to the world of fight clubs. Before this, however, the film has already established a slightly surreal and certainly not literal form of narrative, of which the meeting with Durden is a prime example. Jack, apparently on an internal flight for work purposes, discusses insurance claims with the woman beside him, when the plane crashes and Durden takes her place and they are introduced. Durden is a charismatic and anarchic soap manufacturer and salesman with whom Jack is clearly fascinated. Having parted at the airport, Jack then discovers that his IKEA-laden and consumerist haven of an apartment has been completely destroyed in a gas explosion. On finding a public telephone, it rings and Jack and Tyler Durden arrange a meeting. Following a discussion of the meaninglessness of contemporary consumer society, Durden then lures Jack to fight with him in the street. Jack is initially hesitant and resists, then starts to develop a taste for it and the pair quite literally fight their way into friendship. Having nowhere to live, Jack then follows Tyler Durden to his dilapidated, near derelict and downright dangerous house on a toxic waste site. From this point on, a tense and intense friendship develops between Durden and Jack, further complicated by Jack's jealousy towards Tyler's sexually violent relationship with Singer following her attempted suicide. At the same time, Tyler and Jack form an underground network of fight clubs that spreads and develops with exponential success across the United States, developing into a near Orwellian tale of anarchic uprising against consumer culture called Project Mayhem, and the story progresses in a relatively linear and straightforward fashion until its final and radical twist near the end.

Several themes emerge here as worthy of further discussion. The first is the severe critique of consumerist society and its relationship with masculinity. At the outset and throughout the film, Jack is disillusioned and depressed with the lack of meaning found in contemporary consumerist lifestyles and working in an office. His insomnia seems to imply that he is also verging on mental illness or at least is in crisis. The implication here is that office work and consumerism are 'feminised' practices that fail to satisfy the criteria of a successful and fulfilling masculine identity. As Jack descends into self-destruction, Tyler Durden's violence and physicality come to fill the void. Thus, in essence, Jack's crisis is a crisis of masculinity. More significantly, the clear parallels here with the theories and practices of contemporary men's movements and the philosophy of Robert Bly's work in *Iron John* are striking even to a lay audience (Bly, 1991).

A second theme concerns the role of violence and its relationship to masculinity and society more widely. Durden clearly states his distaste for contemporary consumer society and his desire to reclaim his masculinity through physicality and fighting with other men more specifically. The fights themselves are interesting in their specified rules and codings. The men meet in all-male and clandestine underground environments and networks where discussion or fraternity in the 'real' world is strictly prohibited. This symbolic dimension is also heightened by the 'unreality' of the violence itself – little blood-spilling, minimal injuries, and certainly no hospital trips. On top of this, the men also fight solely one on one and without equipment or clothing, discarding their suits and ties for bare chests and bare-knuckle fist fights that have no rules and no ending other than through one man falling or admitting defeat. This clearly emphasises the physicality of the fighting, its separation from any other form of inter-male intimacy and its relationship to masculine identity.

A third and linked concern here relates to the relationship between the narrator/Jack and Tyler Durden *per se*. The relationship, like the fighting itself, clearly has homoerotic overtones, overtly deflected and indeed repressed through their mutual attraction to Merla Singer and their total avoidance of any more emotional communication of any kind. In addition, given their physicality, secrecy and all-male exclusivity, the fights themselves also work as a clear metaphor for sex, and indeed homosexual sex could easily be substituted for the violence were it not for the stigma of effeminacy attached to it. This would seem to validate the points raised by Steve Neale and others considered earlier (Neale, 1983). However, what confuses this entire discussion is the twist at the end of the film, where it is revealed that the narrator/Jack and Tyler Durden are one and the same person, and that Tyler Durden is, in essence, Jack's idealised alter ego. After an increasingly ludicrous game of cat and mouse between ego and alter ego, the film at this point also tips back into an entirely effects-driven plot concerning blowing up the financial district of the city. In sum, then, *American Psycho* and *Fight Club* both, in different ways and with different outcomes, perceive violence as a response to a crisis in contemporary American masculinity, but where they succeed is in opening up a series of questions concerning the connections of masculinity and contemporary society and where they fail is in finding any more positive or satisfactory answers to these questions.

While *American Psycho* and *Fight Club* both tend to offer negative, even nihilistic, views on the perceived crises of masculinity and the descent of their (anti)heroes into social and self-destruction, Sam Mendes' film *American Beauty* (2000) offers a somewhat more positive view, and indeed outcome. The film tells the story of Lester Burnham, played by Kevin Spacey who, interestingly, narrates the tale posthumously from, as it were, another world.

As a result, the plot works according to the why and how of the ending, which is already known. Burnham lives with his status-seeking, image-conscious and anxious wife, played by a cracklingly uptight Annette Bening, and his rather sulky daughter Jane played by Thora Birch, in what appears to be the epitome of middle-class American suburban perfection, but nothing and no-one in *American Beauty* is quite what it, or they, appear to be. It rapidly becomes apparent that Burnham is far from happy and to all intents and purposes is having a male mid-life crisis. The catalyst in this is his encounter with one of his daughter's school friends, the rather posturing Angela Hayes played by Mena Suvari, for whom he rapidly develops a near adolescent infatuation. However, his fantasies concerning her take on a rather surreal dimension encapsulated in the recurring image of showers of red roses and enhanced through the use of the film's highly effective and successful score. As a result of these epiphanies Lester quits his dull and unsatisfying office job and rather hilariously threatens to accuse his superior of sexual harassment to negotiate a pay-out. He then starts to smoke dope, plays his favourite loud rock music from his youth, works out in the garage, swaps his respectable family saloon for a classic sports car, masturbates and – most absurdly of all – takes a job at a fast-food outlet for a laugh. The film plays heavily on the comedy of all of this and on the various middle-class *faux pas* and embarrassments that Burnham causes – particularly to his wife who then embarks on a rather sycophantic affair with her mentor in real estate.

Given both Mendes' and Spacey's backgrounds in theatre, all of this is handled with a rather stagey sense of satire, yet the film's far darker underside is exposed through the parallel story of the Burnhams' next door neighbours headed by the aggressive and violently repressive retired Marine Corps Colonel Frank Fitts, played by Colin Cooper, who terrorises his long-suffering wife Barbara (Allison Janney) and beats up his dreamily intellectual and dope-smoking son Ricky (Wes Bentley). Ricky meanwhile is having a voyeuristic affair with Jane and also begins supplying his neighbour Lester with dope. Having snooped on his son Ricky, Frank Fitts mistakenly thinks that his son is having a homosexual relationship with Burnham and beats him up. This near farcical story-line is the given a far more ominous twist when Fitts approaches Burnham, who is working out in his garage as usual, while in the style of true cinematic pathetic fallacy it rains torrentially. The audience at this point is clearly expecting Fitts to attack Burnham, but instead he approaches him and attempts to kiss him, revealing his own repressed homosexuality. Burnham gently corrects Fitts and holds him as he breaks down in tears. The stage is now set for the climax of the film, with a cast of characters in highly volatile states, including Burnham's wife who is returning home with a gun to either reclaim her marriage or perhaps end it once and for all. The poignant yet shocking ending is reached as Burnham gazes lovingly at a family photo while a gun is fired from behind his head, blowing his brains across the wall opposite. It is Fitts and not Burnham's wife who has pulled the trigger and the film closes by returning to Burnham's posthumous interior monologue on the inner beauty of American life, otherwise symbolised, or at least captured, in a home video of a paper bag blowing in the wind.

There are a number of themes worthy of discussion and clarification here. The first concerns Lester Burnham's crisis. Though not so much a crisis of masculinity as a more generic mid-life crisis, it is still clearly resolved through his return to earlier, sensual and less materialist values, in many ways summarised and espoused through the practices and politics of the late 1960s and early 1970s, rather than through resorting to violence. Lester's death is the only true scene of violence in the film and this is hardly self-inflicted. There is a clear, if very implicit, message here concerning not only a satire on suburban American lifestyles but on the consumerist and materialist values of the 1980s and 1990s that are upheld by Burnham's wife who, rather symbolically, is pictured as pruning the red roses that Burnham is otherwise so enraptured by. A second thematic concern is more overtly and directly political and relates to the role of Fitts. The clear implication here is that the military masculinity that Fitts encapsulates is morally wrong, repressive and ultimately murderous. At the same time it is also seen as premised on repressed homosexuality and, interestingly, the film also portrays the Burnham family as happily associating with their other overtly gay neighbours. The blistering, if merely implied, assault on US gun laws, the American military and negative attitudes towards homosexuality is undeniable here. A third and more ambivalent issue in *American Beauty* concerns its rather woolly and diffuse stabs at asserting alternative values through the symbolism of roses, simple things like paper bags blowing around, and even perhaps the afterlife. While often hypnotic and indeed beautiful, this isn't entirely convincing and it is left to Spacey's Oscar-winning portrayal of his reclaimed *joie de vivre* to put a smile on one's face when leaving the cinema. What is perhaps more positive here, however, is the fact that the film was an almighty hit with the American box office and critics alike, scooping five Oscars including best picture and six BAFTA awards and vastly enhancing a range of careers, including those of Sam Mendes and Kevin Spacey most particularly. Its imagery and score is now almost routinely referenced in the worlds of advertising and pop music alike. Though in many ways on a similar terrain to the films of David Lynch, whose cult hit *Blue Velvet* most famously exposed the dark underbelly of American suburbia, *American Beauty* perhaps succeeds in making the cross-over to a more mainstream audience.

So what can we conclude from this discussion? First, it is, I think, clear that there is much contemporary and social significance to be found in the analysis of masculinity as it is represented in cinema. More importantly, however, this significance is found through contextualising cinematic representation within wider frameworks and making use of some comparative analysis. Though all of the films mentioned would easily lend themselves to in-depth and intensive individual and psychoanalytically driven media analysis, this tells us little more concerning their wider social significance or indeed concerning their relationship to contemporary masculinities. Although well outside the scope of this particular chapter, much research could be conducted into the varying perceptions of the films mentioned and their relationship to wider patterns of cultural dissemination of issues concerning masculinity. My linked point here is that the vast majority of sociological and social scientific enquiry has completely ignored such questions and left them to the realms of film analysis and media studies alone. This is, I would assert, as much the result of the often high-handed and politically correct stance taken by much social science as 'being above such trivia' and its repeated historic claims to ape the hard sciences, as the increasing specialisation and indeed separation of the disciplines *per se*.

More particularly, several points concerning the perceived crises of masculinity presented in these films are worth discussing. First, they are all examples of a white, Western and often middle-class crisis of masculinity and, more specifically still, primarily its North American variant. Second, cinematic representations of such quasi-existential crises of masculine identity are neither new nor limited to specific films. Of particular interest here are parallel questionings of masculine identity that occur across much contemporary mainstream cinema. The now well established and iconic career of Tom Cruise is a case in point. Many of his films directly throw into jeopardy the very image of successful white Western masculinity that he himself represents. These include legal corruption and the personal price of corporate success (*The Firm*), the crisis of faith engendered in war heroes past and present (*Born on the Fourth of July*, *The Last Samurai*), middle-class crises of personal identity and security (*Eyes Wide Shut*), the questioning of the role of the sports agent and the profit motive (*Jerry Maguire*) or, most recently, alienation itself (*Collateral*, *Vanilla Sky*). All of these films in very different ways see Cruise going into crisis with a given highly successful, white, Western and masculine identity and needing to reconstruct his life according to a series of alternative values and ideals. Third, this leads me to question the significance and value of a purely media-studies-driven analysis of such a widespread and indeed near generic form of representation. The sheer pervasiveness of these representations of masculinity lends itself to wider social and indeed sociological enquiry and research. And, as such, when and why would the representation of masculinity, in or out of crisis, *ever* be a subject best analysed within the confines of media studies *alone*? Ultimately, however, this is, of course, still just my interpretation.

Conclusions: the spectacle of the male

This chapter has had three main intentions and themes: first, to critique the simplicity of Mulvey's influential thesis of gendered viewing relations; second, to discuss applications of media studies to questions of masculinity;

and third, to provide my own case study of the potential – and limits – of such applications. In addition, a more implicit theme has been my exploration of the tension which often exists between media or cultural studies of masculinity in film and more social or sociological accounts of gendered identity. Mulvey's essay on gendered looking relations still exerts a powerful influence across the entire discipline of media studies and gender, yet, despite the severity of its critique and limits, it remains almost wholly ignored within more traditional sociological discussions of gender and masculinity. Neither more established authors such as Connell and Hearn nor more recent contributions from writers such as MacInnes, Petersen, or Whitehead give great, if any, credence to the question of the importance of masculinity and its representation (Connell, 1987, 1995; Hearn, 1987, 1998; MacInnes, 1998; Petersen, 1998; Whitehead, 2002). In addition, while literatures on masculinity and men's fashion – including my own – go some way to investigate the question of gendered looking relations, consideration of cultural texts remains located almost entirely within the domain of cultural studies (Edwards, 1997; Mort, 1996; Nixon: 1996). More fundamentally, consideration of cinematic or other visual forms relating to masculine identity more specifically are rarely addressed within the entire canon of critical studies of men and masculinity. The primary exceptions here are those already working within the arts, media or cultural studies (Buchbinder, 1998; Dyer, 1992; Pfeil, 1995). As outlined in the second section of this chapter, the media and cultural studies literature on masculinity has been critiqued quite severely for its theoretical over-simplification of far more complex phenomena and its textual solipsism yet, in my own short discussion of some contemporary cinematic representations of masculinity, it is, I think, still clear that the questions raised remain entirely relevant to social science and sociological discussions of identity. Consequently, this separation of issues and perspectives on the question of masculinity is ultimately as false as it is unhelpful and it is time for social scientists to take the subject of masculinity, not only in its institutional and practised forms but in terms of its media representations and consumption, seriously.

8   Auto-mechanics
Masculinity, reflexivity and the body

Masculinity would seem to be all about the body. After all, one can hardly be a man without a male body. The problem here, however, is that masculinity does not pertain to male bodies alone and indeed male bodies are not necessarily very 'masculine'. One only has to think of the bodies of young boys, disabled men and elderly or frail men to realise that any such equation is not so simple. Male body does not equal masculine. More problematically still, female bodies can be perceived as masculine or mannish, while a host of chromosomal differences from inter-sex conditions and hermaphroditism to other more social variations such as transvestism and transsexualism, render any simple or dualistic encoding of male–female as masculine–feminine almost nonsensical, even when that dualism appears to be embodied. Studying the body does indeed lead inevitably to an entire series of problematic dualisms: nature versus culture, male versus female, black versus white, active versus passive, mind versus body, to mention only some. Perhaps not surprisingly, it also leads to a variety of encounters with attempts to overcome such dualisms. More importantly, what is also opened up here is the importance of power and processes of normativity, status and the inscription of meaning: what – and who – passes muster in the hierarchy of appearances and physical capacities. Of course none of this necessarily tells us much about masculinities and it remains the task of this chapter to interrogate the connection of the male and the masculine with the physical and the corporeal.

Such an investigation necessarily starts with a consideration of the existing sociology of the body, such as it is, and how this is then applied to questions of masculinity. Secondly, the connections of such studies with wider patterns of performativity, normativity and reflexivity are scrutinised. As a result and following discussions in the preceding two chapters, the question of the relationship of masculinity to patterns of representation is reopened. In the final instance, then, it is asserted that the male body has become a major signifier of masculinity within Western societies and indeed it has become an open cipher for contemporary culture *per se*.

Embodying masculinity: sociology and the body

The body remains a problematic, if not necessarily neglected, subject in sociology and the social sciences more widely and, despite recent theoretical advancements, it is still an awkward object of study for social enquiry. There are a number of reasons for this situation: first and foremost, the body did not become an overt object of enquiry within the social sciences until quite recently and, more particularly, it was not until the publication of Bryan Turner's landmark book *The Body and Society* in 1984 that the body became more formally recognised as a subject worthy of extensive study within sociology (Turner, 1996); secondly, analysis of the body tends to be very interdisciplinary in nature, invoking the work of socio-biologists as much as sociologists and medical critiques as much as media studies; and third, the body arguably not only raises but *forces* a series of wider problematic dualisms within sociology, including the debate between nature and culture, the critique of activity and passivity in understanding human individuality, and the interrogation of the role of wider vectors of power, normativity and social divisions. In this section I consider the significance of the body sociologically and the legacy of some early theories, and indeed theorists, of the body. Following this, I then critique some more contemporary developments in sociology of the body and the growing thesis of embodiment in particular, prior to turning my attention towards the relationship between the body and masculinity.

Though Foucault was not strictly a sociologist of the body, his legacy for the sociology of the body has been immense. In particular, the body is arguably an important sub-theme of many of his major works including *The Birth of the Clinic, Discipline and Punish* and *The History of Sexuality* (Foucault, 1973, 1977, 1978, 1984a, 1984b). In both *The Birth of the Clinic* (1973) and *Discipline and Punish* (1977) Foucault places a heavy emphasis on the role and formation of the modern state in becoming the primary mechanism through which the body and its meanings are regulated. In the former, the concern is with the rise of the mental health institution and indeed the institutionalisation of mental health, while in the latter the concern shifts more directly to the role of the body in the management of crime and deviance. Here his central concern is with the rise of the prison or penal institution coupled with the fall of the *ancien régime* of eighteenth-century France. Foucault's contention is that this development constitutes a qualitative shift, rather than a decline, in the social regulation of the body. This is demonstrated vividly through the lengthy opening description of a public execution via hanging, drawing and quartering, which is then compared with the modern prison order, illustrated in the change from:

> The flesh will be torn from his breasts, arms, thighs and calves with red-hot pincers, his right hand, holding the knife with which he committed the said parricide, burnt with sulphur, and, on those places where the

flesh will be torn away, poured molten lead, boiling oil, burning resin, wax and sulphur melted together and then his body drawn and quartered by four horses and his limbs and body consumed by fire.

(Foucault, 1977: 3)

to:

At the first drum-roll, the prisoners must rise and dress in silence, as the supervisor opens the cell doors. At the second drum-roll, they must be dressed and make their bed. At the third, they must line up and proceed to the chapel for Morning Prayer. There is a five-minute interval between each drum roll.

(Foucault, 1977: 6)

Foucault's key proposition is that the body remains a key site of regulation within both contexts. It is also Foucault's argument that society is increasingly held together not by overt or visible state apparatuses such as the police or the army, but by what he calls 'bio-politics' or the very development of covert or invisible regulations and disciplines practised within and outside such carceral institutions as prisons. There are five key factors in this: first, the continued social function of punishment in maintaining social order; second, the fact that punishment continues to be seen to be done, is applied individually and objectively and is specific or, in short, that it is perceived to fit the crime; third, that the creation of the judiciary is tied to developments in knowledge itself, creating what Foucault calls a new 'juridico-epistemology'; fourth, that the body remains the object of continued regulation whether in its more 'fleshly' or 'mindful' forms; and finally, the role of architectural developments is key and particularly the development of cultures of surveillance through the design of the panopticon by Jeremy Bentham. Within all of this are three key processes: first, the role of hierarchical observation both literally and metaphorically; second, the use of 'normalising' judgements in the allocation of treatments and cures for pre-defined ills; and third, the process of examination and assessment by experts. The importance of such processes for understanding the body are not always made explicit, yet remain significant in reinforcing Foucault's wider emphasis on its construction and regulation. Consequently, the body for Foucault is – by and large – an object to be written on by society rather than some kind of determining or active biological entity in itself. However, it is his savaging of biological determinism that is, for some, Foucault's greatest weakness as well as his strength. Shilling in particular accuses Foucault of rendering the corporeal realities of the body invisible and of imposing an alternative discursive essentialism which simply reinforces the old dualism of nature and culture (Shilling, 1993). I will return to such claims shortly, but it remains necessary in the first instance to consider Foucault's analysis of sexuality.

On the face of it, sexuality is one of the most corporeal aspects of human society, particularly in terms of our experience of it. However, Foucault is at pains to point out that the body does not determine our sexuality or even the meanings that we ascribe to it. Indeed, his entire treatise on the history of sexuality is an overwhelmingly socially constructionist one that argues that sexuality, and indeed all the moral and political baggage that often goes with it, is an invention or the production of discourse (Foucault, 1978). His starting point is his rejection of the notion of repression, most commonly associated with the Victorians. In turning commonsense on its head, Foucault asserts that this was precisely the point at which our modern understanding of sexuality was created, or produced, and its terminology invented. Once again, it is the rise of the state and the role of psychiatry and medicine that are seen as critical in producing what he calls a 'scientia sexualis' or science of sex, later often called sexology. As in earlier works, his focus is primarily epistemological and, to a slightly lesser extent, political. In particular, it is the rise of experts and an expertise concerning sexuality that concerns him and their role in constructing not only an implicitly false notion of sexual 'truth' but a whole series of sexual categories and types. Consequently, the late nineteenth century sees the construction of hysteria, homosexuality and perversion as categories that not only label particular practices or acts but people themselves, which therefore become, as it were, modern identities in themselves. The underlying and more political concern here is of course the sense in which those categories and identities are stacked up hierarchically, divisively and unevenly and ascribed moral overtones of good and bad. Thus, the masturbating child, the homosexual and the sadomasochist are not only 'born' but scientifically and medically condemned at their conception. The legacy and importance of such a thesis for the formation of identity politics cannot be overestimated, and this is considered in more detail in Chapter 5. However, it is its opening of the proverbial can of worms in relation to the body that concerns us here. Later volumes of the *History of Sexuality* see Foucault's attention shift more towards the legacy of classicism and Greco-Roman culture in particular (Foucault, 1984a, 1984b). Here Foucault is once again primarily concerned with the question of regulation, arguing vociferously against any trite notion of pre-modern hedonism and asserting instead that the roots of contemporary moral and political anxieties concerning sexuality were located in early classical dilemmas concerning the role of the body in relation to such factors as the control of pleasure, the importance of duty, the use of diet and notions of physical perfection. In particular, he exposes an entire corpus of moral agonising among classical philosophers from Plato and Plutarch to Aurelius and Seneca, arguing that this growing sense of anxiety concerning uncontrolled bodily desire has had particularly severe consequences for the understanding and development of modern sexuality.

Not surprisingly, Foucault's work has led to much debate, discussion and dissent (Dean, 1999; Mills, 2003; Ramazanoglu, 1993). It is not within the scope of this chapter to discuss this work in detail. Nevertheless, certain key considerations are raised in relation to the body more specifically. The first of these concerns the role of power and the importance of Foucault's work in problematising this as something which both affects and indeed constitutes the body. Foucault's concept of power is radical, for it is seen not as any kind of inherent quality but rather as a force-field of relations powered by discourse. Thus: 'Power is everywhere; not because it embraces everything, but because it comes from everywhere [. . .] it is the name that one attributes to a complex strategical situation in a particular society' (Foucault, 1978: 93). Consequently, the body is not only caught up *within* this set of relations, but its meaning becomes entirely constituted *by* them. Secondly, Foucault's entire canon of work forms an effective and stinging critique of more liberal or benign interpretations of the role of the modern state. Medicine, psychiatry, the judiciary and even sexology are all lambasted for their hidden and not so progressive moral and political agendas. Thirdly, and most controversially, Foucault's underlying theory of discourse and discursive formation is of profound importance in understanding how the body becomes meaningful only through processes of construction and interaction with prevailing epistemologies.

There are a number of well-established points of criticism to be raised here. The first and most frequently cited point is that Foucault renders the body merely a passive object on which social meanings are inscribed and processes of power are acted out *upon* it rather than through interaction *with* it. While this is in some senses the case, to say otherwise would risk collapsing into a new kind of essentialism. To put it more simply, what active or determining role *can* the body have that is *not* biologically driven? While ageing, pain and suffering – or indeed youth, pleasure and enjoyment – are indeed corporeal in many of their aspects, they *mean* little in themselves or outside of the personal, social and historical contexts in which they exist. Second, some authors have argued that Foucault tends to re-work rather than overthrow prevailing dualisms concerning the body and social theory, including the tension between the individual and the social and most notably the Cartesian splitting of mind and body (Shilling, 1993). Thirdly, there is also a more implicit sense in which Foucault invokes a more functionalist understanding of crime and deviance and with it resurrects an understanding of the body and society that is ultimately still teleological in its analysis of cause and effect. Rather than continue to detail these criticisms, which are effectively and fully outlined elsewhere, I wish to assert that the crux of the critique of Foucault's work in relation to the body rests on the unresolved dualism of constructionism and essentialism that continues to be played out in more contemporary sociologies of embodiment. Before conducting this investigation of the sociology of embodiment further, however, it is necessary to consider the work of some other theorists.

Like Foucault, Bourdieu did not label himself a theorist of the body, but his theorising of social reproduction, together with his now classic work

Distinction: a Social Critique of the Judgement of Taste in particular, is perceived as of landmark relevance to its study (Bourdieu, 1984). In the first instance, for Bourdieu, the body is a metaphor or the bearer of symbolic meaning and values and a key site through which social differences are created, perpetuated and reinforced. Central in this is his elaborate theorising of capital and the role of the body as the harbinger of physical capital in particular. Physical capital refers to a range of corporeal skills and human attributes, from the development of manners and deportment through to strength, fitness and sporting prowess. Such capital is both produced, or learned and developed within particular social fields such as education and fashion, and converted into other forms of capital such as economic or material capital, cultural or what one might call 'know-how' capital, and social or status-related capital. A prime example here is the way in which economic and social success in many middle-class and corporate careers is seen to depend on the development of particular skills, from perfecting handshakes to playing golf. Similarly, enhanced working-class status and capital may be gained through participating in sports such as football. Bourdieu elaborates this along with his wider theories of habitus and taste in *Distinction* (1984), a major empirical study of Parisian consumption patterns from housing and schooling through to the arts and fashion. In addition, what is of critical importance to our analysis here is Bourdieu's exposure of the role of the body in these activities and processes. While formal dressing and knowledge of correct dining etiquette are commonly seen as mind over body activities, *individual* bodily management remains profoundly important and, arguably, the body does not become rendered invisible in the more Foucauldian sense.

Of crucial significance, however, is the interaction of such processes with the question of social class. The entire canon of Bourdieu's work is often concerned with the creation and perpetuation of inequalities, most particularly class differences, and his analysis of the body is no exception. In conjunction with this, he argues that the working classes have a fundamentally different relation to their bodies from the dominant or middle classes. The key concern for the working classes is that the body is seen primarily in *instrumental* or mechanical terms as something that is a means to an end or that gets the job done. Strength, health and the ability to labour or achieve practical results are therefore key sites of development. For example, working-class men commonly pride themselves on their ability to build, weld and lift things while working-class women similarly develop skills in managing the home, making up and making do. For the middle or upper classes, however, the concern shifts more towards a *rational* sense of the body's appearance and its role as a project to be kept up and maintained towards higher ends. Consequently, many middle-class men may seek to maintain their fitness through attending gyms while middle-class women more commonly try to look slim and take an interest in fashion. The legacy of Weber's theory of action is clearly apparent here, as is the influence of some more functionalist and Parsonian accounts of social class (Parsons, 1953; Weber, 1946). Bourdieu's concern is also to assert that these types of physical capital are not just different but unequal, and more working-class forms of physical capital typically have a lesser exchange value, in the more Marxist sense, than their middle-class counterparts. More specifically, such factors interact with wider questions of social and geographical location, a habitus and taste or what Bourdieu has occasionally called the 'body nexus'. Also underlying his analysis is a concern with the commodification of the body which, together with his work on the role of cultural intermediaries, has led other theorists to take his ideas in an altogether more postmodern direction (see, for example, Featherstone, 1982).

What are we to make of Bourdieu's theorising around the body for our analysis here? Perhaps the primary point to make is that Bourdieu clearly operates within the legacy of classical sociology and, while his analysis does build on this, it does not entirely break with it. In that sense, the body tends to remain buried under a series of wider concerns with social class, social order and social reproduction. Secondly, though many other theorists have sought to weld Bourdieu's analysis to wider and more postmodern and contemporary concerns such as aestheticisation and commodification or, more empirically, the role of cultural intermediaries in relation to such issues as fashion and advertising, it is difficult to escape the sense that Bourdieu's analysis of class and its relationship to the body is now somewhat dated (Featherstone, Hepworth and Turner, 1991; Nava *et al.*, 1997; Nixon, 1996). The decline of manufacturing renders many traditional working-class notions of labouring as physical capital rather redundant, while the rise of everything from designer fashion and tanning salons to cosmetic surgery to gym memberships as activities for everyone tends to undermine any simple sense of class distinctions in relation to the body. Thirdly, this also tends to lead into the more common criticism that Bourdieu fails to take sufficient account of such factors as gender, let alone racial distinctions in relation to the body (Marshall and Witz, 2004). The blurring of boundaries between career men and women while simultaneously maintaining distinctions in other areas, particularly around the objectification of the black body, are simply absent in most of Bourdieu's sociology. Fourthly, and more theoretically, there is a sense in which Bourdieu's theorising of the body is rather static, and historical change, though acknowledged, tends to exist outside of corporeal limits. Finally, what is also limited here is the sense of individual agency. The more contemporary significance of bodily reflexivity in the work of Giddens and others, though not entirely at odds with the work of Bourdieu, does not entirely sit well with it either (Giddens, 1991). This is a theme I will explore more fully shortly, after first considering the same theme in the more recent work of Turner.

With the possible exception of the work of Bourdieu or Foucault, there has arguably been no sociology of the body and no sociologist of the body prior to the original publication of Bryan Turner's *The Body and Society* in

1984 (Turner, 1996). Turner's work on the body is subtitled 'explorations in social theory' and it is arguably as concerned with sociological theory as much as the body *per se*. As is the case for Bourdieu, the body for Turner is in essence metaphor and it is on this that his concept of a somatic society rests: 'namely a society within which major political and personal problems are both problematised in the body and expressed through it' (Turner, 1996: 1). Turner trawls through an extensive list of sociological, medical, feminist and even religious perspectives on the body, ranging from Malthus to Marxism and from Descartes to Foucault, but the nub of his own argument lies half-way through in his chapter on bodily order. Adapting a Parsonian model of structural functionalism and welding it to the Hobbesian problem of order, Turner posits that the body represents a problem of governance for society in that it encapsulates a wider social need for control of populations according to four factors or dimensions, namely reproduction, restraint, regulation and representation. Reproduction has traditionally been governed through patterns of delayed marriage and patriarchy in order to control fertility and was previously analysed by the eighteenth-century theorist Malthus; restraint is seen to operate primarily in relation to the question of sexual desire and an ideology of asceticism explored most fully in the work of Max Weber; regulation relates to the spatial control of the body, and both Rousseau's argument concerning the moral decay associated with the growth of urbanisation and Foucault's work on the panopticon as a solution to this problem are seen as key here; and the dimension of representation is most contemporary and concerned with changing modes of self-presentation encapsulated most fully for Turner in the work of Erving Goffman. More particularly, each of these dimensions is associated with, or perhaps even epitomised in ideal type form through, a specific illness or medical condition. Consequently, reproduction is linked with onanism, restraint with hysteria, regulation with phobia and representation with anorexia.

As evidenced in the lengthy introduction to the second edition, Turner is also increasingly concerned with the role of commodification in relation to the body, and his argument draws heavily on the later work of Anthony Giddens on reflexivity. It is not within the scope of this chapter to outline in detail Giddens' theory of reflexivity, or Beck's analysis of risk society on which it draws heavily (Beck, 1992; Giddens, 1991). However, the overwhelming thrust of Giddens' analysis is that society is increasingly premised on, and characterised by, patterns of reflexivity that are at once as deeply psychological as they are social and structural. Reflexivity refers to a state of turning inwards or a situation of heightened anxiety and self-absorption varying from deeply personal questions of identity through to global and corporate concerns with negotiating insurance and risk. Of key significance for our analysis here is that these processes are also seen to relate to the body, which becomes a reflexive *project* to be moulded and adapted according to often mounting concerns with self-image, invoking high levels of anxiety and desires for control. While perhaps the most apposite example would be cosmetic surgery, Giddens focuses heavily on anorexia as a primary reflexive phenomenon. Despite the glaring questions of gendered difference and inequality here, Turner tends to endorse such an analysis in his growing concern with wider processes of commodification and the body as a problematic site of increasingly quasi-legal ownership.

Though it is not within the scope of this chapter to consider all of these ideas and their theoretical derivations in detail, it is worth stating some more generic considerations. First, Turner's on occasions dazzling tendency to draw in a wider and wider range of theories and concepts is perhaps its weakness as well as its strength. Though many of his conjunctions and interpretations are telling, many are given insufficiently detailed attention and do not easily assimilate into his overall analysis. His paralleling of the vast complexities of postmodernity with the eighteenth-century's high baroque is one example of a tendency to over-simplify matters, while his near dismissal of feminist concerns surrounding anorexia or the body as merely 'a political manifestation of the underlying economic and social changes taking place' is another that borders on the inflammatory (Turner, 1996: 4). Consequently, his centrifugal attempts to pull things together often have an equally centripetal effect. Second, many critics including Frank and Shilling have pointed out that his theorisation of the body is somewhat one-sided, as he sees it as a problem acted *upon* rather than as an *active* or enabling agent in the formation of embodiment (Frank, 1991; Shilling, 1993). Third, his study is theoretically rather than empirically driven, gaining support precisely through its tendency towards the grandiose and making greater and greater connections. There is clearly a need here for a more specific, and more empirical, focus. Nevertheless, Turner's work remains a path-breaking critique of the Cartesian splitting of mind and body together with other dualisms as yet unresolved within sociology.

One particular legacy of Turner's study is the work of Frank, whose analysis almost can almost be seen to complement that of Turner (Frank, 1991). Frank critiques Turner for his overriding attention to questions of social order and structure, or in short his primarily *external* understanding of the body and then, in effect, turns this on its head to consider what he calls the more *internal* 'action problems' faced by the body itself. Consequently, if Turner considers the problems raised by the body from the outside in, Frank tends to try to consider them from the inside out or, to put it another way, if, for Turner, the body represents a problem for society then, for Frank, society represents a problem for the body. Thus, Turner's four-dimensional model of bodily order is turned into four action problems for the body, namely control, desire, the relation to others, and the relation to oneself. This in turn leads to four bodily styles or ideal types. These are: first, the disciplined body, governed by processes of regimentation and exemplified by the monastic order; second, the mirroring body, typified by processes of consumption and epitomised in the rise of the department store; third, the dominating body, where the key process is one of force, most obviously encapsulated in the pursuit of war; and fourth, the communicative body, governed by processes of recognition and primarily concerned with ritual, care and intimate relationships. Thus Frank and Turner can be seen to quite literally complement or mirror each other in their analysis of the body. Similarly, Frank's emphasis on the mirroring body and consumption more widely has led his analysis to be taken up in some wider accounts of postmodernity. The difficulty here, as is the case with Turner, is that there is an *a priori* assumption about where these bodily problems, whether internal or external, come from, and arguably insufficient attention is paid to questions of history and social, economic or political change.

The question of historical change in relation to the body is addressed most fully in the work of Norbert Elias. Although not a theorist of the body *per se*, Elias's major theorising of the civilising process is fundamental (Elias, 1994). This has already been considered and critiqued in Chapter 3 but it is worth being clear about its more specific relevance to our analysis of the body here. Shilling states that: 'Elias is mostly interested in the body in terms of its relevance to historical transformations in behavioural codes and forms of affect control' (Shilling, 1993: 150). As such, the body is not so much the object of study for Elias, but a key player in the theorising of social and historical change. Having said this, the starting place for Elias's understanding of the body is his rejection of the nature–culture dualism that has beset social science understandings of the body. For Elias, the body is an unfinished biological entity that is both shaped by society and an active player in its formation. A key example here is language, as this is both a socially learned and historically dynamic phenomenon yet one that depends on the development of bodily and cognitive functions to use it. Similarly, birth and death are understood socially, yet remain biological events. Thus, for Elias, the body and society are practicably inseparable and mutually interdependent. The civilising process is then set up on these parameters as Elias argues that the history of modern societies is characterised by an overall move towards or process of civilisation. Particularly significant in this is the social regulation of the body and the growing distaste for many of its functions, from flatulence to defecation. Of primary concern historically is the rise of Court Society and with it, a system of manners and class- and status-related distinctions centred on physical appearances and corporeal controls. With this also comes the increasing separation of the human from the natural or animal and, more domestically, the separation of adults from children, combined with a growing emphasis on children as needing to learn the manners and control, or in short the civilising processes, of their parents. Interestingly, Elias's perspective is thus perhaps as psychologically driven as it is social, as he sees the rise of the civilising process as an internal set of controls centred on such factors as shame, embarrassment and anxiety as much as on external factors of economic growth, class distinction and social order.

As stated in Chapter 3, much Eliasian work has since been concerned with the explanation of reversals of such processes and what are sometimes called 'de-civilising spurts' exemplified in wars and other forms of violence. However, numerous difficulties remain: first, the definition of civilisation is diffuse and heavily value-laden. Though Elias is at pains to point out that he sees civilisation as an ongoing process rather than some kind of end result, it is difficult to escape the sense in which civilised society is valued over and above that which is otherwise implicitly, but inevitably and unavoidably, labelled as savage or primitive. More problematically still, the notion that those in medieval or other societies prior to the rise of Court Society were just a bunch of barbaric yobbos who only learned to do better in the wake of wider changes remains equally inescapable. Second, the sense that such civilising processes remain perilous and open to complete reversal is not explained sufficiently through reference to the notion of de-civilising spurts and opens up the question of other, entirely different, concerns not included in Eliasian analysis, more particularly, the lack of connection of the civilising process to wider economic and political if not social and cultural developments. Third, and most problematically, Eliasian analysis of the body almost unavoidably collapses – somewhat ironically – into asocial and ahistorical essentialism. Most fundamentally, Elias's entire theory of the civilising process depends on, and indeed repeatedly refers to, a series of *a priori* bodily instincts, urges and drives that 'need' on some level to be 'civilised'. More theoretically, to assert that the body enables such developments as language or that birth and death remain biological events does not in fact demonstrate that the biological otherwise drives the social through some kind of interdependent relationship as Elias implies and, more importantly, the mere fact of biological existence does not make it socially meaningful. On top of this, where does the civilising process itself come from and why? There is a sense here that the civilising process is an overwhelmingly totalising concept that is not particularly clearly related to either individual action or its intention. I will return to this question of intention, and indeed meaning, shortly yet it is necessary in the first instance to consider the work of one of Elias's followers on the body, Chris Shilling.

Chris Shilling points out in his theoretical interrogation of the body and social theory, that the body has maintained what he calls an 'absent presence' within sociology: 'Throughout its establishment and development, sociology has adopted a disembodied approach towards its subject matter' (Shilling, 1993: 19). Shilling argues that the body, rather than being entirely neglected within sociology, has in a sense been rendered invisible by it through being invoked by studies of subjects as diverse as class, education and race, yet rarely acknowledged even as the passive object of study, let alone as an active subject of analysis. It is in particular this problem of passivity which undermines still more the study of embodiment, as opposed to the sociology of the body *per se*, or the sense that the body as an active agent in simultaneously empowering and limiting human actions and society is almost wholly neglected. There a few exceptions to this rule, for Shilling, most notably in the work of Bourdieu and Elias. This does, I think, tend to hinge on a wider question of social construction and essentialism, or the dualism of nature versus culture, that Shilling also seeks to address. Shilling argues that Goffman, Foucault, Frank and even Turner in their varying yet consistently socially constructionist arguments end up paying insufficient attention to the body as a corporeal entity and an active agent in the creation of society, thus disembodying social theory and reproducing the dualisms of mind and body, nature and culture. Although not wholly uncritical of Elias's work, the solution for Shilling lies with the Eliasian or figurational notion of historical and social development. As I have already pointed out earlier, however, this tends to collapse back into a form of *a priori* or pre-determining bodily essentialism that reinforces the dualism all over again. Though Foucault and others are often guilty of paying insufficient attention to questions of individual or even collective corporeal or bodily experience, mostly due to an overwhelming lack of empiricism, and more simply neglect the importance of subjectivity *per se*, this does not mean that their assertion that the body is a basically meaningless *tabula rasa* on which the socially meaningful is written is wrong. To argue that the body itself is some kind of active or determining entity is to potentially risk collapsing into a form of biological or fatalistic essentialism and, to be frank, is not very sociological. This is perhaps why so many recent accounts of the body have ended up arguing that social theory needs to widen and change to incorporate the body when arguably it already has done this, just not in the way theorists such as Shilling would like. Despite its expansion, then, the sociology of the body remains almost monotonously in tune with itself and its arguments, pleading for a more embodied form of sociological theory yet offering few solutions that escape old and entrenched dualisms. More importantly, none of this tells us much *at all* about masculinity, to which we now turn.

Bodily absence: masculinity, normativity and the body

If the sociology of the body is arguably still in its infancy and consequently underdeveloped, then the sociology of the body and its relationship to masculinity more specifically has yet to be born and is next to non-existent. Though Connell, Morgan, Whitehead and a few others have started to the address the issue of the embodiment of masculinity, no sociology of men's bodies as yet truly exists (Connell, 1995; Morgan, 1993; Whitehead, 2002). There are perhaps several reasons for this situation: first, men's studies of masculinity were historically so heavily predicated on social constructionist arguments that consideration of the body, because it invoked essentialist questions of male biology, was often flatly denied; second, as we have already seen, the social science understanding of the body is itself inadequate, particularly in terms of its consideration of gender; and third, the body has arguably simply not mattered to studies of masculinity until quite recently. In particular, the increasing contemporary emphasis on the male body within many media and visual cultures alongside its growing significance in lived practices, whether in the guise of the vanity of the New Man or the self-absorption of gym culture, is something the sociology of masculinity has only begun to catch up on and explore. Though studies of the reconstruction of masculinity through consumer culture are increasingly prevalent, these analyses are for the most part 'disembodied', often paying little attention to the body *per se* (Chapman and Rutherford, 1988; Mort, 1996; Nixon, 1996). Rather inevitably, then, it is not only necessary to consider men's studies of masculinity and the body, such as they are, but also more interdisciplinary studies drawing on art, history, media studies and psychoanalytic theory.

One slight exception to the rule of the absent male body within the study of masculinities comes from the work of Connell (Connell, 1995). Connell's starting point is both the predictable critique of essentialist accounts of the body and the problem of its passivity implied by social constructionism. The power of essentialism is seen to come precisely from its 'metaphor of the body as machine' (Connell, 1995: 48). Thus, masculinity is commonly seen by essentialist accounts to emanate from the body and to be driven by it. Connell is equally critical of the likes of Foucault and Turner for their neglect of bodily subjectivity, arguing: 'There is an irreducible bodily dimension in experience and practice; the sweat cannot be excluded' (Connell, 1995: 51). Consequently, he ends up in a similar territory to Shilling in concluding that social theory has yet to get to grips with bodily agency. I have of course critiqued this point already. Where Connell's analysis shifts towards a newer direction is in his consideration of the body's relationship to globalisation. He argues here that the male body, both as an active agent and a bearer of social meaning, has been a central player in many of the key historical developments in, and contemporary problems of, Western civilisation, whittling these down to four key structures of gender: first, *power* and the role of the male body in perpetuating violence; second, *production* and the role of male bodies in both labour and patterns of migration; third, what he calls *cathexis* and the role of the male body in relation to globalised sexualities, from gay culture to sex tourism; and fourth, *symbolisation* or the global economy of images of the male body and masculinity and the dominance of American models of both sportsmen and the thrusting businessman. This culminates in Connell's concept of body-reflexive practice, which he explores in some small-scale qualitative research and interviews through which he exposes the role of the body in both potentially shoring up notions of masculinity and contradicting them. Crucial here are men's subjective experiences of their bodies, which are frequently at odds with their ideals and indeed hegemonic masculinity. While this is useful more schematically, it remains rather under-developed.

Much the same applies to David Morgan's analysis of the body in his essay 'You Too Can Have a Body like Mine' (Morgan, 1993). Morgan notes the comparative lack of embodiment of masculinity relative to the embodiment of femininity, consequently re-invoking the sense in which masculinity is bound up more with conceptions of culture and femininity than with notions of nature. He also argues that much representation of the male body seeks to present an 'over-phallicized picture of man' while often denying its bodily realities (Morgan, 1993: 70). Though the overall thesis here perhaps holds purchase, the examples given are less than apt. In particular, Morgan asserts that most masculine dress codes hide the male body according to a classical, and perhaps even stereotypical, notion of masculinity as premised on rationality and mind over body. As I have pointed out elsewhere, suits and other uniforms, let alone other more casual clothes, do not necessarily seek to hide the male body as much as heighten many of its more phallic connotations in emphasising the shoulders and chest, while the tie traditionally points to the two main bodily symbols of masculinity, the Adam's apple and the penis (Edwards, 1997). It is in fact this question of power that constitutes the main thrust of Morgan's analysis, elucidating the way in which masculinity is premised on the bodily taking-up of space, often exemplified in the splaying of legs and swaggering walks. Consequently, this leads Morgan to consider the sense in which the body and masculinity are connected according to four key dimensions: first, the oppressing and violent body; second, the body as a site of emotional expression or repression; third, the body's role in formal and informal practices of male fraternity; and fourth, its connections to questions of health. In following Featherstone, Morgan also once again refers to its increasing commodification in consumer culture (Featherstone, 1982). This is perhaps an effective platform on which to build an analysis of masculinity and the body, yet has been little utilised since.

A somewhat more developed account of the relationship between masculinity and the body is provided by Stephen Whitehead (Whitehead, 2002). Whitehead notes the increasing theoretical attention given to the male body and indeed the comparative explosion in its media representations, ranging from *The Full Monty* to the scandals surrounding the former President of the United States Bill Clinton, and from the rising participation of men in more feminised forms of consumption to the increasing importance attached to men's health and the significance of gym cultures. All of this leads Whitehead to conclude that the body symbolises or at least encapsulates the very 'materiality of masculinities' or the sense that masculinity is embodied (Whitehead, 2002: 183). This embodiment of masculinity is seen to take three forms: first, in terms of experience and as it were the very physicality of masculinity; second, the sense in which the male body is inscribed with meaning and becomes a template for a series of signifiers; and third, through the male body's relationship to the social world and its, as it were, spatial role. As a result, the male body becomes a site 'from which masculinities appear both as illusion and as materiality' (Whitehead, 2002: 186). Interestingly, in returning to the work of Foucault, Whitehead goes in the reverse direction to many other theorists in the area. His argument rests on a critique of the Enlightenment and Cartesian understandings that seek to split mind and body in relation to masculinity. Thus masculinity is primarily conceived in

Foucauldian terms as a discursive construct given varying social and cultural meanings according to context, which in turn intersects with its incomplete, fragmented and shifting material existence. Thus in accepting the material embodiment of masculinities yet rejecting any *a priori* association of meaning, Whitehead starts to disrupt the collapse into essentialism associated with the work of Elias and Shilling while developing the potential of Foucauldian analysis and particularly the importance of what he calls the panoptic gaze. Also drawing on the feminist work of Young and Butler, he argues that the panoptic gaze is most importantly racialised, sexualised and aged as well as gendered (Butler, 1993; Young, 1990). Consequently black men, gay men and older or infirm men and their bodies are inscribed with meanings that are ideological and political: 'Thus the gaze is not simply about reifying bodies; the gaze politicizes bodies, rendering them into numerous political fields of truth and knowledge of which race, sexuality and age are but three' (Whitehead, 2002: 203).

Clearly underlying Whitehead's analysis is a concern with the role of the male body in relation to questions of masculinity and normativity or, to put it more simply, the importance of the body in forming and maintaining inequalities and social divisions between men. This is a theme taken up in the work of Gerschick on disability and Ekins and King on transgenderism (Gerschick, 2004; Ekins and King, 2004). Gerschick argues that bodies, male and female, are stratified according to a host of factors including age, weight, height, colour and size, into a kind of pecking order through which 'people are privileged by the degree to which they approximate cultural ideals' (Gerschick, 2004: 372). In addition, the increasing attention paid to questions of bodily modification, from diet and exercise regimes through to cosmetic surgery, means that people are going to ever-increasing extremes not only to 'discipline' their own bodies but to discipline others through processes of stigmatisation and valorisation. A prime example here, though not mentioned by Gerschick, is the rise of celebrity cultures and the increasingly visceral attacks made on those caught on camera who do not pass muster, varying from long lens shots of celebrities with cellulite to article-length obsessions with their weight and muscularity. Such attention is no longer restricted to women, and contemporary headline examples have included George Clooney's weight and Colin Farrell's hair colour, drinking and penis size. Gerschick gives the telling, if amusing, examples of oil rigger Stodder's regular abuse on an oil rig, being dangled above the floor and threatened with anal rape with a 'tarred implement', all apparently 'in jest', while Perry is cited in telling the tale of the extreme vigilance employed to hide his manhood from others, feeling himself to be 'hung like a hamster' (Stodder, 1979; Perry, 1992). The sense that men who do not conform to cultural ideals are quite simply rendered laughing stocks and game for abuse is, to say the least, cause for concern here. Similarly, Ekins and King document in detail the numerous ways in which, within medical, academic and feminist circles alike, transsexual and transgender men are seen to renounce, suspend, reject or transcend masculinity and in short to do everything but have any (Ekins and King, 2004).

Of implicit importance here of course is the question of representation. Australian academics McKay, Mikosza and Hutchins begin to address this question in their article amusingly titled 'Gentlemen, the Lunchbox has Landed', derived from the film *The Full Monty* (McKay, Mikosza and Hutchins, 2004). They note that the male body occupies an ambiguous position of being present but not visible and they go on to argue that, despite its expansion: 'The bulk of the research on men's bodies, especially the body image literature, tends to be theoretically unsophisticated, uncritical, and essentialist' (McKay, Mikosza and Hutchins, 2004: 275). Seen to be particularly absent are analyses of cyber bodies, subordinated masculinities, non-Western male bodies, and the local–global nexus in relation to masculinity. As I have suggested already, the sociology of the male body and masculinity is indeed lacking. Of more concern is their proposed solution to this situation through the deployment of Johnson's concept of the circuit of culture, also taken up extensively by Paul du Gay and colleagues at the Open University (Du Gay *et al.*, 1997). This is a heuristic device designed to aid the understanding of the ways in which any given cultural artefact becomes meaningful in relation to the articulation, or connection, of five interrelated processes of production, consumption, identity, representation, and regulation. This is then applied to the construction and indeed articulation of masculinity through the rise of men's style magazines. As these are considered in detail in Chapter 2, it is not appropriate to consider this analysis here. However, what remains of concern are the conclusions they draw from this discussion: first, that the media simultaneously reinforce and destabilise prevailing conceptions of masculinity and male bodies; second, that there is a cultural economy, or an enmeshed system of cultural and economic production, of gender which also relates to men's bodies; and third, that this leads to a need for research that is relational, seeing such factors as production and consumption, and more specifically masculinity and femininity, as completely interlinked. In conjunction with this, they also stress the ongoing importance of anxieties concerning sexuality in relation to the male body and conclude that: 'the time when we see a front-on pan of a row of 'full monties' in the popular media is still some way off' (McKay, Mikosza and Hutchins, 2004: 284).

Though all of the aforementioned and primarily sociological studies of masculinity in relation to the male body offer interesting insights into the construction of its meanings and start to develop models that may enhance its understanding, this is a literature that remains in its infancy and that is often hampered by an overly theoretical agenda. There is indeed an increasing need here to start to pull together some of the rather disparate and not always entirely helpful fragments that constitute the sociology of the body and, more importantly, to become more interdisciplinary in focus. One vehicle for doing this is to address more directly the question of representation and how the male body has been presented and understood over time.

Masculinity, reflexivity and representations of the male body

Analyses of the male body and its representation are, rather like fashion, often not located within the confines of sociology and social science at all, but rather under the auspices of art history and more contemporarily media studies. Also invoked here is psychoanalytic theory, yet it is perhaps worth starting with history itself. The most cursory of glances at history reveals some connection of the male body with wider and more social shifts in masculinity. From the setting-up of Greco-Roman ideals, now somewhat echoed in an increasingly visual and media culture of men's naked musculature, to the sense of an increasingly set of powerful internal and external restraints imposed on men's bodies and minds in the wake of the Industrial Revolution, the male body has often come to form a cipher or symbol for many, much wider cultural processes concerning masculinity. In an edited collection on the representation of the male body, Judith Still notes that there is an important trajectory, particularly artistically, in representations of passive, boyish or even feminised male bodies being conjoined with their more obvious active, muscular and assertive forms (Still, 2003). While Elias and Bourdieu and, more recently, Featherstone and Giddens, have gone some way to documenting the body's wider cultural and historical significance, the lack of a more specifically gendered focus tends to lead us more towards feminism (Bourdieu, 1984; Elias, 1994; Giddens, 1991).

While feminist accounts of the female body and the sexual objectification of femininity are now numerous, undoubtedly the most fully developed, and arguably the *only*, feminist account of the male body comes from Susan Bordo (Bordo, 1993, 1999; Orbach, 1978, 1986; Wolf, 1991). Bordo's book *The Male Body*, in blending – to a degree – a cultural history with media studies and feminist theory as well as autobiography, provides an eclectic yet focused concern with the relationship of the male body to questions of masculinity. Crucial to Bordo's analysis is the increasing commodification of the male body under the guise of consumer culture and, in particular, the importance of the phallus and the reworking of sexual anxieties concerning male genitalia:

> Five years after the Reynolds centrefold made its appearance, Hollywood put its first hunk in (discreetly black) briefs on the screen (John Travolta, playing Tony Manero in *Saturday Night Fever*), and Calvin Klein, inspired by muscular yet sinewy gay male aesthetics, brought the beauty of men in tight jeans – and a bit later, clinging underwear – to a mass market. No naked penises true. But a new willingness to visually foreground the sexuality of male hips and buttocks and, ultimately, male

genitals. The representational frontiers of the male body have been expanded; geographically, it now included the southern hemisphere. Consumer culture had discovered and begun to develop the untapped resources of the male body.

(Bordo, 1999: 18)

Covering everything from viagra and the phallus to Tom of Finland and gay culture, and from 1950s Hollywood to contemporary advertising, Bordo concludes that gender politics remain much intact. In particular, she deconstructs the dual marketing approach of advertisers as a form of homophobia that addresses gay men 'in a way that the straight consumer will not notice' (Bordo, 1999: 183) and parallels gym culture, or what she calls 'bigorexia', with anorexia and gloomily surmises that she 'never dreamed that "equality" would move in the direction of men worrying *more* about their looks rather than women worrying less' (Bordo, 1999: 217). Tellingly, she also reveals the puritanism of much contemporary culture and the 'ugh' factor involved in the increasingly extreme concern with looks, weight and corporeal discipline. Thus the lithe and slightly feminised John Travolta of *Saturday Night Fever* is transformed into the pumping, grinding-body-obsessed gym bunny of *Staying Alive*. What Bordo begins to document quite formidably here is a contemporary shift towards an increasingly anxious, image-centred and strangely gender-blurred but still reactionary and overwhelmingly commodified culture of bodily obsession. What she wrestles with rather less successfully are the explanations for this situation.

To begin to provide such an explanation does I think require an overwhelmingly interdisciplinary analysis that also seeks to bring together a number of disparate points made by authors in different arenas. First, and perhaps foremost, the contemporary obsession with the male body in consumer culture is not only a reflection of wider patterns or what Featherstone has called the aestheticisation and commodification of everyday life, but a more specifically historical phenomenon (Featherstone, 1982, 1991). The primary issue here is that gendered difference has, since the industrial revolution, functioned and developed not only through the sexual division of labour but through the bodily enactment of that division. Consequently, the working man was defined as masculine not only through a notion of going to work, which has now largely imploded through the increasing participation of women, but also through the bodily markers that came with working. Labouring and mechanical work was also defined as 'masculine' through its relationship to the male body, requiring or developing musculature and strength and adding further signatures of physical labour and skill or quite simply getting one's hands dirty as 'masculine' activities set apart from those of the home or service industries. The decline of manufacturing is not, I think, hardly coincidental with the rise of gym cultures and weight-training as popular activities for working-class men. Similarly, the increasingly thrusting and phallocentric displays and assertions of masculinity within white-collar and corporate and office cultures provides a more middle-class yet similarly corporeal assertion of masculinity and sexual difference.

A second factor here is that of the notion of reflexivity. Though Giddens and others often fail to connect such concepts to questions of masculinity, there is clearly a sense in which the self-absorption and anxiety commonly associated with anorexia is applicable to the increasingly commodified and image-obsessed world of the male body, as Bordo has noted (Bordo, 1993; Featherstone, 1991; Giddens, 1991).

A third factor here remains the legacy of Foucauldian analysis of the body as a site for and of internal and external discipline and control. Concerns with diet and exercise, often seen masquerading as health and fitness, are all intensive forms of physical control and discipline. In addition, as Whitehead has noted, these processes are deeply subject to and inscribed by the panoptic gaze of normalising judgements (Whitehead, 2002). While Elias's notion of the civilising process has some purchase here, it lacks both the theoretical sophistication and the sense of contemporary specificity and political edge of Foucault's account of bodily discipline (Elias, 1994; Foucault, 1977). While neither approach properly accounts for the role of subjectivity, or indeed gender, the overarching notion of a civilising process is just too cumbersome.

Fourthly, what also lurks under the surface here is the need for a greater understanding not of the objective state of the body and its meanings but its subjective experiences. Interestingly, there is much untapped potential in psychoanalytic work here and, in particular, the legacy of Freud or at least a Freudian understanding of the role of the phallus and indeed the phallo-centric in creating the centrepiece of the relationship between masculinity and the body (Freud, 1977). Though strictly Freudian accounts are now frequently dismissed as anachronistic or sexist, Freud nevertheless provided a theory of the development of masculine identity and even masculinity *per se* in relation to the body, and moreover the most fundamental question of gendered difference through the possession of a penis, a theory that remains both unique and largely untapped. One exception is the work of Chodorow, yet this tends to move away from the body as the baseline for its analysis (Chodorow, 1978).

More widely, any explanation of more contemporary concerns with the male body requires both a feminist input as well as an analysis of media representation. Far too many attempts to theorise the body lack *any* kind of gendered perspective. The concern with class and status invoked most particularly in the work of Bourdieu is striking here, as the body – while clearly still performing the function of signifying social class – is a far more *obvious* signifier of gender and indeed race, as well as age. As Whitehead notes, accounts of globalisation and the body also do not go nearly far enough to relate it fully to questions of race and ethnicity (Whitehead, 2002). Consequently, there is clearly a need to develop new directions of enquiry into the male body and masculinity as well as pull together the differing accounts as they currently stand.

One tentative example of such an exploration and development is Laurence Goldstein's edited collection titled *The Male Body*, which includes contributions as diverse as they are numerous ranging from poetry and fiction through to illustrations and essays from authors working in a variety of disciplines (Goldstein, 1994). The volume acts as a companion to an earlier collection on the female body and argues that:

> If recent writings, including those in this collection, are any indication, the task of men's studies is to recover from history, and from empirically-observed behaviours in the present day, that sense of choice and variety in self-definition that so many women have embraced as a means of personal and social liberation.
>
> (Goldstein, 1994: vii/viii)

While the influence of second-wave feminism is overwhelming, finding common or recurrent themes is necessarily not easy in such a diverse collection yet, certain points crop up repeatedly: first, the role of the Cartesian mind–body split in constructing masculinity historically as an increasingly rational achievement of mind over body, whether through self-restraint or disciplines of power and strength; secondly, and in addition to this, the example of musculature as reinforcing the sense of masculinity as hardness; third, the repeated invocation of anxieties concerning sexuality and the weakness of the penis in relation to the phallus; fourth, the sense that certain contemporary developments such as gym culture would appear to move in a more postmodern direction of a concern with bodily surface rather than substance; fifthly, the important ways in which many of these developments also centre on factors of race as the over-sexualised and hyper-masculine black male body is particularly caught up in processes of subordination to a supposedly rational white and Western male body. The lack of a wider literature on the black male body apart, these are points well demonstrated throughout the preceding analysis and it remains to reaffirm the rather glib point that far more research on the relationship between the male body and masculinity is needed.

Conclusions: auto mechanics

During the writing of this book I became 40, or effectively over the hill, redundant and fit for the scrap heap as far as many gay, or many other media informed definitions of masculine sex appeal and attractiveness are concerned. A recent edition of one celebrity magazine, for example, featured an article, subtly titled 'Phwoar at 40', concerning men still deemed sexually attractive over the age of 40, as Tom Cruise, Johnny Depp and Brad Pitt inevitably age like the rest of us – well, sort of. There are perhaps several points to be raised here. One is the implied discourse that 'phwoar' doesn't usually apply to a man over forty. Another point is that what makes these men exceptional are their bodies, given that they are seen as being blessed with unusually good looks. Of course the fact that they are celebrities with a history of being sex symbols is hardly coincidental. Conversely, the near character assassination of Ben Affleck in the media recently as a man apparently completely losing the plot in the appearance department following a nose-dive in his movie career and his break-up with Jennifer Lopez reinforces the gold standard that now exists concerning men's looks. In particular, Affleck was plastered across numerous media in increasingly ludicrous states of poor dress, messy dress and even undress. The TV programme Queer Eye for the Straight Guy *in both its UK and USA variants similarly squeals, often literally, at the appalling states of such men who do not 'measure up'. More particularly, this tyranny of appearances now often applies to men as much as to women although the criteria, justifications and ramifications frequently remain markedly different. For example, while dieting retains a near Orwellian control over most women's lives, the increasing emphasis on muscularity and fitness for men now has them scurrying to the gym in their millions. There are a number of factors to consider here. One is the sheer plethora of images of male attractiveness equated with men's bodies that now exist – even newsreaders and weather reporters now look like style-conscious Hollywood wannabes, let alone actors and pop stars, while not a single soap opera or drama in the US, UK or Europe fails to have its quotient of guys who look good with their shirts off. A second factor is the overwhelming equation of such images with health –* Men's Health *magazine and similar titles whether in the US or UK promote the same impossibly gleaming pumped and chiselled blow-up doll version of masculinity on their front covers and then pack their pages with a 1001 ways you could look like that too if only you swap your Mars bars for bar bells, keep your woman – or maybe your man – regularly satisfied and work out just like they tell you in page after page after page . . . All of this hard work highlights the third factor, namely the overwhelming puritanical-cum-fascist thrust of the underlying discourse – fat fuzzy and furry are 'out' and what's more downright bad; while slim, toned and hard are not only 'in' but desirable, essential to self-esteem and even heroic. Consequently, many Western governments are now banging their tambourines and joining in the religious zeal of banning obesity for fear of the escalating catastrophe. Fat is indeed a purist issue – George Michael recently closed down his fans' website forum due to the slagging off he was getting for being insufficiently glamorous, fat and simply over forty – if that is fan worship I dread to think what the fickle non-fans think. This is a frankly frightening state of affairs.*

It's particularly alarming here that gay men and gay culture are often the worst of all gladiatorial arenas of male bodily spectacle. I have not met a single gay man in the past ten years at least who does not suffer from major hang-ups concerning his appearance, from weight and musculature to grey hair, no hair or hair in the wrong places, to style, dress, demeanour and confidence, let alone cock size and sexual performance. The anxiety invoked, the lowness of self-confidence and the degree of self-loathing is crippling. Yet the gay press, gay bars, gay shops, gay websites and most other gay institutions, formal or informal, promote if not flagellate their clientele with relentless imagery of the often white, usually toned, frequently naked and – above all – youthful model. All of this is perhaps understandable, given the prevalence of such imagery more widely, yet gay men's inability to resist or to come up with other options given over thirty years of political mobilising is galling. I have also had numerous conversations with gay men deeply aware of these external pressures and contradictions, often even showing feminist awareness and wider understandings of body fascism yet, when confronted with the local totty, they resort without fail to the tried and trusted habits of desire and longing. One friend, now in his fifties who suffers from some particular physical disabilities of his own, still fails to make such connections and castigates all those more than three pounds overweight as chronically fat and all those over 35 as over the hill – consequently both porn star Steve Hooper and actors John Travolta and Matt le Blanc are now fat and past it in his opinion.

During the writing of this book I also broke my hand – it was initially terrifying and an immense nuisance, hampering dressing, washing and even eating, yet I cannot say that it of itself *meant anything*. Its meaning, conversely, came entirely from my own personal position and perception. I like to dress well and couldn't, I am rather fastidious and felt I couldn't keep clean; I'm also independent and couldn't drive. Consequently, I was frustrated and angry and rather depressed – not surprising really – but it would have been very different if I had been a different kind of person, for example a complete slob or a sportsman. All of this tends to undermine the notion that any kind of meaning resides *within the body* – even pain and injury is open to personal interpretation. Moreover, meaning does still overwhelmingly come from outside and the media in particular, with divisive and even derisive consequences. Consequently, if one can make predictions concerning the future direction of masculinity, it would seem to be towards an increasingly self-absorbed and anxious state of being concerned with how one looks as much if not necessarily more than what one does or, in short, the auto mechanic's masculinity is now increasingly auto-mechanical.

Conclusion

The social and cultural theory of men and masculinities

> Gender is thus a construction that regularly conceals its genesis; the tacit collective agreement to perform, produce, and sustain discrete and polar genders as cultural fictions is obscured by the credibility of those productions – and the punishments that attend not agreeing to believe in them; the construction 'compels' our belief in its necessity and naturalness.
>
> (Butler, 1990: 140)

The recent massacring of Oliver Stone's movie *Alexander* in the United States and the almost simultaneous vaulting of Scorsese's *The Aviator* tells us something concerning contemporary men and masculinities, namely that good old God Save America is not ready for psychologically complex studies of sexually ambiguous heroes from antiquity and would rather stick to the comfort of heterosexual rags-to-riches stories and the mastery of technology. While critics will try to defend their slaughtering of *Alexander* and, in the end, the Academy did not reward Scorsese either – nothing in the name of movie critique can justify or explain the extraordinary jeers of derision that were levelled at the lead actor, Colin Farrell, his co-stars, or the director Oliver Stone. Indeed, some of the premieres across the world and reports in the press resembled public spectacles more suited to Salem's witch-burning trials in the seventeenth century – they too, of course, were all about sexuality and gender deviance, with a hefty dose of God thrown into the flames with them. It tells us *something*, yes. Yet it hardly tells us everything or even a lot concerning contemporary masculinities.

Similarly, no end of statistics and discussion showing that men earn more than women, that men are more violent than women, or that men dominate nearly every Western institution – or that men could change or more often *should* change – tells us everything, or even much, and this has been the dilemma of this book. The picture is incomplete, the story half told, the sight only partial in either case. However, if all sides are considered, it is perhaps a little less partial, a little more told, a little more complete.

Whatever the assessment of its outcomes, one of the key successes of second-wave feminism was that it sought, in a myriad of forms, to articulate women's experience – a case of saying 'no, it's not like that, it's like this'. And this is what the newly formed critical studies of men and masculinities has mostly failed to do – tell it like it is *for* men not *about* men, *of* men and not *at* men, and *by* men – the good, the bad and the ugly. This is not a call for yet more attempts at consciousness-raising or autobiography, but for more research and particularly more qualitative research that actually listens to men as not only the primary makers of masculinity but its principal consumers. Ask them what it's *like*, whether at home or work – or even at the movies. While there is now some more empirical work on men and masculinities, it is still drowned ten-fold by theorisation and politicisation, whether in culturalist analysis and media studies or sociology and social science. Indeed, if the project of any critical studies of men and masculinities is for men to increasingly recognise themselves *as* men, then perhaps we need to start listening more and telling less, and encourage dialogue academically as well as personally in an attempt to articulate our experience.

Bibliography

Adam, B. D. (1987) *The Rise of a Gay and Lesbian Movement*, Boston, Mass.: Twayne Publications.

Adams, M. and Coltrane, S. (2004) 'Boys and men in families: the domestic production of gender, power and privilege', in M. S. Kimmel, J. Hearn and R. W. Connell (eds) *Handbook of Studies on Men and Masculinities*, London: Sage.

Ainsworth, P. B. (2000) *Psychology and Crime: Myths and Reality*, Harlow: Longman/Pearson Education.

Altman, D. (1971) *Homosexual: Oppression and Liberation*, Sydney: Angus & Robertson.

Altman, D. (1986) *AIDS and the New Puritanism*, London: Pluto Press.

Altman, D. (2001) *Global Sex*, Chicago: Chicago University Press.

Anderson, B. (1983) *Imagined Communities*, London: Verso.

Arnot, M., David, M. and Weiner, G. (1999) *Closing the Gender Gap: Post-war Education and Social Change*, Cambridge: Polity.

Austin, J. (1962) *How To Do Things With Words*, Oxford: Clarendon Press.

Badinter, E. (1995) *XY: On Masculine Identity*, New York: Colombia University Press.

Bandura, A. (1973) *Aggression: A Social Learning Analysis*, Englewood Cliffs, NJ: Prentice-Hall.

Bandura, A. (1977) *Social Learning Theory*, Englewood Cliffs, NJ: Prentice-Hall.

Barrett, M. (1980) *Women's Oppression Today: Problems in Marxist Feminist Analysis*, London: Verso.

Barthes, R. (1977) *Image, Music, Text: Essays Selected and Translated by Stephen Heath*, London: Fontana.

Baudrillard, J. (1983) *Simulacra and Simulations*, New York: Semiotext(e) (orig. pub. 1981).

Bech, H. (1997) *When Men Meet: Homosexuality and Modernity*, Cambridge: Polity.

Beck, U. (1992) *The Risk Society: Towards a New Modernity*, London: Sage.

Beck, U. *et al.*, (1994) *Reflexive Modernization*, Cambridge: Polity.

Bem, S. (1974) 'The measurement of psychological androgyny', *Journal of Consulting and Clinical Psychology* 42: 155–62.

Bennett, A. (2000) *White Identities: Historical and International Perspectives*, Harlow: Prentice Hall.

Benwell, B. (2000) 'Ironic discourse: masculine talk in men's lifestyle magazines', unpublished conference paper for 'Posting the Male', Liverpool: John Moores University.

Benwell, B. (ed.) (2003) *Masculinity and Men's Lifestyle Magazines*, Oxford: Blackwell.

Berger, M. (*et al.*) (eds) (1995) *Constructing Masculinity*, London: Routledge.

Bersani, L. (1988) 'Is the rectum a grave?' in D. Crimp (ed.) *AIDS: Cultural Analysis, Cultural Activism*, London: MIT Press.

Bersani, L. (1995) 'Loving men', in M. Berger *et al.* (eds) *Constructing Masculinity*, London: Routledge.

Beynon, J. (2002) *Masculinities and Culture*, Milton Keynes: Open University Press.

Blachford, G. (1981) 'Male dominance and the gay world', in K. Plummer (ed.) *The Making of the Modern Homosexual*, London: Hutchinson.

Bly, R. (1991) *Iron John: A Book about Men*, Shaftsbury, Dorset: Element.

Bordo, S. (1993) *Unbearable Weight: Feminism, Western Culture, and the Body*, Berkeley, Calif.: University of California Press.

Bordo, S. (1999) *The Male Body: A New Look at Men in Public and in Private*, New York: Farrar, Straus & Giroux.

Bourdieu, P. (1984) *Distinction: A Social Critique of the Judgement of Taste*, London: Routledge & Kegan Paul.

Bowker, L. H. (ed.) (1998) *Masculinities and Violence*, London: Sage.

Bowlby, R. (1993) *Shopping with Freud*, London: Routledge.

Box, S., Hale, C. and Andrews, G. (1988) 'Explaining fear of crime', *British Journal of Criminology* 28(3): 340–56.

Bray, A. (1982) *Homosexuality in Renaissance England*, London: Gay Men's Press.

Breward, C. (1999) *The Hidden Consumer: Masculinities, Fashion and City Life 1860–1914*, Manchester: Manchester University Press.

Bristow, J. (1989) 'Homophobia/Misogyny: sexual fears, sexual definitions', in S. Shepherd and M. Wallis (eds) *Coming On Strong: Gay Politics and Culture*, London: Unwin Hyman.

Bristow, J. and Wilson, A. (eds) (1993) *Activating Theory: Lesbian, Gay, Bisexual Politics*, London: Lawrence & Wishart.

Brittan, A. (1989) *Masculinity and Power*, Oxford: Blackwell.

Brod, H. (ed.) (1987) *The Making of Masculinities: The New Men's Studies*, London: Hutchinson.

Brod, H. and Kaufman, M. (eds) (1994) *Theorising Masculinities*, London: Sage.

Bronski, M. (1984) *Culture Clash: The Making of a Gay Sensibility*, Boston, Mass.: South End Press.

Brownmiller, S. (1975) *Against Our Will: Men, Women and Rape*, New York: Simon & Schuster.

Brownmiller, S. (1984) *Femininity*, New York: Simon & Schuster.

Bruzzi, S. and Gibson, P. C. (eds) (2000) *Fashion Cultures: Theories, Explanations and Analysis*, London: Routledge.

Buchbinder, D. (1994) *Masculinities and Identities*, Victoria: Melbourne University Press.

Buchbinder, D. (1998) *Performance Anxieties: Re-Producing Masculinity*, St Leonards, NSW: Allen & Unwin.

Butler, J. (1990) *Gender Trouble: Feminism and the Subversion of Identity*, London: Routledge.

Butler, J. (1993) *Bodies That Matter: On the Discursive Limits of Sex*, London: Routledge.

Butler, J. (1995) 'Melancholy gender/refused identification', in M. Berger *et al.* (eds) *Constructing Masculinity*, London: Routledge.

Califia, P. (1994) *Public Sex: The Culture of Radical Sex*, San Francisco, Calif.: Cleiss Press.

Campbell, B. (1993) *Goliath: Britain's Dangerous Places*, London: Penguin.

Canaan, J. E. and Griffen, C. (1990) *The New Men's Studies: Part of the Problem or Part of the Solution?*, in J. Hearn and D. Morgan. (eds) *Men, Masculinities and Social Theory*, London: Unwin Hyman.

Caplan, P. (ed.) (1987) *The Cultural Construction of Sexuality*, London: Tavistock.

Carbado, D. W. (ed.) (1999) *Black Men on Race, Gender, and Sexuality: A Critical Reader*, New York: New York University Press.

Carpenter, E. (1908) *The Intermediate Sex: A Study of Some Transitional Types of Men*, London: Mitchell Kennedy.

Carrigan, T., Connell, R. W. and Lee, J. (1985) 'Toward a new sociology of masculinity', *Theory & Society* 14: 551–604.

Cashmore, E. (2002) *Beckham*, Cambridge: Polity.

Chaney, D. (1996) *Lifestyles*, London: Routledge.

Chapman, R. and Rutherford, J. (eds) (1988) *Male Order: Unwrapping Masculinity*, London: Lawrence & Wishart.

Chesney-Lind, M. (1997) *The Female Offender: Girls, Women, and Crime*, London: Sage.

Chodorow, N. (1978) *The Reproduction of Mothering: Psychoanalysis and the Sociology of Gender*, Berkeley, Calif.: University of California Press.

Clare, A. (2000) *On Men: Masculinity in Crisis*, London: Chatto & Windus.

Cockburn, C. (1983) *Brothers*, London: Pluto.

Cohan, S. and Hark, I. A. (eds) (1993) *Screening the Male: Exploring Masculinities in Hollywood Cinema*, London: Routledge.

Cohen, P. (1997) 'Laboring under whiteness', in R. Frankenberg (ed.) (1997) *Displacing Whiteness: Essays in Social and Cultural Criticism*, New York: Duke University Press.

Cohen, S. (1972) *Folk Devils and Moral Panics: The Creation of Mods and Rockers*, London: Martin Robertson.

Cole, S. (2000) *'Don We Now Our Gay Apparel': Gay Men's Dress in the Twentieth Century*, Oxford: Berg.

Collins, P. H. (1991) *Black Feminist Thought: Knowledge, Consciousness, and the Politics of Empowerment*, London: Routledge.

Connell, R. W. (1987) *Gender and Power*, Cambridge: Polity.

Connell, R. W. (1995) *Masculinities*, Cambridge: Polity.

Connell, R. W. (2000) *The Men and the Boys*, Cambridge: Polity.

Cooley, C. H. (1902) *Human Nature and the Social Order*, New York: Schribner's.

Cornwall, A. and Lindisfarne, N. (eds) (1994) *Dislocating Masculinity: Comparative Ethnographies*, London: Routledge.

Craig, S. (ed.) (1992) *Men, Masculinity and the Media*, London: Sage.

Craik, J. (1994) *The Face of Fashion: Cultural Studies in Fashion*, London: Routledge.

Creed, B. (1993) 'Dark desires: male masochism in the horror film' in S. Cohan and

I. R. Hark (eds) *Screening the Male: Exploring Masculinities in Hollywood Cinema*, London: Routledge.

Crenshaw, K. W. (1999) 'Foreword – Why we can't wait: integrating gender and sexuality into antiracist politics', in D. Carbado (ed.) *Black Men on Race, Gender and Sexuality: A Critical Reader*, New York: New York University Press.

Crewe, B. (2003) 'Class, masculinity and editorial identity in the reformation of the UK men's press', in B. Benwell (ed.) *Masculinity and Men's Lifestyle Magazines*, Oxford: Blackwell.

Crimp, D. (ed.) (1988) *AIDS: Cultural Analysis, Cultural Activism*, London: MIT Press.

Crisp, Q. (1968) *The Naked Civil Servant*, Glasgow: Collins.

Crompton, R. (1997) *Women and Work in Modern Britain*, Oxford: Oxford University Press.

Crompton, R, Gallie, D. and Purcell, K. (1996) *Changing Forms of Employment: Organisation, Skills and Gender*, London: Routledge.

Daly, M. (1979) *Gyn/Ecology: The Metaethics of Radical Feminism*, London: Women's Press.

Daly, M. and Wilson, M. (1988) *Homicide*, New York: Aldine de Gruyter.

David, D. S. and Brannon, R. (eds) (1976) *The Forty Nine Percent Majority: The Male Sex Role*, Cambridge, Mass.: Addison-Wesley.

Davidoff, L. and Hall, C. (1987) *Family Fortunes: Men and Women of the English Middle Class*, London: Hutchinson.

Dean, M. (1999) *Governmentality: Power and Rule in Modern Society*, London: Sage.

De Beauvoir, S. (1953) *The Second Sex*, New York: Alfred A. Knopf.

Delph, E. W. (1978) *The Silent Community: Public Sexual Encounters*, Beverly Hills, Calif.: Sage Publications.

De Man, P. (1979) *Allegories of Reading: Figural Language in Rousseau, Nietzsche, Rilke and Proust*, London: New Haven.

Derrida, J. (1982) *Margins of Philosophy*, Chicago: University of Chicago Press.

Dobash, R. E. and Dobash, R. (1979) *Violence Against Wives*, New York: Free Press.

Dobash, R. E. and Dobash, R. (1992) *Women, Violence and Social Change*, London: Routledge.

Dobash, R. E. *et al.* (2000) *Changing Violent Men*, London: Sage.

Dollimore, J. (1991) *Sexual Dissidence: Augustine to Wilde, Freud to Foucault*, Oxford: Clarendon Press.

Dollimore, J. (1997) 'Desire and difference: homosexuality, race, masculinity', in H. Stecopoulos and M. Uebel (eds) *Race and the Subject of Masculinities*, Durham: Duke University Press.

Donald, R. R. (1992) 'Masculinity and machismo in Hollywood's war films', in S. Craig (ed.) *Men, Masculinity and the Media*, London: Sage.

Douglas, Lord A. B. (1983) 'Two loves', in S. Coote (ed.) *The Penguin Book of Homosexual Verse*, London: Penguin (orig. pub. 1894).

Dowsett, G. (1987) 'Queer fears and gay examples', *New Internationalist* 175: 10–12.

Du Gay, P. *et al.* (1997) *Doing Cultural Studies: The Story of the Sony Walkman*, London: Sage.

Du Gay, P. *et al.* (eds) (2000) *Identity: A Reader*, London: Sage.

Dunning, E. (1999) *Sport Matters: Sociological Studies of Sport, Violence and Civilization*, London: Routledge.

Dunning, E. and Rojek, C. (eds) (1992) *Sport and Leisure in the Civilizing Process: Critique and Counter-Critique*, London: Macmillan.

Durkheim, E. (1951 [1897]) *Suicide: A Study in Sociology*, Glencoe: Free Press.

Dworkin, A. (1981) *Pornography: On Men Possessing Women*, London: Women's Press.

Dyer, R. (1985) 'Male sexuality in the media', in A. Metcalf and M. Humphries (eds) *The Sexuality of Men*, London: Pluto.

Dyer, R. (1989) 'Don't look now: the instabilities of the male pin-up', in A. McRobbie (ed.) *Zoot Suits and Second-Hand Dresses: An Anthology of Fashion and Music*, London: Macmillan.

Dyer, R. (1992) *Only Entertainment*, London: Routledge.

Dyer, R. (1993) *The Matter of Images: Essays on Representation*, London: Routledge.

Dyer, R. (1997a) *White*, London: Routledge.

Dyer, R. (1997b) 'The white man's muscles', in H. Stecopoulos and M. Uebel (eds) *Race and the Subject of Masculinities*, Durham, NC: Duke University Press.

Edley, N. and Wetherell, M. (1995) *Men in Perspective: Practice, Power and Identity*, London: Harvester Wheatsheaf.

Edwards, T. (1990) 'Beyond sex and gender: masculinity, homosexuality and social theory', in J. Hearn and D. Morgan (eds) *Men, Masculinities and Social Theory*, London: Unwin Hyman.

Edwards, T. (1992) 'The AIDS dialectics: awareness, identity, death and sexual politics', in K. Plummer (ed.) *Modern Homosexualities: Fragments of Lesbian and Gay Experience*, London: Routledge.

Edwards, T. (1994) *Erotic & Politics: Gay Male Sexuality, Masculinity and Feminism*, London: Routledge.

Edwards, T. (1997) *Men in the Mirror: Men's Fashion, Masculinity and Consumer Society*, London: Cassell.

Edwards, T. (1998) 'Queer fears: against the cultural turn', *Sexualities* 1(4): 471–84.

Edwards, T. (2000) *Contradictions of Consumption: Concepts, Practices and Politics in Consumer Society*, Buckingham: Open University Press.

Edwards, T. (2003) 'Sex, booze and fags: masculinity, style and men's magazines', in B. Benwell (ed.) *Masculinity and Men's Lifestyle Magazines*, Oxford: Blackwell.

Edwards, T. (2004) 'Queering the pitch: gay masculinities', in M. S. Kimmel, J. Hearn and R. W Connell (eds) *Handbook of Studies on Men and Masculinities*, London: Sage.

Eglinton, J. Z. (1971) *Greek Love*, London: Neville Spearman.

Eisenstein, H. (1984) *Contemporary Feminist Thought*, London: Unwin.

Ekins, R. and King, D. (2004) 'Transgendering, men, and masculinities', in M. S. Kimmel, J. Hearn and R. W. Connell (eds) *Handbook of Studies on Men and Masculinities*, London: Sage.

Elias, N. (1994) *The Civilizing Process: The History of Manners and State Formation and Civilization*, Oxford: Blackwell.

Elias, N. and Dunning, E. (1986) *Quest for Excitement: Sport and Leisure in the Civilizing Process*, Oxford: Blackwell.

Elliott-Major, L. (2000) 'Ladies first', *Guardian Education* 16 (January): 9.

Ellis, B. E. (1985) *Less Than Zero*, London: Picador.

Ellis, B. E. (1987) *The Rules of Attraction*, London: Picador.

Ellis, B. E. (1991) *American Psycho*, London: Picador.

Ellis, J. (1982) *Visible Fictions*, London: Routledge.

Ennew, J. (1986) *The Sexual Exploitation of Children*, Cambridge: Polity.

Epstein, S. (1987) 'Gay politics, ethnic identity: the limits of social constructionism', *Socialist Review* 17: 9–54.

Epstein, S. (1988) 'Nature vs. nurture and the politics of AIDS organising', *Out/Look* 1(3): 46–50.

Evans, D. (1993) *Sexual Citizenship: The Material Construction of Sexualities*, London: Routledge.

Faderman, L. (1981) *Surpassing the Love of Men: Romantic Friendship and Love Between Women from the Renaissance to the Present*, New York: William Morrow.

Faludi, S. (1992) *Backlash: The Undeclared War Against Women*, London: Vintage.

Faludi, S. (2000) *Stiffed: The Betrayal of Modern Man*, London: Vintage.

Fanon, F. (1970) *Black Skin White Masks*, London: Paladin.

Faraday, A. (1981) 'Liberating lesbian research', in K. Plummer (ed.) *The Making of the Modern Homosexual*, London: Hutchinson.

Farrell, W. (1974) *The Liberated Man Beyond Masculinity: Freeing Men and Their Relationships with Women*, New York: Random House.

Farrell, W. (1993) *The Myth of Male Power: Why Men Are the Disposable Sex*, New York: Simon & Schuster.

Featherstone, M. (1982) 'The body in consumer culture', *Theory, Culture And Society* 1: 18–33.

Featherstone, M. (1991) *Consumer Culture and Postmodernism*, London: Sage.

Featherstone, M., Hepworth, M. and Turner, B. S. (eds) (1991) *The Body, Social Process and Cultural Theory*, London: Sage.

Fejes, F. J. (1992) 'Masculinity as fact: a review of empirical mass communication research on masculinity', in S. Craig (ed.) *Men, Masculinity and the Media*, London: Sage.

Firestone, S. (1970) *The Dialectic of Sex: The Case For Feminist Revolution*, New York: Bantam Books.

Fletcher, A. (1995) *Gender, Sex and Subordination in England 1500–1800*, New Haven, CT: Yale University Press.

Flügel, J. C. (1930) *The Psychology of Clothes*, London: Hogarth Press.

Foucault, M. (1973) *The Birth of the Clinic: An Archaeology of Medical Perception*, London: Tavistock.

Foucault, M. (1977) *Discipline and Punish: The Birth of the Prison*, Harmondsworth: Penguin.

Foucault, M. (1978) *The History of Sexuality – Volume One: An Introduction*, Harmondsworth: Penguin.

Foucault, M. (1984a) *The Use of Pleasure: The History of Sexuality – Volume Two*, Harmondsworth: Penguin.

Foucault, M. (1984b) *The Care of the Self: The History of Sexuality – Volume Three*, Harmondsworth: Penguin.

Francis, B. (1998) *Power Plays: Primary School Children's Constructions of Gender, Power, and Adult Work*, Stoke on Trent: Trentham Books.

Francis, B. (2000) *Boys, Girls and Achievement: Addressing the Classroom Issues*, London: Routledge.

Frank, A. (1991) 'For a sociology of the body: an analytical review', in M. Featherstone, M. Hepworth and B. Turner (eds) *The Body, Social Process and Cultural Theory*, London: Sage.

Frankenberg, R. (1993) *White Women, Race Matters: The Social Construction of Whiteness*, London: Routledge

Frankenberg, R. (ed.) (1997) *Displacing Whiteness: Essays in Social and Cultural Criticism*, New York: Duke University Press.

Franz, M. L. von (1981) *Puer Aeternus*, Santa Monica, Calif.: Sigo Press (2nd edn; orig. pub. 1970).

Freud, S. (1977) *On Sexuality: Three Essays on the Theory of Sexuality and Other Works*, London: Penguin (orig. pub. 1905).

Friedan, B. (1963) *The Feminine Mystique*, London: Victor Gollancz.

Fuchs, C. J. (1993) 'The buddy politic', in S. Cohan and I. R. Hark (eds) *Screening the Male: Exploring Masculinities in Hollywood Cinema*, London: Routledge.

Furlong, A. (1991) *Sado-Masochism and the Law: Consent versus paternalism*, published as *Legal Notes No. 12*, London: The Libertarian Alliance.

Gaillie, D., Marsh, C. and Vogler, C. (eds) (1994) *Social Change and the Experience of Unemployment*, Oxford: Oxford University Press.

Gaines, J. (1986) 'White privilege and looking relations: race and gender in feminist film theory', *Cultural Critique*, Fall: 59–79.

Game, A. and Pringle, R. (1984) *Gender at Work*, London: Pluto.

Gardiner, J. K. (ed.) (2002) *Masculinity Studies and Feminist Theory: New Directions*, New York: Columbia University Press.

Gerschick, T. J. (2004) 'Masculinity and degrees of bodily normativity in Western culture', in M. S. Kimmel, J. Hearn and R. W. Connell (eds) *Handbook of Studies on Men and Masculinities*, London: Sage.

Giddens, A. (1991) *Modernity and Self-Identity: Self and Society in the Late Modern Age*, Cambridge: Polity Press.

Gilbert, R. and Gilbert, P. (1998) *Masculinity Goes To School*, London: Routledge.

Gilroy, P. (1987) *There Ain't No Black in the Union Jack: The Cultural Politics of Race and Nation*, London: Hutchinson.

Gilroy, P. (2000) *The Black Atlantic: Race, Identity and Nationalism at the End of the Colour Line*, London: Allen Lane.

Ginsburg, E. and Lerner, S. (1989) *Sexual Violence Against Women: A Guide to the Criminal Law*, London: Rights of Women.

Goldberg, H. (1976) *The Hazards of Being Male: Surviving the Myth of Masculine Privilege*, New York: Nash.

Goldman, R. (1992) *Reading Ads Socially*, London: Routledge.

Goldstein, J. H. (1989) 'Beliefs about human aggression', in J. Groebel and R. A. Hinde (eds) *Aggression and War: Their Biological and Social Bases*, Cambridge: Cambridge University Press.

Goldstein, L. (ed.) (1994) *The Male Body: Features, Destinies, Exposures*, Ann Arbor: University of Michigan Press.

Gough, J. (1989) 'Theories of sexual identity and the masculinization of the gay man', in S. Shepherd and M. Wallis (eds) *Coming On Strong: Gay Politics and Culture*, London: Unwin Hyman.

Grace, D. (1993) 'Dynamics of desire', in V. Harwood *et al.* (eds) *Pleasure Principles: Politics, Sexuality, and Ethics*, London: Lawrence & Wishart.

Green, I. (1984) 'Male function: a contribution to the debate on masculinity in the cinema', *Screen* 25(4–5): 36–48.

Greenberg, D. F. (1988) *The Construction of Homosexuality*, London: University of Chicago Press.

Greer, G. (1971) *The Female Eunuch*, London: Paladin.

Greer, G. (2000) *The Whole Woman*, London: Anchor.

Gregory, J. and Lees, S. (1999) *Policing Sexual Assault*, London: Routledge.

Halberstam, J. (1998) *Female Masculinity*, Durham, NC: Duke University Press.

Hall, S. (ed.) (1997) *Representation: Cultural Representation and Signifying Practices*, London: Sage.

Hall, S. and Du Gay, P. (eds.) (1996) *Questions of Cultural Identity*, London: Sage.

Hall, S. *et al.* (eds) (1978) *Policing the Crisis: Mugging, the State, and Law and Order*, London: Macmillan.

Hanmer, J. and Maynard, M. (eds) (1987) *Women, Violence and Social Control*, Basingstoke: Macmillan.

Hanmer, J. and Saunders, S. (1984) *Well-founded Fear: A Community Study of Violence To Women*, London: Hutchinson.

Harding, S. (ed.) (1987) *Feminism and Methodology: Social Science Issues*, Buckingham: Open University Press.

Hargreaves, J. (1992) 'Sex, gender and the body in sport: has there been a civilizing process?', in E. Dunning and C. Rojek, (eds) *Sport and Leisure in the Civilizing Process: Critique and Counter-Critique*, London: Macmillan.

Hargreaves, J. (1994) *Sporting Females: Critical Issues in the History and Sociology of Women's Sports*, London: Routledge.

Hark, I. R. (1993) 'Animals or Romans: looking at masculinity in spartacus', in S. Cohan and I. R. Hark (eds) *Screening the Male: Exploring Masculinities in Hollywood Cinema*, London: Routledge.

Harwood, V. *et al.* (eds) (1993) *Pleasure Principles: Politics, Sexuality, and Ethics*, London: Lawrence & Wishart.

Hatty, S. E. (2000) *Masculinities, Violence, and Culture*, London: Sage.

Haywood, C. and Mac an Ghaill, M. (2003) *Men and Masculinities: Theory, Research and Social Practice*, Buckingham: Open University Press.

Hearn, J. (1987) *The Gender of Oppression: Men, Masculinity and the Critique of Marxism*, Brighton: Wheatsheaf.

Hearn, J. (1998) *The Violences of Men: How Men Talk About and How Agencies Respond To Men's Violence To Women*, London: Sage.

Hearn, J. and Morgan, D. (eds) (1990) *Men, Masculinities and Social Theory*, London: Unwin Hyman.

Hearn, J. and Parkin, W. (1987) *'Sex' at 'Work'. The Power and Paradox of Organisation Sexuality*, Brighton: Wheatsheaf.

Hearn, J. and Parkin, W. (2001) *Gender, Sexuality and Violence in Organizations: The Unspoken Forces of Organization Violations*, London: Sage.

Hebdige, D. (1979) *Subculture: The Meaning of Style*, London: Routledge.

Heidensohn, F. (1996) *Women and Crime*, Basingstoke: Macmillan.

Hoch, P. (1979) *White Hero, Black Beast: Racism, Sexism and the Mask of Masculinity*, London: Pluto.

Hocquenghem, G. (1972) *Homosexual Desire*, London: Allison and Busby.

Hollander, A. (1994) *Sex and Suits*, New York: Knopf.

Holmlund, C. (1993) 'Masculinity as masquerade: the 'mature' Stallone and the Stallone clone', in S. Cohan and I. R. Hark (eds) *Screening the Male: Exploring Masculinities in Hollywood Cinema*, London: Routledge.

hooks, B. (1982) *Ain't I a Woman: Black Women and Feminism*, London: Pluto Press.

hooks, B. (1992) *Black Looks: Race and Representation*, Boston, MA: South End Press.

hooks, B. (1994) *Outlaw Culture: Resisting Representations*, New York: Routledge.

hooks, B. (2004) *We Real Cool: Black Men and Masculinity*, London: Routledge.

Horrocks, R. (1994) *Masculinity in Crisis: Myths, Fantasies, Realities*, Basingstoke: Macmillan.

Hough, M. (1995) *Anxiety about Crime: Findings from the British Crime Survey*, London: Home Office.

Hutchings, P. (1993) 'Masculinity and the horror film', in P. Kirkham and J. Thumin (eds) *You Tarzan: Masculinity, Movies and Men*, London: Lawrence & Wishart.

Jackson, P. *et al.* (2001) *Making Sense of Men's Magazines*, Cambridge: Polity.

Jardine, A. and Smith, P. (eds) (1987) *Men in Feminism*, London: Methuen.

Jay, K. and Young, A. (1979) *The Gay Report*, New York: Summit Books.

Jeffords, S. (1994) *Hard Bodies: Hollywood Masculinity in the Reagan Era*, New Brunswick, NJ: Rutgers University Press.

Jeffreys, S. (1985) *The Spinster and Her Enemies: Feminism and Sexuality 1890–1930*, London: Pandora.

Jeffreys, S. (1990) *Anticlimax: Feminist Perspectives on the Sexual Revolution*, London: Women's Press.

Katz, J. (1976) *Gay American History: Lesbians and Gay Men in the USA*, New York: Thomas Y. Crowell.

Keen, S. (1991) *Fire in the Belly: On Being a Man*, New York: Bantam.

Kelly, L. (1988) *Surviving Sexual Violence*, Cambridge: Polity.

Kemp, S. and Squires, J. (eds) (1997) *Feminisms*, Oxford: Oxford University Press.

Kenway, J. (1995) 'Masculinities in schools: under siege, on the defensive and under reconstruction?', *Discourse: Studies in the Cultural Politics of Education* 16(1): 59–80.

Kimmel, M. S. (1987a) 'The contemporary "crisis" of masculinity in historical perspective', in H. Brod (ed.) *The Making of Masculinities: The New Men's Studies*, London: Hutchinson.

Kimmel, M. S. (ed.) (1987b) *Changing Men: New Directions in Research on Men and Masculinity*, Beverly Hills, Calif.: Sage.

Kimmel, M. S. (1994) 'Masculinity as homophobia: fear, shame, and silence in the construction of gender identity', in H. Brod and M. Kaufman (eds) *Theorizing Masculinities*, London: Sage.

Kimmel, M. S. and Kaufman, M. (1994) 'Weekend warriors: the new men's movement', in H. Brod and M. Kaufman (eds) *Theorizing Masculinities*, Thousand Oaks, Calif.: Sage.

Kimmel, M. S., Hearn, J. and Connell, R. W. (eds) (2004) *Handbook of Studies on Men and Masculinities*, London: Sage.

Kinsey, A. F. *et al.* (1948) *Sexual Behaviour in the Human Male*, Philadelphia: W. B. Saunders.

Kirkham, P. and Thumin, J. (eds) (1993) *You Tarzan: Masculinity, Movies and Men*, London: Lawrence & Wishart.

Kirsta, A. (1994) *Deadlier Than the Male: Violence and Aggression in Women*, London: HarperCollins.

Kramer, L. (1978) *Faggots*, London: Methuen.

Kramer, L. (1983) '1,112 and counting', *New York Native* 59: 14–27.

Kramer, L. (1986) *The Normal Heart*, London: Methuen.

Kristeva, J. (1982) *Powers of Horror: An Essay on Abjection*, New York: Columbia University Press.

La Fontaine, J. (1990) *Child Sexual Abuse*, Cambridge: Polity.

Lacan, J. (1977) *Ecrits: A Selection*, London: Tavistock (orig. pub. 1966).

Lee, C. and Owens, R. G. (2002) *The Psychology of Men's Health*, Buckingham: Open University Press.

Lee, J. A. (1978) *Getting Sex: A New Approach – More Fun, Less Guilt*, Ontario: Mission Book Company.

Lees, S. (1996) *Ruling Passions: Sexual Violence, Reputation, and the Law*, Buckingham: Open University Press.

Lees, S. (1997) *Carnal Knowledge: Rape on Trial*, London: Penguin.

Le Vay, S. (1993) *The Sexual Brain*, London: MIT Press.

Liddle, M. (1993) 'Masculinity, "male behaviour" and crime: a theoretical investigation of sex-differences in delinquency and deviant behaviour', in *Masculinity and Crime: Issues of Theory and Practice – Conference Report*, Brunel: The Centre for Criminal Justice Research.

Lightfoot, L. (2000) 'Black culture holding back boys', *Daily Telegraph*, 21 August.

Lindsay, L. A. and Miescher, S. F. (eds) (2003) *Men and Masculinities in Modern Africa*, Portsmouth, NH: Heinemann.

Lingard, B. and Douglas, P. (1999) *Men Engaging Feminisms: Pro-feminism, Backlashes and Schooling*, Buckingham: Open University Press.

London Consortium (2000) *Whiteness*, London: Lawrence & Wishart.

Lury, C. (1996) *Consumer Culture*, Cambridge: Polity.

Mac an Ghaill, M. (1994) *The Making of Men: Masculinities, Sexualities and Schooling*, Buckingham: Open University Press.

Mac an Ghaill, M. (ed.) (1996) *Understanding Masculinities*, Buckingham: Open University Press

MacInnes, J. (1998) *The End of Masculinity: The Confusion of Sexual Genesis and Sexual Difference in Modern Society*, Buckingham: Open University Press.

MacKinnon, C. A. (1987) *Feminism Unmodified: Discourses on Life and Law*, Cambridge, Mass.: Harvard University Press.

MacKinnon, K. (1997) *Uneasy Pleasures: The Male as Erotic Object*, London: Cynus Arts.

Maccoby, E. and Jacklin, C. (1974) *The Psychology of Sex Differences*, Stanford, Calif.: Stanford University Press.

Mains, G. (1984) *Urban Aboriginals: A Celebration of Leathersexuality*, San Francisco, Calif.: Gay Sunshine Press.

Marriott, D. (2000) *On Black Men*, Edinburgh: Edinburgh University Press.

Marshall, B. and Witz, A. (2004) *Engendering the Social: Feminist Encounters With Sociological Theory*, Buckingham: Open University Press.

Marsiglio, W. and Pleck, J. H. (2004) 'Fatherhood and masculinities', in M. S. Kimmel, J. Hearn and R. W. Connell (eds) *Handbook of Studies on Men and Masculinities*, London: Sage.

McClintock, A. (1995) *Imperial Leather*, London: Routledge.

McDowell, D. E. (1997) 'Pecs and reps: muscling in on race and the subject of masculinities', in H. Stecopoulos and M. Uebel (eds) (1997) *Race and the Subject of Masculinities*, Durham: Duke University Press.

McIntosh, M. (1968) 'The homosexual role', *Social Problems* 16(2): 182–92.

McKay, J., Mikosza J. and Hutchins, B. (2004) '"Gentlemen, the lunchbox has landed": representations of masculinities and men's bodies in the popular media', in M. S. Kimmel, J. Hearn and R. W. Connell (eds) *Handbook of Studies on Men and Masculinities*, London: Sage.

McMahon, A. (1999) *Taking Care of Men: Sexual Politics in the Public Mind*, Cambridge: Cambridge University Press.

McRobbie, A. (ed.) (1989) *Zoot Suits and Second-Hand Dresses: An Anthology of Fashion and Music*, Basingstoke: Macmillan.

McRobbie, A. (1991) *Feminism and Youth Culture: From 'Jackie' to 'Just Seventeen'*, Basingstoke: Macmillan.

McRobbie, A. (1998) *British Fashion Design: Rag Trade or Image Industry?* London: Taylor & Francis.

Mead, G. H. (1934) *Mind, Self and Society*, Chicago: University of Chicago Press.

Mead, M. (1977) *Sex and Temperament in Three Primitive Societies*, London: Routledge and Kegan Paul (orig. pub. 1935).

Mercer, K. and Julien, I. (1988) 'Race, sexual politics and black masculinity: a dossier', in R. Chapman and J. Rutherford (eds) *Male Order: Unwrapping Masculinity*, London: Lawrence & Wishart.

Messerschmidt, J. W. (1993) *Masculinities and Crime: Critique and Reconceptualization of Theory*, Lanham, MD: Rowan & Littlefield.

Messerschmidt, J. W. (1997) *Crime as Structured Action: Gender, Race, Class, and Crime in the Making*, London: Sage.

Messner, M. A. (2004) 'Still a man's world? Studying masculinities and sport', in M. S. Kimmel, J. Hearn and R. W. Connell (eds) *Handbook of Studies on Men and Masculinities*, London: Sage.

Messner, M. A. and Sabo, D. (1994) *Sex, Violence and Power in Sports: Rethinking Masculinity*, Freedom, CA: Crossing Press.

Miedzian, M. (1991) *Boys Will Be Boys: Breaking the Links Between Masculinity and Violence*, New York: Anchor Books.

Mieli, M. (1980) *Homosexuality and Liberation: Elements of a Gay Critique*, London: Gay Men's Press.

Miles, M. (2003) 'Ghetto culture', *Axm* 6(1): 32–4.

Millett, K. (1971) *Sexual Politics*, London: Sphere.

Millett, K. (1984) 'Beyond politics? Children and sexuality', in C. S. Vance (ed.) *Pleasure and Danger: Exploring Female Sexuality*, London: Routledge & Kegan Paul.

Mills, S. (2003) *Michel Foucault*, London: Routledge.

Mitchell, J. (1971) *Woman's Estate*, Harmondsworth: Penguin.

Mooney, J. (2000) *Gender, Violence, and the Social Order*, Basingstoke: Macmillan.

Morgan, D. (1992) *Discovering Men*, London: Routledge.

Morgan, D. (1993) 'You too can have a body like mine: reflections on the male body and masculinities', in S. Scott and D. Morgan (eds) *Body Matters: Essays on the Sociology of the Body*, London: Falmer Press.

Mort, F. (1996) *Cultures of Consumption: Masculinities and Social Space in Late Twentieth-Century Britain*, London: Routledge.

Mosse, G. L. (1996) *The Image of Man*, Oxford: Oxford University Press.

Moynihan, D. (1965) *The Negro Family: The Case For National Action*, Washington: US Department of Labor.

Mulvey, L. (1975) 'Visual pleasure and narrative cinema', *Screen* 16(3): 6–18.

Mulvey, L. (1981) 'Afterthoughts . . . inspired by *Duel in the Sun*', *Framework* 15, 16, 17.

Muñoz, J. E. (1997) 'Photographies of mourning: melancholia and ambivalence in Van Der Zee, Mapplethorpe, and *Looking For Langston*', in H. Stecopoulos and M. Uebel (eds) *Race and the Subject of Masculinities*, Durham, NC: Duke University Press.

Nardi, P. (ed.) (2000) *Gay Masculinities*, London: Sage.

Nava, M. (1992) *Changing Cultures: Feminism, Youth and Consumerism*, London: Sage.

Nava, M. *et al.* (eds) (1997) *Buy This Book: Studies in Advertising and Consumption*, London: Routledge.

Neale, S. (1982) 'Images of Men', *Screen* 23(3–4): 47–53.

Neale, S. (1983) 'Masculinity as spectacle: reflections on men and mainstream cinema', *Screen* 24(6): 2–16.

Newburn, T. and Stanko, E. (eds) (1994) *Just Boys Doing Business? Men, Masculinities and Crime*, London: Routledge.

Nicholson, L. and Seidman, S. (eds) (1995) *Social Postmodernism: Beyond Identity Politics*, Cambridge: Cambridge University Press.

Nixon, S. (1996) *Hard Looks: Masculinities, Spectatorship and Contemporary Consumption*, London: UCL Press.

Oakley, A. (1972) *Sex, Gender and Society*, London: Temple Smith.

O'Connell-Davidson, J. and Layder, D. (1994) *Methods, Sex and Madness*, London: Routledge.

Orbach, S. (1978) *Fat Is a Feminist Issue: How To Lose Weight Permanently – Without Dieting*, London: Paddington Press.

Orbach, S. (1986) *Hunger Strike: The Anorectic's Struggle as a Metaphor for Our Age*, London: Faber.

Osgerby, B. (2001) *Playboys in Paradise: Masculinity, Youth and Leisure-Style in Modern America*, Oxford: Berg.

Osgerby, B. (2003) 'A pedigree of the consuming male: masculinity, consumption and the American "leisure class"', in B. Benwell (ed.) *Masculinity and Men's Lifestyle Magazines*, Oxford: Blackwell.

Owens, C. (1987) 'Outlaws: gay men in feminism', in A. Jardine and P. Smith (eds) *Men in Feminism*, London: Methuen.

Palahnuik, C. (1996) *Fight Club*, New York: Hyperion Books.

Parsons, T. (1953) 'A revised analytical approach to the theory of stratification', in R. Bendix and S. M. Lipset (eds) *Class, Status and Power: A Reader in Social Stratification*, Glencoe: Free Press.

Pateman, C. (1988) *The Sexual Contract*, Cambridge: Polity.

Patton, C. (1985) *Sex and Germs: The Politics of AIDS*, London: South End Press.

Patton, C. (1990) *Inventing AIDS*, London: Routledge.

Pease, B. (2000) *Recreating Men: Postmodern Masculinity Politics*, London: Sage.

Perry, G. (1992) 'Hung like a hamster: the heavy weight of a small penis', in C. Harding (ed.) *Wingspan: Journal of the Male Spirit*, New York: St. Martin's.

Person, E. S. (1980) 'Sexuality as the mainstay of identity: psychoanalytic perspectives', *Signs* 5(4): 605–30.

Petersen, A. (1998) *Unmasking the Masculine: 'Men' and 'Identity' in a Sceptical Age*, London: Sage.

Pfeil, F. (1995) *White Guys: Studies in Postmodern Domination and Difference*, London: Verso.

Phizacklea, A. (1990) *Unpacking the Fashion Industry*, London: Routledge.

Plummer, K. (ed.) (1981) *The Making of the Modern Homosexual*, London: Hutchinson.

Plummer, K. (1984) *Telling Sexual Stories: Power, Change and Social Worlds*, London: Routledge.

Pollak, M. (1985) 'Male homosexuality – or happiness in the ghetto', in P. Aries and A. Bejin (eds) *Western Sexuality: Practice and Precept in Past and Present Times*, Oxford: Basil Blackwell.

Pollard, A. (1985) *The Social World of the Primary School*, London: Cassell.

Pope, H. G., Phillips, K. A. and Olivardia, R. (2000) *The Adonis Complex: The Secret Crisis of Male Body Obsession*, New York: Free Press.

Radclyffe Hall, A. (1982) *The Well of Loneliness*, London: Virago (orig. pub. 1928).

Ramazanoglu, C. (ed.) (1993) *Up Against Foucault: Explorations of Some Tensions Between Foucault and Feminism*, London: Routledge.

Rechy, J. (1977) *The Sexual Outlaw: A Documentary*, London: W. H. Allen.

Rich, A. (1984) 'Compulsory heterosexuality and lesbian existence', in A. B. Snitow *et al.* (eds) *Desire: The Politics of Sexuality*, London: Virago.

Riley, D. (1988) *Am I That Name? Feminism and the Category of 'Women' in History*, New York: Macmillan.

Rodowick, D. (1982) 'The difficulty of difference', *Wide Angle* 5(1): 4–15.

Rubin, G. (1975) 'The traffic in women: notes on the "political economy" of sex', in R. Reiter Rayner (ed.) *Toward an Anthropology of Women*, New York: Monthly Review Press.

Rubin, G. (1984) 'Thinking sex: notes for a radical theory of the politics of sexuality', in C. S. Vance (ed.) *Pleasure and Danger: Exploring Female Sexuality*, London: Routledge & Kegan Paul.

Russell, D. E. H. (1984) *Sexual Exploitation: Rape, Child Sexual Abuse, and Workplace Harassment*, London: Sage.

Russo, V. (1987) *The Celluloid Closet: Homosexuality in the Movies*, New York: Harper & Row.

Sabo, D. (2004) 'The study of masculinities and men's health: an overview', in M. S. Kimmel, J. Hearn and R. W. Connell (eds) *Handbook of Studies on Men and Masculinities*, London: Sage.

Sabo, D. and Gordon, D. F. (eds) (1995) *Men's Health and Illness: Gender, Power and the Body*, Thousand Oaks, CA: Sage.

Said, E. W. (1995) *Orientalism: Western Conceptions of the Orient*, London: Penguin (orig. pub. 1978).

Sartre, J. P. (1969) *Being and Nothingness: An Essay on Phenomenological Ontology*, London: Methuen (orig. pub. 1943).

Savage, J. (1996) 'What's so new about the new man? Three decades of advertising to men', in D. Jones (ed.) *Sex, Power and Travel: Ten Years of Arena*, London: Virgin.

Schoene-Harwood, B. (2000) *Writing Men: Literary Masculinities from Frankenstein to the New Man*, Edinburgh: Edinburgh University Press.

Scott, S. and Morgan, D. (eds) (1993) *Body Matters: Essays on the Sociology of the Body*, London: Falmer Press.

Sedgwick, E. K. (1985) *Between Men: English Literature and Male Homosexual Desire*, New York: Columbia Press.

Sedgwick, E. K. (1990) *Epistemology of the Closet*, Berkeley, Calif.: University of California Press.

Sedgwick, E. K. (1995) 'Gosh, Boy George, you must be awfully secure in your masculinity!', in M. Berger *et al.*, *Constructing Masculinity*, London: Routledge.

Segal, L. (1987) *Is the Future Female? Troubled Thoughts on Contemporary Feminism*, London: Virago.

Segal, L. (1990) *Slow Motion: Changing Masculinities, Changing Men*, London: Virago.

Segal, L. (1994) *Straight Sex: The Politics of Pleasure*, London: Virago.

Segal, L. (1999) *Why Feminism? Gender, Psychology, Politics*, Cambridge: Polity.

Segal, L. and McIntosh, M. (eds) (1992) *Sex Exposed: Sexuality and the Pornography Debate*, London: Virago.

Seidler, V. J. (1989) *Rediscovering Masculinity: Reason, Language and Sexuality*, London: Routledge.

Seidler, V. J. (1991) *Achilles Heel Reader: Men, Sexual Politics and Socialism*, London: Routledge.

Seidler, V. J. (1994) *Unreasonable Men: Masculinity and Social Theory*, London: Routledge.

Seidman, S. (1995) 'Deconstructing queer theory or the under-theorization of the social and ethical', in L. Nicholson and S. Seidman (eds) *Social Postmodernism: Beyond Identity Politics*, Cambridge: Cambridge University Press.

Shiers, J. (1980) 'Two steps forward and one step back', in Gay Left Collective (ed.) *Homosexuality: Power and Politics*, London: Allison & Busby.

Shilling, C. (1993) *The Body and Social Theory*, London: Sage.

Shilling, C. (1997) 'The body and difference', in K. Woodward (ed.) *Identity and Difference*, London: Sage.

Shilts, R. (1987) *And the Band Played On: Politics, People, and the AIDS Epidemic*, London: Penguin.

Silverman, K. (1992) *Male Subjectivity at the Margins*, London: Routledge.

Simmel, G. (1904) 'Fashion', *International Quarterly* 10.

Simpson, M. (1994) *Male Impersonators: Men Performing Masculinity*, London: Routledge.

Simpson, M. (1996) *It's a Queer World*, London: Vintage.

Smart, C. (1978) *Women, Crime and Criminology: A Feminist Critique*, London: Routledge.

Smith, D. E. (1988) *The Everyday World as Problematic: A Feminist Sociology*, Milton Keynes: Open University Press.

Solomon-Godeau, A. (1997) *Male Trouble: A Crisis in Representation*, London: Thames & Hudson.

Spada, J. (1979) *The Spada Report*, New York: Signet.

Spillers, H. J. (1984) 'Interstices: a small drama of words', in C. S. Vance (ed.) *Pleasure and Danger: Exploring Female Sexuality*, London: Routledge.

Stanko, E. A. (1994) 'Challenging the problem of men's individual violence', in

T. Newburn and E. A. Stanko (eds) *Just Boys Doing Business?* London: Routledge.

Stanko, E. A. and Hobdell, K. (1993) 'Assault on men: masculinity and male victimisation', *British Journal of Criminology* 33(3): 400–15.

Stanley, L. (1982) 'Male needs: the problems and problems of working with gay men', in S. Friedman and E. Sarah (eds) *On the Problem of Men: Two Feminist Conferences*, London: Women's Press.

Stanley, L. (1984) 'Whales and minnows: some sexual theorists and their followers and how they contribute to making feminism invisible', *Women's Studies International Forum* 7(1): 53–62.

Staples, R. (1982) *Black Masculinity: The Black Male's Role in American Society*, San Francisco: Black Scholar's Press.

Stecopoulos, H. and Uebel, M. (eds) (1997) *Race and the Subject of Masculinities*, Durham, NC: Duke University Press.

Stevenson, N., Jackson, P. and Brooks, K. (2003) 'Reading men's lifestyle magazines: cultural power and the information society', in B. Benwell (ed.) *Masculinity and Men's Lifestyle Magazines*, Oxford: Blackwell.

Still, J. (ed.) (2003) *Men's Bodies*, Edinburgh: Edinburgh University Press.

Stodder, J. (1979) 'Confessions of a candy-ass rough-neck', in E. Shapiro and B. Shapiro (eds) *The Women Say, The Men Say*, New York: Delacorte.

Stoltenberg, J. (2000) *Refusing To Be a Man: Essays on Sex and Justice*, London: UCL Press (revised edition, orig. pub. 1989).

Swain, J. (2000) '"The money's good, the fame's good, the girls are good": the role of playground football in the construction of young boys' masculinity in a junior school', *British Journal of Sociology of Education* 21: 95–109.

Tasker, Y. (1993) 'Dumb movies for dumb people: masculinity, the body, and the voice in contemporary action cinema', in S. Cohan and I. R. Hark (eds) *Screening the Male: Exploring Masculinities in Hollywood Cinema*, London: Routledge.

Taylor, I. (1999) *Crime in Context: A Critical Criminology of Market Societies*, Cambridge: Polity.

Taylor, Y. and Sunderland, J. (2003) '"I've always loved women": the representation of the male sex worker in *Maxim*', in B. Benwell (ed.) *Masculinity and Men's Lifestyle Magazines*, Oxford: Blackwell.

Thewelheit, K. (1987) *Male Fantasies*, Cambridge: Polity.

Tolson, A. (1977) *The Limits of Masculinity*, London: Tavistock.

Turner, B. S. (1996) *The Body and Society: Explorations in Social Theory*, London: Sage (2nd edn).

Uebel, M. (1997) 'Men in order: introducing race and the subject of masculinities', in H. Stecopolous and M. Uebel (eds) *Race and the Subject of Masculinities*, Durham: Duke University Press.

Vance, C. S. (ed.) (1984) *Pleasure and Danger: Exploring Female Sexuality*, London: Routledge & Kegan Paul.

Wallace, M. (1990) *Black Macho and the Myth of the Superwoman*, London: Verso (2nd edn, orig. pub. NY: Dial Press, 1979).

Walter, A. (ed.) (1980) *Come Together: The Years of Gay Liberation (1970–73)*, London: Gay Men's Press.

Watney, S. (1987) *Policing Desire: Pornography, AIDS and the Media*, London: Comedia.

Watson, J. (2000) *Male Bodies: Health, Culture and Identity*, Buckingham: Open University Press.

Weber, M. (1946) *From Max Weber: Essays in Sociology*, eds. H. H. Gerth and C. W. Mills, London: Routledge & Kegan Paul.

Weeks, J. (1977) *Coming Out: Homosexual Politics in Britain from the Nineteenth Century to the Present*, London: Quartet.

Weeks, J. (1981) *Sex, Politics and Society: The Regulation of Sexuality Since 1800*, London: Longman.

Weeks, J. (1985) *Sexuality and Its Discontents: Meanings, Myths and Modern Sexualities*, London: Routledge & Kegan Paul.

Wellings, K. *et al.* (1994) *Sexual Behaviour in Britain: The National Survey of Sexual Attitudes and Lifestyles*, London: Penguin.

Wells, P. (1993) 'The Invisible Man: shrinking masculinity in the 1950s science fiction B-movie', in P. Kirkham and J. Thumin (eds) *You Tarzan: Masculinity, Movies and Men*, London: Lawrence & Wishart.

West, C. (1992) 'Identity: a matter of life and death', *October* 61: 20–23.

Wheaton, B. (2003) 'Lifestyle sport magazines and the discourses of sporting masculinity', in B. Benwell (ed.) *Masculinity and Men's Lifestyle Magazines*, Oxford: Blackwell.

Whelehan, I. (2000) *Overloaded: Popular Culture and the Future of Feminism*, London: Women's Press.

White, E. (1986) *States of Desire: Travels in Gay America*, London: Picador.

Whitehead, S. M. (2002) *Men and Masculinities: Key Themes and New Directions*, Cambridge: Polity.

Whitehead, S. M. and Barrett, F. J. (eds) (2001) *The Masculinities Reader*, Cambridge: Polity.

Wilde, O. (2000) *The Picture of Dorian Gray*, London: Penguin (orig. pub. 1891).

Willemen, P. (1981) 'Anthony Mann: looking at the male', *Framework* 15, 16, 17.

Willis, P. (1977) *Learning To Labour: How Working Class Kids Get Working Class Jobs*, Farnborough, Hants: Saxon House.

Willott, S. and Griffin, C. (1996) 'Men, masculinity and the challenge of long-term unemployment', in M. Mac an Ghaill (ed.) *Understanding Masculinities*, Buckingham: Open University Press.

Wilson, E. (1985) *Adorned in Dreams: Fashion and Modernity*, London: Virago.

Winship, J. (1987) *Inside Women's Magazines*, London: Pandora Press.

Wittig, M. (1997) 'One is not born a woman', in S. Kemp and J. Squires (eds) *Feminisms*, Oxford: Oxford University Press (orig. pub. 1981).

Wolf, N. (1991) *The Beauty Myth*, London: Vintage.

Wollstonecraft, M. (1992) *A Vindication of the Rights of Woman*, London: Penguin (orig. pub. 1792).

Woodward, K. (ed.) (1997) *Identity and Difference*, London: Sage.

Young, I. M. (1990) *Throwing Like a Girl and Other Essays in Feminist Philosophy and Social Theory*, Bloomington and Indianapolis: Indiana University Press.

Index